Aboutness

Carl G. Hempel Lecture Series

Aboutness

Stephen Yablo

PRINCETON UNIVERSITY PRESS

PRINCETON AND OXFORD

Copyright © 2014 by Princeton University Press
Published by Princeton University Press, 41 William Street,
Princeton, New Jersey 08540
In the United Kingdom: Princeton University Press,
6 Oxford Street, Woodstock, Oxfordshire OX20 1TW

press.princeton.edu

Jacket illustration: "Birds of a Feather" © Oleg Shuplyak

Library of Congress Cataloging-in-Publication Data
Yablo, Stephen.
Aboutness / Stephen Yablo.
pages cm. — (Carl G. Hempel lecture series)
Includes bibliographical references and index.
ISBN 978-0-691-14495-5 (hardcover)
1. Semantics (Philosophy)   2. Definition (Philosophy)
3. Meaning (Philosophy)   I. Title.
B840.Y33 2014
110—dc23
2013049375

British Library Cataloging-in-Publication Data is available

This book has been composed in Sabon Next LT Pro

Printed on acid-free paper. ∞

Typeset by S R Nova Pvt Ltd, Bangalore, India
Printed in the United States of America

1   3   5   7   9   10   8   6   4   2

Contents

Contents

- 10 -

- 11 -

- 12 -

Preface

This book is based on my 2008 Hempel Lectures. Chapters 1 to 3 and 5 "were" the first lecture, chapters 8 and 9 were the second, and chapters 10 to 12 were the third. Chapters 6 and 7 grow out of remarks scattered throughout. Chapter 4, on truthmakers, is the newest and, may I say, the least fun. How a few hours of spoken word turned into so many pages of text, I don't know. Either the lectures were incomprehensibly dense, or the book overexplains things, I suppose; maybe both. For their comments and kindness on that occasion, I would like to thank Sarah McGrath, Bas van Fraassen, John Burgess, Tom Kelly, Elizabeth Harman, Dan Garber, Tori McGeer, Phillip Pettit, Paul Benacerraf, and Harry Frankfurt. Michael Smith interpreted Princeton for me from Australia. Conversations with Gideon Rosen on truthmaking were a huge influence. I have benefited as much from Gideon's input as anyone's.

The Hempel ideas were reworked (in one case, preworked) for presentation at the University of Michigan (Nelson Lectures, 2007), Barcelona University (a minicourse in fall 2008), Stanford (Kant Lectures, 2011), and Oxford (Locke Lectures, 2012). I owe thanks, at Michigan, to Jim Joyce, Thony Gillies, Eric Swanson, Allan Gibbard, Andy Egan, Sarah Buss, Richmond Thomason, and Peter Railton; at Barcelona, to Miquel Miralbés del Pino, Manuel Garcia-Carpintero, José Diez, Gemma Celestino, Dan López da Sa, Max Kölbel, Pablo Rychter, Therese Marques, Genoveva Marti, Sven Rosenkranz, and Manolo Martínez; at Stanford, to Mark Crimmins, Debra Satz, Alexis Burgess, Krista Lawlor, Tamar Schapiro, Ken Taylor, Solomon Feferman, David Hills, Wes Holliday, and Johan van Benthem; and at Oxford, to Cian Dorr, Daniel Rothschild, Anandi Hattiangadi, Ofra Magidor, Scott Sturgeon, Maya Spener, John Broome, Jessica Moss, Jeremy Goodman, Jennifer Nagel, Alan Code, and Ian Rumfitt. Cian and Daniel were particularly generous with ideas and time.

Kit Fine assigned the manuscript in his spring 2013 semantics seminar at NYU, and invited me down for discussion. There were questions—more like polite advisories, in some cases—from Yu Gao, Martin Zavaleta, Vera

Flocke, Martin Glazier, Erica Schumener, and Joshua Armstrong, some of which led to changes in the text, others of which should have but didn't.

I first encountered Kit's work in this area at the "Because II" conference on noncausal explanation (Humboldt University, 2010). His paper was "Truthmaker Semantics," mine "A Semantic Conception of Truthmakers." Having a topic in common with Kit is one of the better fates that can befall a philosopher. I highly recommend it. Any number of points and examples trace back in some way to Kit. I tried to hold the line at six acknowledgments; it could have been dozens.

I arrived at MIT a fictionalist, or figuralist, about various matters. One makes as if to assert that *A*, on this view, in order to really assert that *R*—*R* being the real-world condition that authorizes the feigned assertion. The linguistics colleagues who did not succeed in avoiding me found this fanciful, and I resolved to put the project on a more respectable footing. A paper of Kai von Fintel's on (what I call) noncatastrophic presupposition failure pointed the way (von Fintel 2004). Ideas about presupposition and implicature were batted around with, and occasionally down by, Danny Fox. I benefitted as well from a stint as head of P when Irene Heim was head of L. (Ours is the department of L&P—Linguistics and Philosophy.)

I owe thanks, on the philosophy side, to Robert Stalnaker, for the stimulus of his work and his openness to ideas of which he does not necessarily approve. I am grateful to Agustín Rayo for manifold inter-locutory contributions and comments on an early draft. Richard Holton worked through, and taught, some of this material, and threw a number of ideas my way, like the idea of subject-matter-directed attitudes: wondering about, knowing about, being deceived about, and so on. Brad Skow, Sally Haslanger, Vann McGee, Rae Langton, Roger White, Alex Byrne, and Caspar Hare all made comments that changed the book in some way.

In the category of seminar exchanges, miniconferences, work in progress sessions, and drunken misunderstandings, the thankees are Brian Hedden, Rae Langton, Dan Greco, Ekaterina Vavova, Frank Arntzenius, Melissa Schumacher, David Liebesman, Mark Richard, Andrew Graham, Rebecca Millsap, Eric Swanson, Ruth Chang, Andy Egan, Benjamin Schnieder, Shamik Dasgupta, Seth Yalcin, Alejandro Pérez-Carballo, Ephraim Glick, Elizabeth Barnes, Mahrad Almotohari, Bernhard Salow, Anne Bezuiden-hout, Susanna Rinard, Ross Cameron, Paolo Santorio, and Sarah Moss. Thanks, all.

For correspondence and discussion, I am grateful to Hartry Field, Matti Eklund, L. A. Paul, Jonathan Schaffer, Timothy Williamson, Louise Antony, Carlotta Pavese, Stew Cohen, Jonathan Vogel, Levi Spectre, Delia Graff Fara, David Kaplan, Jim Pryor, Gerhard Nuffer, Ted Sider, David Lewis, Frank Jackson, Francois Reçanati, Zoltan Szabo, Lloyd Humberstone, Brian Weatherson, Chris Peacocke, Jason Stanley, Karen Bennett, Keith DeRose, Bob Hale, Charles Parsons, Amie Thomasson, Crispin Wright, Mark Colyvan, and John MacFarlane.

Johan van Benthem read the whole manuscript and sent comments from China. This was unexpected and wonderful.

I owe thanks to two anonymous referees for Princeton University Press for their ideas and advice. One asked, reasonably enough, what subject-matters are "of," on my account. I *think* the answer is sentences in context, as suggested originally by Kaplan. Another asked how the views expressed here relate to my earlier fictionalism/figuralism. I chose to interpret this as a question not about myself, but figuralism and presuppositionalism as such. The answer is found in the last few chapters: figuralism wins on power, presuppositionalism on plausibility. Both referees thought the book was too complicated. I wish I could have fixed that.

A different sort of debt is owed to Ken Gemes and Lloyd Humberstone, for creating, with their work on content-parts (Gemes 1994, Gemes 1997, Gemes 2007a, Gemes 2007b, among many others), subject matter (Humberstone 2000), partial truth (Humberstone 2003), and logical subtraction (Humberstone 1981, Humberstone 2011, 657–687), the present area of study.

This work was supported by the National Endowment for the Humanities, the Guggenheim Foundation, and the American Council of Learned Societies. My thanks to the people who made that possible. Rob Tempio, Karen Carter, and Ryan Mulligan, at Princeton University Press, were terrific throughout.

As explained on the first page, it all ultimately goes back to Zina. I thank her for the things she wasn't talking about, and the things she was. Schooling me on aboutness went better than teaching me how to Dougie, but thank you, Zina, for both, and the concerts and long drives and stories. My son is no longer a boy, but thank you, Isaac, for your boyish ways, and grasp of situations, and for coming home on holidays. Sally knows how I feel.

How to Read This Book

The book is demanding in places. You should definitely not take on too much at a time. I suggest the following seven-day program, if you're up for it. Alternatively you could do the first n days for any $n > 2$. Day 4 can be skipped without loss of continuity. Otherwise each day depends on the ones before it.

Day 1: Basics
  1.1–1.5; 5.1; whichever of 5.2–5.8 you like
Day 2: Subject Matter
  2.1–2.8
Day 3: Inclusion
  3.1–3.4; 3.5 if you're a detail person; 4.1; 4.8–4.10
Day 4: Epistemology
  Your pick: 6.1–6.6 for confirmation; 7.1–7.5 and 7.7–7.9 for knowledge
Day 5: Extrapolation
  8.1–8.6; 9.1–9.4; 9.6–9.9
Day 6: Bridging Logical Gaps
  11.1–11.4
Day 7: Real Content
  10.1–10.4; 12.1–12.4

Whatever is missing from this list you should read only if possessed by some powerful urge. Chapter 4 gets into the weeds on truthmakers. The appendix to chapter 5 suggests a way to think about impossible worlds. Section 6.7 sets out a Popperian theory of verisimilitude, based on work of Ken Gemes. Section 7.6 relates the hyperintensionality of knowledge to that of permission and desire. Section 12.5 muses on the (un)avoidability of philosophy.

Aboutness

Introduction

"Aboutness" is a grand-sounding name for something basically familiar. Books are on topics; portraits are of people; the *1812 Overture* concerns the Battle of Borodino. Aboutness is the relation that meaningful items bear to whatever it is that they are *on* or *of* or that they *address* or *concern*.

Aboutness has been studied before. Brentano made it the defining feature of the mental (Brentano 1995). Phenomenologists attempt to pin down the aboutness-features of particular mental states (Husserl 1970). Materialists sometimes claim to have grounded aboutness in natural regularities (Fodor 1987). Medieval grammarians distinguished what we are talking about from what is said about it, and linguists have returned to this theme (Hajicová et al. 1998, Beaver and Clark 2009). Historians ask what the Civil War was about. *Report from Iron Mountain: On the Possibility and Desirability of Peace* asks this about war in general (Lewin et al. 1996). Attempts have even been made, by library scientists and information theorists, to operationalize aboutness (Hutchins 1978, Demolombe and Jones 1998).

And yet the notion plays no serious role in philosophical semantics. This is surprising—sentences have aboutness properties, if anything does— so let me explain. One leading theory, the truth-conditional theory, gives the meaning of a sentence, *Quisling betrayed Norway*, say, by listing the scenarios in which it is true, or false. Nothing is said about the principle of selection, about *why* the sentence would be true, or false, in those scenarios. Subject matter is the missing link here. A sentence is true because of how matters stand where its subject matter is concerned.

According to the other leading theory, *Quisling betrayed Norway* expresses an amalgam of Quisling, betrayal, and Norway. One imagines that sentences are about whatever makes its way into the corresponding amalgam. This lets too much in, however. *Quisling did NOT betray Norway* is about Quisling and Norway, and perhaps betrayal. It is not about **NOT**, the logical operation of negation. Yet **NOT** is just as much an element of the amalgam as Quisling (Armstrong and Stanley 2011).

1

This book makes subject matter an independent factor in meaning, constrained but not determined by truth-conditions. A sentence's meaning is to do with its truth-value in various possible scenarios, *and* the factors responsible for that truth-value. No new machinery is required to accommodate this. The proposition that S is made up of the scenarios where S is true; S's reasons for, or ways of, being true are just additional propositions. When Frost writes, *The world will end in fire or in ice*, the truth-conditional meaning of his statement is an undifferentiated set of scenarios. Its "enhanced" meaning is the same set, subdivided into fiery-end worlds and icy-end worlds.

Now you know the plan: to make subject matter an equal partner in meaning. I have not said why this would be desirable.

The initial motivation comes from our sense of when sentences say the same thing. The truth-conditional theory does not respect the intuitive appearances here. Mathematicians know a *lot* of truths; metaphysicians know a lot of others. These truths are all identical if we go by truth-conditions, since they are true in the same cases: all of them.[1] *Here is a sofa* does not seem to say the same as *Here is the front of a sofa, and behind it is the back*, but they are (or can be understood to be) truth-conditionally equivalent. *All crows are black* cannot say quite the same as *All non-black things are non-crows*, for the two are confirmed by different evidence. Subject matter looks to be the distinguishing feature. One is about crows, the other not.

Aboutness is interesting in its own right; that is the first reason for caring about it. The second is that it helps us to make sense of *other* notions interesting in their own right.

So, for instance, one hypothesis can seem to *include* another, or to have the other as a *part*. Part of what is required for all crows to be black is that this crow here should be black. It is not required that all crows be black or on fire, though this is also implied by the blackness of crows. The idea is elusive, but we rely on it all the time. What does it mean to *unpack* an assertion? Unpacking is teasing out the asserted proposition's various parts. What does it mean for your position to in certain respects *agree* with mine? We agree to the extent that our views have content in common; part of what you say is identical to part of what I say. What does it mean for a claim that

---

[1] This is an aspect of the problem of logical omniscience.

is overall mistaken to get *something* right? You got something right if your claim was partly true, in the sense of having wholly true parts. How right you were depends on the size of those parts.

Content-inclusion is elusive, I said, but this might be questioned. *A* includes *B*, one might think, just if *A* implies *B*. The argument *A* ∴ *B* is in that case valid. Every third logic book explains a valid argument as one whose conclusion was already there in the premise(s). For *B* to be already there in *A* is for *B* to be *included* in *A*, surely.

Suppose this were right; inclusion was implication. There would then be truth in every hypothesis whatsoever, however ridiculous, for there is no *A* so thoroughly false as not to imply a true *B*. (*Snow is hot and black* gets something right by this standard, namely, that snow has these properties, or else boiled tar does.) *A* contains *B*, I propose, if the argument *A*, *therefore B*, is both truth-preserving *and subject-matter-preserving*. *Snow is hot and black* ∴ *Snow is hot and black, or boiled tar is hot and black*, though not truth-conditionally ampliative, does break new ground on the aboutness front.

Why assert false sentences with truth in them, rather than just the true bits? I am moved by a remark of William James's: "a rule of thinking which would absolutely prevent me from acknowledging certain kinds of truth if those kinds of truth were really there, would be an irrational rule." If truth-puritanism is the rule *Insist on pure truths; accept no substitutes*, then it threatens to be irrational, for there might be truths accessible only as parts of larger falsehoods. Dallying with the larger falsehoods would be good policy in such cases. The proper rule allows us to stretch the truth, if we make clear that our interest and advocacy extend only to the part about thus and such.

A lot of philosophical problems take the form: Such and such has GOT to be true. But how CAN it be? *Pegasus does not exist*, we say, and this is surely correct. How can it be, though, when there is no Pegasus for it to be true *of*? Again, a color shift too small to notice cannot possibly make the difference between red and not red. But it sometimes must, or a slippery slope argument forces us to extend redness even to green things. The number of Martian moons is indisputably two. How is that possible, when it is disputed whether numbers even exist?

Philosophy is shot through with this sort of conundrum. Subject matter enables a new style of response. The statements seem clearly correct, because the controversial bits are, in Larry Horn's phrase, assertorically inert. It is the rest, the part we care about and stand behind, that is clearly correct. If the number of Martian moons strikes us as undoubtedly two, that is because we look past the numerical packaging to the part about Mars and its moons. If subliminal color differences seem like they cannot affect whether a thing is red, that is because we see through to the part about *observational* red. Observational red really is tolerant in this way. Our mistake, which is understandable given that red was *supposed* to be observational, is to think that the observational part is the whole.

One way of cutting a claim down to size is to focus on the part about thus and such. Another is to strip away one of its implications, in an operation called *logical subtraction*. Will Rogers was engaged in subtraction when he said (of some public figure), "It's not what he doesn't know that bothers me; it's what he does know, that just isn't true." Rogers is bothered by what the public figure "knaws," where to "knaw" a thing is like knowing it, except for one detail: it might be false. Law books that define duress as "like necessity, except for the element of coercive pressure" are representing duress as the result of subtracting coercion from necessity. Cookbooks that define a gratin as a quiche that is not made in a shell are explaining *This is a gratin* as $(Q-S)\&\neg S$.[2]

Subtraction offers an alternative to the standard method of analysis, which approaches target contents from below (knowledge is belief plus truth plus...). One can also approach "from above," overshooting the target and then backtracking as necessary. Plantinga, for instance, defines warrant as whatever it is that knowledge adds to true belief. Intending to raise one's arm has been explained as raising it, minus the fact that the arm goes up. A statement is lawlike, for Goodman, if it is a law, except it might not be true.

Subtraction is a powerful operation, but a perilous one. Ask yourself what drinking adds to ingesting, or scarlet adds to red. Subject matter can be helpful here. To each B corresponds the matter of whether or not B is the case. If we understand $A-B$ as the part of A that is not about whether B,

---

[2] Where Q says it is a quiche, and S that it is made in a shell. The example is from Fuhrmann (1999). See also Fuhrmann (1996).

a story emerges about why red is more extricable from red-and-round than it is from scarlet. *B* is more or less extricable depending on how much damage is done to *A*, when we prescind from the issue of whether *B*. Not much is left of a tomato being scarlet, when we abstract away from its redness. Plenty is left of the tomato's being round and red; there is still the fact of its shape.

Assertive content—what a sentence is heard as saying—can be at quite a distance from compositional content. One would like to know how this comes about. Perhaps, as Stalnaker has suggested, assertive content is *incremental*. It is what literal content adds to information that is already on the table, or information that is backgrounded. Well, what does it add? This is a job for logical subtraction. *A*'s incremental content is *A–B*, where *B* is the background against which *A* is meant to be understood. But, while we know what this means when *B* is implied by *A*, background assumptions are oftentimes independent of *A*. (As *That guy murdered Smith* is independent of *Smith's murderer is insane*.) We are thus led to consider what *A–B* might mean in general, that is, dropping the requirement on *B* that it should follow from *A*. That *A* is heard to say that *A–B* makes for a new kind of linguistic efficiency. An overtly indexical sentence can, as we know, be made to express a variety of propositions, by shifting the context of utterance. If assertive content is incremental, then any sentence whatever can be made to do this, by varying background assumptions.

Nobody wakes up thinking, today would be a good day to cram subject matters into meanings. If they *are* to be introduced, the conservative choice would be Lewisian subject matters (Lewis 1988b): equivalence relations on, or partitions of, logical space. I will argue for going one step further, to similarity relations on, or "divisions" of, logical space. These allow us to deal—since similarity is intransitive, and a division's cells can overlap—with sentences (such as *Snow is white or cold*) whose truth-value is overdetermined: sentences true in two ways at once.

Overdetermination is not the only challenge we face. A division's cells are incomparable, so allowance has not been made for "nested" truthmakers: truthmakers some of which are stronger than others. *There are infinitely many moments of time* is true because t_0, t_1, t_2, t_3, etc. are moments of time. But the fact that t_1, t_2, t_3, etc. are moments of time, which is weaker but still sufficient, ought presumably to be a truthmaker as well. It seems we need to loosen up still further, and allow as a possible subject matter for A any old sets of worlds that cover between them the A-worlds—any old "cover" of the A-region, in the jargon.[3]

No doubt further refinements are possible. One has to stop somewhere, though, and we stop in this book at divisions, leaving covers for another day.[4] Such a compromise won't please everyone, but it makes for a cleaner and clearer picture, albeit slightly more complicated than Lewis's picture. Details are given in "Aboutness Theory" (available via http://press.princeton.edu/titles/10013.html).

---

[3] I am thinking here of sets that sum to *exactly* the A-worlds. Normally the sum would be expected only to include the A-worlds.

[4] Occasional note will be made of them in the text, and we allow ourselves the occasional sample sentence whose subject matter is likelier a cover than a division. Certain cases of part-whole require them too. Not every truthmaker for *Tom is red* (Tom is crimson, e.g.) is implied by a truthmaker for *Tom is scarlet*. But, truthmakers enough to cover the region where Tom is red have this property. Thanks to Brad Skow, Cian Dorr, Johan van Benthem, and Kit Fine for discussion.

- 1 -

I Wasn't Talking about That

1.1 EXCUSES

Carl Hempel, in whose honor these lectures are given, once wrote of some other lectures, given by Rudolf Carnap at Harvard in the 1930s. Carnap is supposed to have introduced his topic as follows:

> Let *A* be some physical body, such as a stone, or a tree, or—to borrow an example from Russell—a dog.[1]

I wish I could explain my topic the way Carnap explained his, with an example devised by Russell. But I am going to be talking about subject matter, meaning, truth, reasons for truth, contents, parts of contents, extricability of one content from another—as in Wittgenstein's famous example of subtracting *My arm went up* from *I raised my arm*—and philosophical applications of the above. These sorts of notions do not especially lend themselves to introduction by example, or to the extent they do, the examples won't mean much except surrounded by so much commentary as to defeat the purpose.[2]

I will try to set the mood with some stories. They are, to begin with anyway, on the theme of semantic excuses—excuses that might be given for saying things that are or may be untrue.

"You never take me out for ice cream any more," Zina complained recently. I observed that we had been out for ice cream the day before, on her birthday. "I know," she said, "I wasn't talking about that."

---

[1] Hempel (1975, 262). The story is meant to illustrate Carnap's "punctiliousness."
[2] Russell does comment in one place on partial truth, in a spirit of parody. Certain philosophers, he says, having "arrived at results incompatible with the existence of error, ... have then had to add a postscript explaining that what we call error is really partial truth. If we think it is Tuesday when it is really Wednesday, we are at least right in thinking that it is a day of the week. If we think America was discovered in 1066, we are at least right in thinking that something important happened in that year" (Russell 1910, 88).

This struck me at the time as not a very convincing reply.[3] If you advance a generalization, and there are counterexamples, it seems a lame defense to say that you weren't talking about them. Later, though, I realized matters were not so simple. For I was reminded of another story in which a basically similar excuse did not seem so lame.

The second story concerns a metaphysician named Sally. Her dissertation was on the same sort of topic as Carnap's lectures: physical objects and their identity over time. This presented a problem when it came to applying for jobs, for one invariably speaks in this area about persistence through gain or loss of *properties*. And Sally didn't want to take a position on the metaphysics of properties, or even on whether such things existed. She would explain at her interviews that when she spoke, for instance, of a tomato "losing the property of being green and gaining the property of being red," this was not meant to express any sort of ontological commitment to redness as an entity in its own right. The issue was really to do with the tomato and its changing color. One of the interviewers took issue with this approach. Properties are not real, he said. To speak of "them" as gained or lost is just false; it is advisable at a job interview to stick to the truth.

I will leave the rest of the story to a footnote,[4] because the aspect that matters to us is this: Sally made a statement implying the existence of properties, a statement that she knew to be false if properties didn't exist. But she was absolutely unbothered by the possibility that properties didn't exist. Her excuse for this insouciance was that her topic was material objects and how they persist through change—not the properties, if such there be, of those objects.

But, how is it an excuse for asserting falsehoods (or potential falsehoods) to explain that one was talking about such and such? How is

---

[3] I may have been influenced by the memory of an earlier exchange. "Isaac got a bag of popcorn. That's not fair." "Huh? You got one, too." "I wasn't talking about that." You can't make things unequal by refusing to talk about one of them. The example in the text is not so silly.

[4] Interviewer: "We on the East Coast have arguments disproving the existence of properties." Sally: "This isn't really my battle, but why don't you tell me what the arguments are, and we can take it from there." Interviewer: "I shouldn't have to tell you what our East Coast arguments are. You're applying for a job in metaphysics; you should know them." Sally: "I see. Well, we on the West Coast have replies to your East Coast arguments. I won't repeat them here since they will be old news to a pro like yourself."

misrepresenting the facts in the course of addressing a certain topic any better than misrepresenting them with topic unspecified?

An answer is suggested by my third story. The third story is due to Nelson Goodman and Joseph Ullian, in a paper called "Truth about Jones" (Ullian and Goodman 1977). Jones is on trial for murder and Falstaff is chief witness for the defense. Jones's attorney concedes there is a problem with Falstaff's testimony: It is false. That would seem to make the testimony worthless, but the attorney (Lupoli, he's called) thinks he sees a way out. The testimony was indeed about his client Jones—no getting around that. And it was false—no getting around that, either. But, Lupoli insists, the testimony was not *false about Jones*. The judge calls this nonsense and declares a recess, threatening Lupoli with contempt unless he can explain how the very same sentences can be (i) false, and (ii) about Jones, yet not (iii) false about Jones.

I hope you see a connection with the earlier stories. Just as Zina and Sally were not concerned if their statements were strictly speaking false, Lupoli does not care if Falstaff's testimony was false. It is enough for Lupoli if the testimony was *partly* true—true in what it said about Jones. Maybe that should be Zina's excuse, too. "You never take me to Friendly's" may not have been true overall, but it was true about what *usually* happens, birthdays aside. And maybe it should be Sally's excuse; it is enough for her if "The tomato lost one property and gained another" was true in what it said *about the tomato*. Maybe it is enough, in some contexts, if a statement is *partly* true—true in what it says about the subject matter under discussion.

1.2 PURITANISM

This idea of being *partly* true is apt to arouse suspicion. It is hard not to share the judge's frustration when he threatens Lupoli with contempt. The phrase "partly true" is perfectly good English, of course. Apparently it was decent Greek too; the creation myth in the Phaedrus is described by Socrates as "partly true and tolerably credible." When Cratylus tells Socrates it would be "nonsensical" to address him using somebody else's name, Socrates responds, "Well, but [it] will be quite enough for me, if you will tell me whether the nonsense would be true or false, or partly true and partly false:—which is all that I want to know." That is actually not a bad statement of one theme of these lectures: sometimes whether a statement is *partly* true is all that we want to know.

Why, then, do I say that it doesn't come naturally to us to settle for partial truth? Consider a fourth story, this one due to the psychoanalyst Melanie Klein. (She didn't consider it just a story, of course.) Newborns, in Klein's view, face an enormous cognitive challenge—they have to put the things that gratify them together with the things that frustrate them into a single world. They must take it on board, as Klein put it, that the good breast, which turns up when they're hungry, and the bad breast, which is withheld, are the very same breast. This hurdle is usually cleared at around four months, she thinks, at which point the infant moves from the paranoid-schizoid position to the apparently far preferable depressive position.

That, anyway, is the normal case. Occasionally, the integration challenge proves too great, and the individual never really wraps their mind around the fact that a thing can have good and bad in it. The result is the cognitive style known as "black/white thinking" or "polarized thinking." A black/white thinker is the type of person who loves you or hates you, according to how recently you've disappointed them. They're the type of person, more generally, who insists on dividing the world up into good, full stop, and bad, full stop.

This kind of attitude is familiar with kids, of course, and forgivable there. I recall my son Isaac squirming around in his seat at the movie *Shrek*, unable to settle down until he knew whether Donkey (the Eddie Murphy character) was a *good* donkey or a *bad* donkey.

But imagine you're watching the news with full-grown neighbors, and all they want to talk about is: Is this Hugo Chávez fellow a good man or a bad man? When you try to suggest it's more complicated than that, they reject this as spineless evasion. Answer the question, they say. That is black/white thinking, and it surely deserves its reputation as pathological.

Our assessment changes, though, when the focus shifts from goodness to truth. Demanding to know whether a statement is true, full stop, or false, full stop, is considered forthright and healthy minded, not pathological in the least. It is almost as if, having lost our Kleinian paranoia about goodness, there was no energy left to outgrow the analogous attitude about truth. A second theme of these lectures is that this is nevertheless worth doing, or insofar as we've already done it, owning up to doing. Let us put the paranoid-schizoid position on truth behind us, and go boldly forth to the depressive position. (I admit it's not the best rallying cry.)

1.3 PARTIAL TRUTH AS TRUTH OF A PART

There are two questions at this point: What is partial truth? And why would we be willing settle for it? The second question I want to leave until later. The quick answer is that there are areas where if it wasn't for partial truth, we wouldn't, or might not, have any truth at all.[5]

But that, as I say, I want to leave aside the time being, to focus on the other question. What is it for a hypothesis to be partly true?[6] Here is the naivest possible idea about this:

> 1 A hypothesis is partly true iff it has parts that are wholly true.

Now we must ask what is meant by *part* of a hypothesis. The naivest possible idea about part/whole as a relation on hypotheses is

> 2 One hypothesis is part of another iff it is implied by the other.[7]

A includes *B*, in other words, just if it implies *B*.

The naivest possible idea about partial truth is on the right track, I think; something is partly true to the extent it has (nontrivial) parts that are wholly true.[8] But the naivest possible idea about what it takes for *A* to include *B* is questionable.

A paradigm of inclusion, I take it, is the relation that simple conjunctions bear to their conjuncts—the relation *Snow is white and expensive* bears,

---

[5] Adapted from "Born Under a Bad Sign" (Booker T. Jones and William Bell): "if it wasn't for bad luck, I wouldn't have no luck at all."

[6] I use the word "hypothesis" ambiguously for a sentence or its propositional content.

[7] Consider the version of (2) that focuses on propositional contents, rather than sentences. If we think of contents the way Lewis does, as sets of possible worlds, then (2) says one hypothesis includes another iff it is a subset of the other. Lewis in effect proposes this at one point, in "Statements Partly about Observation" (Lewis 1988b). He also notices that it doesn't sit very well with his view that subsets are parts of the sets they sub—which leads him to define contents, for these purposes, as the set of worlds ruled out rather than in. I don't want to dwell on these issues since (2) strikes me as pretty clearly mistaken.

[8] Perhaps the true part should be to meet other conditions besides nontriviality: it should be relevant to the matter at hand, and not overshadowed by wholly false parts of a similar form. I will stick with the pure notion that abstracts away from such issues.

for example, to *Snow is white*. A paradigm of noninclusion is the relation disjuncts bear to disjunctions; *Snow is white* does not have *Snow is white or expensive* as a part. This is not predicted by (**2**). Disjuncts imply their disjunctions every bit as much as conjunctions imply their conjuncts. There is more to inclusion than implication, apparently.

You might say that paradigm case intuitions are a poor basis for theory. But the intuitions here are systematic. A number of things suggest that parthood has an explanatory role to play that requires it to be more than mere implication.

> *Saying*: Someone who says that snow is white and expensive has said, among other things, that snow is white. This is not all they've said, but they have said it. To describe snow as white, however, is not to say inter alia that it is white or expensive. Why, when there is implication in both cases? Saying-that transmits down to the parts of what is said more easily than to "mere consequences," meaning by this consequences that are not also parts.[9]

> *Agreement*: If I describe snow as white and expensive, and you reply that it is white, but not expensive, then we agree on our statements' shared content, namely that snow is white. The content p shares with q has sometimes been defined as the strongest statement they imply in common, which is easily seen to be $p \lor q$.[10] But then, we would still have agreed on something if I had called snow white and you had called it black, namely that it is one or the other. This is not how we ordinarily think of it. Statements agree to the extent they have *parts* in common.

> *Musts*: Ordering Smith to eat pork chops is ordering her to eat pork. Ordering her to eat pork is not ordering her to eat pork or human flesh,

---

[9] "[C]onsider the case of a conjunctive sentence *Sam is at work and Susan is at the market.* Someone who assertively utters this sentence asserts the conjunctive proposition that Sam is at work and Susan is at the market. But surely such a person also asserts the proposition that Sam is at work.... . The reason the speaker is counted as asserting that Sam is at work is that this proposition is a trivial consequence of the conjunctive proposition the speaker asserts" (Soames 2002, 61). Soames probably does not mean to be suggesting that trivial consequences are always asserted. My own view is that they are typically not asserted, unless they are parts.

[10] Hempel says, for instance, that a disjunction "expresses the common content" of its disjuncts (Hempel 1960, 465).

though eating pork or human flesh is no less implied by eating pork than eating pork is by eating pork chops. One commands (normally) the parts of what one commands, but not its implications more generally. A similar pattern obtains with "must" and "required": I must do the parts of what's required of me, not random consequences.

Mights: If Smith and Jones might have pork chops for dinner, then they might have pork for dinner. That they might have pork does not similarly entail that Smith and Jones might have pork for dinner or human flesh. Epistemic possibility extends to the parts of a hypothesis, as opposed to its consequences more generally.

Priority: Conjuncts are apt strike us as prior to—preconditions of—the conjunctions in which they figure, while disjunctions are posterior to—consequent on—their disjuncts. p must hold before $p \& q$ can hold, but it is not the case that $p \lor q$ must hold before p can hold. A similar pattern obtains with generalizations. Parts are prior to their implying wholes, it seems, while other consequences—"mere consequences"—are posterior to, or logically downwind from, their impliers.

Explanation: The falsity of a conjunct p explains the falsity of $p \& q$. But the falsity of a disjunction $p \lor q$ only guarantees, without explaining, the falsity of its disjunct p. Why? If S has a false part, S will be false due to the falsity of that part. A part's falsity is well positioned to explain the falsity of the whole. But for a mere consequence to be false is a symptom of S's falsity, not the reason for it.

Confirmation: A well-known model of confirmation says that theories T are confirmed by their true consequences. If this includes *mere* consequences, then every truth helps with the confirmation of every theory, for T entails its disjunction with that truth. Parts confirm better than mere consequences. *All ravens are black* is better confirmed by *This raven is black* than by *All ravens are black, or all are white, or all are red, and so on*.[11]

---

[11] This relates to the "tacking by disjunction" problem in confirmation theory (see Hempel 1960, Grimes 1990, Gemes 1998, Moretti 2006).

Knowledge: Looking at a ripe tomato tells me that it is red, but not, it seems, that the tomato does not misleadingly appear to be red. The calendar tells me I'll be teaching logic next fall, but not that I won't die in the meantime.[12] Is it a coincidence that the elusive implications here are not included in their impliers? The counterexamples that have been suggested to epistemic closure principles all share this feature. Perhaps knowing a thing suffices, not for knowing its consequences generally, but only for knowing its parts.

And then, of course

Partial truth: *Snow is white and expensive* is made partly true by the fact that snow is white. *Snow is expensive* is not made partly true by the fact that snow is white or expensive. Again, *Everything ages* is partly true by virtue of the fact that *Wood ages*, whereas *Wood is edible* is not made partly true by the fact that *Something is edible*. Why these differences? True parts confer partial truth on their wholes. Other true implications lack this power.

More is involved, it seems, in B's being part of A than B's being implied by A; parts are special and behave differently from mere consequences. What is the missing ingredient? What is the X such that

$$Parthood = implication + X?$$

The stories we began with suggest an answer. Falstaff's testimony is partly true because *the part that concerns Jones* is wholly true. Zina's statement to the effect that I never take her for ice cream is partly true because the part about what *usually* happens—what happens birthdays aside—is wholly true. Sally's statement about the tomato retaining its identity as its properties change is partly true because *it is true as far as the tomato is concerned*. A statement's parts are identified in all of these cases by looking for an implication *whose subject matter is part of the subject matter of the original statement*.

The proposal is that for B to be part of A involves, in addition to A implying B, that B's subject matter be part of A's subject matter. Conversely, the reason A's implications are sometimes *not* included in A is that they

[12] Vogel (1990), Cohen (2002).

bring in alien subject matter, subject matter foreign to A. *Grass is green* does not include *Grass is green or radioactive* because the latter brings in the matter of radioactivity, which is absent from *Grass is green.*

Content-inclusion is implication plus subject-matter inclusion. Both of these are relations in which a semantically important property is preserved: truth, in the one case, and aboutness, in the other. So the proposal can be put like this:

3 *B* is part of *A* iff the inference from *A* to *B* is

    (i) truth-preserving—*A* implies *B*
    (ii) aboutness-preserving—*A*'s subject matter includes that of *B*.

For this to work, however, we will need a notion of *overall sentential subject matter*—of what a sentence is overall about—such that each sentence winds up with just one of them. There will have to be such a thing as *the* subject matter of *S*.[13] We return to this issue in section **2.7** and chapter **4**.

1.4 ABOUTNESS IN HISTORY

Contents have parts. Identifying them will require us to broaden our focus from truth-conditions to what sentences are about, their subject matters. (A third theme of these lectures is that there are *lots* of things to understand which it helps to look beyond truth-conditions to subject matters.)[14]

To speak of "broadening" our focus suggests that subject matter has been neglected in philosophy. This is true, I think (some exceptions will be noted below). How many times have you heard a philosopher reject the analysis of *P* as ϕ on the grounds that their truth-conditions differ; *P* can be true when ϕ is false, or vice versa? (Plato on justice, Gettier on knowledge, Frankfurt on freedom and responsibility,...) Broadening the focus from truth-conditions gives us another way to challenge proposed philosophical analyses. *P* and ϕ may be true in the same cases, but ϕ gets the subject

---

[13] Or, *S*'s subject matter in a particular context of utterance.
[14] The first two were: whether a statement is *partly* true may be all that we want to know; and, acknowledging this is difficult but worth doing, or insofar as we've already done it, owning up to doing.

matter wrong; P is about one thing, ϕ is about something else. How many times have you heard a philosopher argue like *that*?

Subject matters have been relatively neglected, not completely neglected. One example of non-neglect is Frege's work on informative identity statements. He initially held that "Hesperus = Phosphorus" says of the words "Hesperus" and "Phosphorus" that they refer to the same object. His reason for rejecting this early account was *not* that it assigned the wrong truth-values—"Hesperus = Phosphorus" is indeed true if and only if "Hesperus" and "Phosphorus" have a shared referent—but that it gets the subject matter wrong. "Hesperus = Phosphorus" is about the planets Hesperus and Phosphorus, not our devices for picking those planets out. Frege's new explanation in terms of sense arguably runs into a similar problem. It is certainly not trivial that the sense of *Hesperus* picks out the same object as that of *Phosphorus*. But this, it may be felt, cannot explain the informativeness of *Hesperus = Phosphorus* unless the sentence *says* of the two senses that they pick out the same object. And *Hesperus = Phosphorus* does not say anything about senses; it's about planets.[15]

Frege's theory of existence-claims has been questioned on a similar basis. The theory treats existence as a property, not of the things we call existent, but of *concepts* instantiated by those things. *Biden exists* says of our Biden-concept that it has instances. That is certainly not how it feels! In attributing existence to a thing x, we speak of x, not some concept it falls under.[16]

Or consider Kripke's famous objection to counterpart theory. Humphrey is in despair, because he lost an election he could have won. Counterpart theory understands his possibly winning the election as the winner being, in some other world, a man who suitably resembles Humphrey. But, Kripke suggests, "Humphrey could care less whether someone else ... would have been victorious in [another] world" (Kripke 1980, 45). This has been called an argument from *concern*—Humphrey doesn't *care* about the someone else—but that doesn't really get to the heart of the matter. The lack of concern stems from a prior circumstance that would be just as problematic if Humphrey did care:

> if we say, *Humphrey might have won the election* ... we are not [according to counterpart theory] talking about something that might have

---

[15] Perry (2011).
[16] Quine's adaptation of Frege is an improvement in this respect: *Something bidenizes* has the truth-conditions Frege wanted, but without the allusion to concepts.

happened to Humphrey but to someone else, a "counterpart." (Kripke 1980, 45)

Humphrey doesn't care about what the counterpart-theorist is offering him, because it has the wrong subject matter; the winner is someone else.[17] Kripke himself appears to get the subject matter wrong in places. Consider how he explains the intuition that heat might have been low mean molecular energy (Kripke 1980, 131). The problem is that we confuse *that* putative possibility with the possibility that *low molecular energy could have felt this way to creatures with different neural wiring.*[18] But, the thought that this heat I am now feeling could have been low energy is a thought about this heat I am now feeling, not the way it feels to local observers whomever they may be. The possibility Kripke points to *might* explain the intuition that low molecular energy could have felt a certain way *to us*, if, as he imagines, it's a contingent fact about us to have this particular neural structure. But the intuition that this thing we are sensing could have been low molecular energy is not an intuition about us. One imagines a switcheroo *out there*, where the heat is, not back here where it is being observed.[19]

Constructive empiricists maintain that science aims, not at true theories, but empirically adequate ones. A theory is empirically adequate if its observational content is true. What is observational content? Earlier

---

[17] The Humphrey objection has been called unconvincing on the ground that it is *Humphrey himself*, not his counterpart, who is a possible president on the counterpart-theoretic account. But I hear the objection differently. Kripke is complaining, not that *Humphrey could have won* winds up *not* being about the guy it intuitively *does* concern (Humphrey), but that it winds up *also* being about a guy it intuitively *doesn't* concern (a guy only resembling Humphrey).

[18] "It seems to me that any case which someone will think of, which he thinks at first is a case in which heat—contrary to what is actually the case—would have been something other than molecular motion, would actually be a case in which some creatures with different nerve endings from ours inhabit this planet (maybe even we, if it's a contingent fact about us that we have this particular neural structure), and in which these creatures were sensitive to that something else, say light, in such a way that they felt the same thing that we feel when we feel heat" (Kripke 1980, 131–132).

[19] A proper Kripke-style explanation of the intuition that *that* (heat) could have been low molecular energy would invoke a doppelganger of heat with low molecular energy as its underlying constitution. It would appeal to the possibility of substituting low energy for high while retaining outward appearances. There is no such possibility, however (Yablo 2006a)! Which is presumably why Kripke posits a switcheroo on the observer side rather than the observed.

empiricists had sought to explain it as content expressible in observational *vocabulary*. Van Fraassen argues that it is not a distinctive vocabulary we should be appealing to here, but a distinctively observational *subject matter*. A theory's observational content is not what *part* of the theory, formulated in a restricted vocabulary, says about *all* of reality; it's what *all* of the theory says about *part* of reality, the observable part.[20] Elliott Sober notes that van Fraassen is employing here an undefined notion:

> Our total body of beliefs is empirically adequate if all its claims about observables are true.... [But] van Fraassen never provides a characterisation of the aboutness relation (Sober 1985, 14).

This is no idle worry, because some very common ideas about aboutness lead to results van Fraassen would not accept. Dirt is observable, surely. Why wouldn't a claim about its subatomic structure be a claim about observables, then, so that getting that structure wrong makes it empirically inadequate? Subatomic structure is the paradigm, of course, of an issue that empirically adequate theories can afford to get wrong. If van Fraassen is not to deny the observability of dirt, he had better deny that *S is a claim about such and such* and *Such and such is observable* imply *S is a claim about observables*. This is none too easy a thing to do. The point for now is that the proper formulation of constructive empiricism turns on how we understand aboutness.

Our final example concerns epistemic modality rather than metaphysical. The standard analysis of *It might be that φ* has it expressing something in the neighborhood of *I don't know that not-φ*. But that cannot be right. Suppose Mary asks Jen where Bob is, and receives the answer, *He might be in his office*. This statement Mary receives in reply is directed at the very same issue as her question: Bob and his location. It is *not* about the extent of Jen's knowledge.[21] There is a concern aspect here, too. Imagine that the building has caught fire and we are out on the sidewalk looking around for colleagues. Bob is nowhere to be seen. I am worried that he might be still in his office. The limited extent of my information does not worry me in

---

[20] This is ignoring van Fraassen's conception of theories as sets of models. He himself would explain the observational part of a theory semantically, in terms of model extensions. Muller and van Fraassen (2008) is an interesting recent discussion.

[21] If it were, the following would be a much less ridiculous conversation. Mary: *Where is Bob?* Jen: *Bob might be in his office.* Mary: *Will you please get over yourself?*

the slightest; it plays a role in *why* I am worried, perhaps, but it is not what I am worried *about*.[22]

These sorts of examples notwithstanding, subject matter has often been dismissed as just a way station on the road to truth-conditions. And a somewhat arbitrary way station at that, because, as many authors have been concerned to emphasize, one can scramble what subsentential expressions refer to while leaving truth-conditions the same. This is argued, for instance, in Quine, "Ontological Relativity" (Quine 1996), Davidson, "Reality without Reference" (Davidson 2007), and Putnam, "Models and Reality" (Putnam 1980). Quine seems to suggest that not much would be lost if we assigned numbers to every material object and read statements seemingly about the latter as really about the associated numbers; "I am hungry" would say of the number 18 that it is hungry*, where to be hungry* is to have your associated person be hungry.

A sentence's truth-conditions underdetermine its subject matter; they can be arrived at via any number of reference-assignments, as long as compensating changes are made in the interpretation of predicates. This might be taken to show that subject matter is less well grounded than truth-conditions, or even somehow less real. But the more natural conclusion is that we have in subject matter a potentially independent factor in overall meaning, one that can vary even as truth-conditions remain the same.

1.5 HEMPEL'S RAVENS

A good, anyway tempting in the present context, illustration is Hempel's raven paradox. *All ravens are black* is true in the same circumstances as *All nonblack things are nonravens*. One would expect, then, that data confirming the one should equally confirm the other. And yet a black raven seems more confirmationally relevant to *All ravens are black* than to *All nonblack things are nonravens*, while a nonblack nonraven seems (if anything) more confirmationally relevant to *All nonblack things are nonravens* than to *All ravens are black*. Fruit bats seem to bear more directly on *No fructivores are ungulates* than herbivorous cows; with *No ungulates are fructivores*, which is equivalent, it's the other way around.

---

[22] Veltman (1996), Yalcin (2007), Yablo (2011).

Here is what I think we are tempted to say, before the confirmation theorists get to us. *No Fs are Gs* and *No Gs are Fs* are true in the same scenarios, but they are about different things. One is about the world's *Fs* and which if any are *G*; the other is about its *Gs* and which if any are *F*. To confirm a hypothesis about the properties of one kind of thing, one should look at examples of that kind of thing, while to confirm hypotheses about another kind of thing's properties, one should look at examples of that other kind of thing.[23]

This is not a very sophisticated or well-developed reply. And there's an obvious objection. How can a difference in subject matter make for a confirmational difference, when confirmation is to do with likelihood of truth, and the statements are truth-conditionally equivalent?

Goodman distinguishes two ways a generalization can be confirmed by its instances. There's first the basic, boring kind of confirmation you get by eliminating a potential counterexample—the way my being born on a Tuesday confirms that all of us here were born on a Tuesday. Then there's the kind of confirmation that is supposed to occur in induction, where the fact that this *P* before us is *Q* makes it likelier that other *Ps*, not yet observed, are *Q*. For an instance to *inductively* confirm a hypothesis it has to bear favorably on—increase the likelihood of—the hypothesis's *other* instances, especially the untested ones.[24]

Now, a generalization's instances might well be considered *parts* of that generalization; let's assume that is right and see where it gets us.[25] Inductive confirmers should increase the likelihood, not only of the generalization itself (that much occurs already in content-cutting), but also its parts, especially the untested parts. Inductive confirmation so understood has nothing syntactic about it. We can ask of any kind of hypothesis, and any evidence, whether *E* confirms *H* "pervasively," in a way that penetrates down to (bubbles up from?) its parts.

An *E* that confirms *H* in the basic sense may well count *against* a lot of *H*, as long as the net effect is positive. *Rudy looks black* may not seem

---

[23] Hempel floats a similar idea: "Perhaps the impression of the paradoxical character of [these cases] may be said to grow out of the feeling that the hypothesis that *All ravens are black* is about ravens, and not about non-black things, nor about all things" (Hempel 1945a, 17).
[24] Ken Gemes calls the boring kind of confirmation "mere content-cutting"; see Gemes (1998) and Gemes (2007b).
[25] See section **6.5** for discussion.

like evidence for *Rudy looks black but is white*. It is, though, if it's only the net effect that matters. *Rudy looks black but is white* is, taken in its entirety, likelier conditional on *Rudy looks black* than absolutely. If the case still bothers us, that's because we are thinking of inductive/pervasive confirmation. *E* does not pervasively confirm *H* because the latter has a part, namely *Rudy is white*, that is not confirmed (in the basic sense) by Rudy looking black.

Now we are getting somewhere. If to inductively confirm a hypothesis involves probabilifying its parts, then hypotheses differing in their parts are going to differ confirmationally as well—even if, like *All ravens are black* and *All nonblack things are nonravens*—they're true in the same scenarios.[26]

Parthood is defined in terms of subject matter, and inductive/pervasive confirmation is to do with parts. Subject matter differences make for mereological differences make for confirmational differences. This is what we find with *All ravens are black* and *All nonblack things are nonravens*: the color of ravens is a different matter than the biological type of nonblack things. Rudy's color speaks only to the first of these.

So that's the fourth theme: subject matters are an important and potentially independent factor in meaning, over and above truth-conditional content.[27] The fifth theme is that they are not as independent a factor as all that, because what a sentence is about is deeply tied up with its ways (in this world and others) of being true.[28] *All ravens are black* is about ravens and how they are colored, not how writing desks are colored or whether

---

[26] Instance confirmation is mostly ignored these days, for good reason: instances are identified syntactically, and, Hempel's early hopes notwithstanding, syntactic views of confirmation have not panned out. And yet confirmation by positive instances remains the intuitive paradigm; ravens and emeralds are wheeled out on the first day of class. This is puzzling. Why mention the instantiation relation at all, if it is syntactic and marginal to the project of confirmation theory? I suspect that we see through it to another relation—that of part to whole—that is (a) central to the project of confirmation theory and (b) in a good sense syntax-free.

[27] The first three were: whether a statement is *partly* true may be all that we want to know; acknowledging this is difficult but worth doing, or insofar as we've already done it, owning up to doing; to understand content-parts we have to broaden our focus from truth-conditions to subject matter.

[28] By a sentence's truth-conditional content, I have in mind a Lewis-style proposition—a set of possible worlds, or, to allow for partial propositions, a (not necessarily total) function from worlds to truth-values. Propositions equipped with corresponding subject matters will be called *directed* contents, or sometimes *thoughts*. (Other terms sometimes used for directed and truth-conditional contents are *thick* and *thin*.)

nonblack things fail to be ravens. This seems not unconnected to the fact that it is true in a world because, or by way of, or in virtue of, what that world's *ravens* are like, not the properties of writing desks or nonblack things. Which seems in turn not unconnected to the fact that its way of being true *changes* when we move to a world with different ravens, but not (or not necessarily) when we move to a world with different writing desks, and so forth.

1.6 SUMMING UP

Partial truth is apt to strike us as sneaky, unclean, the last refuge of a scoundrel. But, whether a statement is partly true, or true in what it says about BLAH, may be all that we want to know. A statement S is partly true insofar as it has wholly true parts: wholly true implications whose subject matter is included in that of S. An account of subject matter will thus be needed, and of the relation ("aboutness") that sentences bear to their subject matters, if we want to understand partial truth.

Aboutness has been somewhat neglected in philosophy. But not entirely; think of Frege on identity, Kripke on counterparts, van Fraassen on empirical adequacy, Yalcin on epistemic modals, and Hempel on confirmation. Subject matter will be treated here as an independent factor in meaning, over and above truth-conditional content. Not completely independent, though, for what a sentence is about is tied up with its ways of being true and false.

- 2 -

Varieties of Aboutness

2.1 EXISTING PROPOSALS

A few philosophers have tried to think systematically about subject matter, starting with Gilbert Ryle in his 1933 *Analysis* paper "About" (Ryle 1933). Nelson Goodman tries to improve on Ryle in a 1961 paper of the same name (Goodman 1961).[1] The best and most thorough account to date is David Lewis's in "Statements Partly about Observation" (Lewis 1988b).[2]

A sentence is about whatever it mentions, Ryle proposes, where to mention an item k is to contain a word or phrase k that designates it.[3] *Jones climbed Helvellyn* is about Jones and Helvellyn, because it contains *Jones* and *Helvellyn*. There is a danger now of *Jones climbed Helvellyn* coming out with the same aboutness-properties as *Jones mined Helvellyn*; this leads Ryle to extend the account

> to cover parts of speech which are not nouns. . . . A conversation would be "about" climbing, although the noun "climbing" nowhere occurred, but verbs such as "climbed" and adjectives such as "climbable" were common to all or most of the sentences. (Ryle 1933, 11)

Goodman objects that a statement is not only about what is mentioned in it. *Everyone has their secrets* is in part about the author, despite not containing any expressions designating the author. *Maine is prosperous* is about New England, though nothing in it designates New England. His first proposal is this: S is about k if k is mentioned either in S or in a statement R it suitably implies. *Everyone has a secret* implies *The oldest person*

---

[1] See also Carnap (2002), 284–292, Putnam (1958), Putnam and Ullian (1965), and Perry (1989). Perry discusses a suggestion of Barbara Partee's about the recovery of subject matter from truth-conditions.

[2] See also Lewis (1988a). Lewis's account is further developed in Humberstone (2000). Two influential papers in library science/information theory are Hutchins (1977) and Demolombe and Jones (1998).

[3] Atlas (1988) holds that this gets things backwards: mentioning is to be explained rather in terms of aboutness.

has a secret, *The second oldest person has a secret*, and so on; and eventually we reach an implication in which I am mentioned. *Maine is prosperous* is about New England, because it implies *Of the New England states, at least one is prosperous*.

Goodman's trick is *too* powerful, one might think, for *Maine is prosperous* implies statements mentioning whatever you like. Surely it does not get to be about Texas just by implying *Maine is prosperous or Texas is*! Remember, though, S must "suitably" imply a statement mentioning k. Suitable implication is *selective* implication; S should imply $R(k)$ without implying that $R(x)$ holds for every x whatsoever. Texas doesn't come into it, for what *Maine is prosperous* implies about Texas it implies about everything. Selective implication swings too far in the other direction, however. *Everything ages* is about everything, me included. But *Yablo ages* is not selectively implied. Goodman has an idea about this, too, but we've probably seen enough to want to explore other options.

Anyway, there is from our present perspective a more basic problem. Each sentence S is, in Goodman's view, about a *lot* of things. And we need a *single* subject matter (call it s) to slot into our proposed definition (**3**) of content-part.

Could s be built somehow out of S's Goodmanian subject matters, say, as their set, or sum? There is a difficulty about any approach that tries to build S's subject matter up out of the items mentioned in it. A sentence's subject matter has to do with what it *says*; and what it says depends not just on the words employed, but how the words are ordered.

> When a dog bites a man, that is not news, because it happens so often.
> But if a man bites a dog, that is news. (John B. Bogart, editor of the
> *New York Sun*)

Why is MAN BITES DOG a better headline than DOG BITES MAN? One thing we can certainly say here is that it is on a more interesting topic. A more interesting topic is a different topic. And yet the same items are mentioned in both.

A sentence's subject matter depends on what it says, because subject matter is to do with ways of being true, and the ways a sentence can be true depend on what it says. Perhaps we can turn this into a definition: the subject matter of S is the (smallest?) m such that facts about m determine whether the sentence is true.

Unfortunately, the question of when a *fact* is about such and such is not much easier than the corresponding question about sentences. Is the idea that m's *properties* determine the sentence's truth-value? This is trivial unless the properties are somehow restricted. (Texas has the property of coexisting with unprosperous Maine.) Maybe what we are after is an item whose *intrinsic* properties determine truth-value, as the nineteenth century's intrinsic properties settle the truth-value of sentences entirely about goings on in that century.

The nineteenth century is for Lewis a *kind* of subject matter; it's the kind he calls *parts-based*. m is parts-based, if for worlds to be alike with respect to m is for corresponding parts of those worlds to be intrinsically indiscernible. The nineteenth century is parts-based because worlds are alike where it is concerned if and only if the one's nineteenth century is an intrinsic duplicate of the other's nineteenth century. Note that the nineteenth century ≠ the nineteenth century. The first is a part of one particular world (ours), or of its history. The second is a way of *grouping* worlds according to what goes on in their respective nineteenth centuries.

This approach is not sufficiently general. Take the matter of how many stars there are. Astronomers have not discovered a "star-counter" part of the universe, such that worlds agree in how many stars they contain if and only if the one's counter is an intrinsic duplicate of the other's. Facts about how many stars there are not stored up in particular spatiotemporal regions.

Or consider the matter of observables,[4] mentioned above in connection with constructive empiricism. This is prima facie a parts-based subject matter, like the biggest star. Worlds are observationally equivalent just if their observables—whatever in them can be seen, heard, and so on— are intrinsically just alike. But again, dirt can be seen, and among dirt's intrinsic properties are some that are highly theoretical, for instance, the property of being full of quarks. It is not supposed to count against a theory's empirical adequacy that it gets subatomic structure wrong.

Observables—what an empirically adequate theory should get right— is better regarded as a *non*-parts-based subject matter, like the number of stars. Worlds are alike with respect to observables if they're observationally indistinguishable; they look and feel and sound (etc.) the same. But now a question arises. What becomes of the idea, seemingly essential to

---

[4] Lewis calls it observation.

constructive empiricism, that T need only be true to the observable part of reality, if observables does not correspond to a part of reality? Something is said about this in section **2.3**.

2.2 FROM PARTS TO PARTITIONS

A parts-based subject matter, whatever else it does, induces an equivalence relation on, or partition of, "logical space."[5] Worlds are equivalent, or cell-mates, if corresponding parts are intrinsically alike.

A *non*-parts-based subject matter, however, *also* induces an equivalence relation on logical space: worlds are equivalent, or cell-mates, just in case they are indiscernible where that subject matter is concerned. If m is the number of stars, $\equiv_m$ is the relation one world bears to another just if they have equally many stars. But then, if one wants a notion of subject matter that works for both cases, let them be not *parts* but *partitions*. The second notion subsumes the first while exceeding it in generality.

To review—one starts out thinking of subject matters as parts of the world, like the western hemisphere or Queen Victoria or the nineteenth century. These then give way to world-*partitions*, which are ways of grouping worlds. Should the grouping be on the basis of goings on in corresponding world-parts, we get a kind of subject matter that, although still thoroughly partitional, looks back to world-parts for its identity-conditions. The distinction here, between part and part-based partition, is subtle and easy to lose track of. We have the good fortune of an Oscar Wilde story to help us remember it.

Wilde offered on some occasion to construct a pun on any subject. What about the queen? someone suggested. "The Queen is not a subject," he replied. Our theory supports Wilde on this point. Consider Albert, prince consort. He lived in the nineteenth century. The nineteenth century is a thing in, or part of, the world. Living in the nineteenth century is not the same as living in an equivalence relation. The subject matter that groups

---

[5] Lewis (1988b). An equivalence relation $\equiv$ is a binary R that's reflexive (everything bears R to itself), symmetric (if x bears R to y, then y bears R to x), and transitive (if x bears R to y and y bears it to z, then x bears R to z). A partition is a decomposition of some set into mutually disjoint subsets, called cells. Equivalence relations are interdefinable with partitions as follows: x's cell $[x]$ is the set of ys equivalent to x; $x \equiv y$ if they lie in the same cell.

worlds on the basis of how well their nineteenth centuries match up is the nineteenth century. Again, Albert was married to the queen. The queen is a thing in, or part of, of the world. The queen is a relation or partition; it groups worlds on the basis of their queen-parts. Albert was married to a person, not a subject matter. The queen is not a subject (matter). That would be the queen.

A subject matter—I'll sometimes say *topic*, or *matter*, or *issue*—is a system of differences, a pattern of cross-world variation.[6] Where the identity of a set is given by its members, the identity of a subject matter m is given by the pattern of trans-world changes where m is concerned:

> 4 $m_1 = m_2$ iff worlds differing where the first is concerned differ also with respect to the second, and vice versa.

This might seem too abstract and structural. To know what m_1 is as opposed to m_2 doesn't seem to tell us what goes into a world's m_1-condition, as opposed to its m_2-condition. Shouldn't we know, to grasp a subject matter m, the proposition $m(w)$ that specifies how matters stand in w where m is concerned?

But, subject matters as just explained *do* tell us what w is like where m is concerned. The proposition we're looking for is meant to be true in all and only worlds in the same m-condition as w; on an intensional view of propositions, it *is* the set of worlds in the same m-condition as w. That proposition is already in our possession. To be in the same m-condition as w is to be m-equivalent to w, and the set of worlds m-equivalent to w is just w's cell in the partition. A world's m-cell is thus the proposition saying how matters stand in it m-wise.

Lewis writes nos for the number of stars. How do we find the proposition specifying how matters stand in a world where nos is concerned? Well, w has a certain number of stars, let's say a billion. Its nos-cell is the set of worlds with exactly as many stars as w. The worlds with exactly as many stars as w are the ones with a billion stars. The worlds with a billion stars compose the proposition that there are a billion stars. That it contains

---

[6] Linguists have their own notion of topic; a sentence's topic/focus structure is something like its subject/predicate structure. Topics in the linguist's sense may or may not be reflected in a sentence's subject matter. (Note, sentential subject matter as we'll be thinking of it is still a ways off; we make a start on it in section **2.6**.)

one billion stars sums up w's nos-condition quite nicely. By transitivity of identity, its nos-cell sums up its nos-condition quite nicely.

Let's take stock. The subject matters in (4) seemed too abstract and structural to tell us what was going on m-wise in a given world. But each m determines a function m(...) that encodes precisely that information. It works backward, too; one can recover the equivalence relation from the function, by counting worlds m-equivalent if they are mapped to the same proposition.[7] m can thus be conceived as (i) an equivalence relation—that's what it is "officially"—or (ii) a partition, or (iii) a specification for each world of what is going on there m-wise. The number of stars, for instance, can be construed as a function taking each *k*-star world w to the proposition There are exactly *k* stars.

The problem may seem to recur at a deeper level. How are we to get an intuitive handle on the function m(...) taking worlds to their m-conditions? It's one thing if m(...) is introduced in the first place as specifying how many stars a given world contains. But all we know of specification functions considered in themselves is that they are mathematical objects (sets, or partial sets) built in such and such ways out of worlds. It is not clear how we are to think about sets like this, other than by laying out the membership tree and describing the worlds at terminal nodes as best we can.

Each specification function m(...) has associated with it a set of propositions, expressing between them the various ways matters can stand where m is concerned. (A proposition goes into the set if it is m(w) for some world w.) The operation is again reversible: to find m(w), look for the proposition to which w belongs.

A subject matter can also be conceived, then, as (iv) a set of propositions. Sets of this type function in semantics as what is expressed by sentences in the interrogative mood. *Questions*, as they are called, stand to interrogative mood sentences Q as propositions stand to sentences S in the indicative mood.[8] To find a Q expressing a particular set of propositions, we look for one to which those propositions are the possible answers. This Q then gives

---

[7] This won't work with just any old function from worlds to propositions. The proposition associated with w should be true in it; the propositions associated with different worlds should be identical or incompatible.

[8] I will sometimes use "question" sloppily as standing also for the sentences.

us an immediately comprehensible designator for the set of propositions at issue.[9]

What, for instance, is the Q to which There are exactly k stars, for specific values of k, are the possible answers? It is *How many stars are there?* We are dealing, then, with the issue or matter of how many stars there are. What is the question addressed by You did BLAH last summer, for specific values of BLAH? It is *What did you do last summer?* Thinking how to answer *What did you do last summer?* is considering the matter of what you did last summer.

2.3 MEREOTOPICOLOGY

One benefit of understanding subject matters this way is that lots of relations now become definable. m is *orthogonal* to n iff each cell of m overlaps each cell of n. What this means at an intuitive level is that how matters stand m-wise puts no constraints on how they stand n-wise, or vice versa. The number of stars is orthogonal to the number of comets, because any number of stars is compatible with any number of comets. m is *connected* to n—you don't need to know this!—iff they are not orthogonal, that is, one has a cell that does not overlap every cell of the other; they're *interwoven* if no cell of one overlaps every cell of the other. n is *part* of m iff ... that's what we're coming to. m is *disjoint* from n iff they have no nontrivial parts in common; otherwise they *overlap*.[10]

The relation of interest to us is *part-of*, along with its converse *inclusion*. The nineteenth century surely includes the 1820s, and what you did last summer includes what you did last July. Claims of this sort are intuitive in themselves, and required by clause (ii) of our schematic account of

---

[9] By pointing us to the corresponding indirect question. The indirect question corresponding to *Do cats paint?* is *whether cats paint*. The indirect question corresponding to *Why do they paint?* is *why cats paint*.

[10] Overlapping subject matters are always connected, Lewis shows; but connected subject matters need not overlap. Lewis says he cannot think of an intuitive counterexample, but he had one under his nose. The number of stars is connected to the number of planets, if we assume that planets have got to revolve around stars, for then the number of stars constrains how many planets there are; you can't have zero stars and three planets. How many stars exist is connected to the number of planets, but they have no parts in common.

29

content-part, according to which B is part of A only if B's subject matter is included in that of A. But what is the definition?

One sees what subject-matter inclusion would be on the parts-based conception. Chunks of reality stand in inclusion relations right out of the box. But m doesn't have to be part-based to include another subject matter n. The number of stars includes whether there are any stars, and is itself included in the number of stars and their ages. How are we to make sense of this on the present conception?

The larger subject matter is the one it is easier for worlds to disagree on, Lewis suggests. Considered as an equivalence relation, it is the *stricter* of the two. Considered as a partition, it's the one with the smaller cells. You may recognize this from algebra as the *refinement* relation. But we will need to define it in a slightly nonstandard way, to allow for the possibility that m and n are not defined on the same worlds.

5 n is part of m iff

    (i) each n-cell includes an m-cell,
    (ii) each m-cell is included in an n-cell.[11]

The number of stars includes (has as a part) the matter of whether the stars number more than a billion, because, on the one hand, worlds agreeing in how many stars exist are bound to agree in whether they number a billion, and on the other hand, worlds agreeing in whether they contain at least a billion stars are going to be subdivisible into worlds agreeing in how many stars they contain. What you did last summer includes what you did last July because worlds agreeing on what you did last summer are bound to agree on what you did last July, and the worlds in which you, say, slept through July can be further classified according to what you did in them last June and August.

Let's return now to a question left hanging at the end of section **2.1**. The observable is not a parts-based subject matter. It groups worlds together

---

[11] This requirement is waived for m-cells containing worlds on which n is not even defined. An example may help. m and n are everyone's life span and my life span. m ought surely to have n as a part. But, everyone's life span has cells where I do not exist. These can hardly be expected to lie within cells of my life span; I have a life span only where I exist. Cells where I fail to exist are exempted from the requirement, on account of containing worlds on which my life span is not defined.

which *look* the same, and looking the same is not a matter of having indiscernible corresponding parts. The question was this: A theory is meant to be empirically adequate if it is true, not perhaps about the world as a whole, but the observable part of it. What could it mean for a theory to be true to the observable part of the world, if the observable is not a part of the world at all (but rather an aspect of it)?

Just as the queen has to be distinguished from the queen, the world—that all-inclusive object—has to be distinguished from the world— the all-inclusive subject matter.[12] The observable may not be part of the world, but it is part of the world. And how matters stand observationally is part of how they stand overall. An empirically adequate theory is supposed to be true about that portion of how matters stand overall consisting of how they stand observationally.

2.4 TRUTH ABOUT A SUBJECT MATTER

A lot of philosophical problems take the form: Such and such has GOT to be the case.[13] But how CAN it be? *Pegasus does not exist*, we say, and this seems true. How can it be, when there is no Pegasus for it to be true of? A color shift too small to notice cannot possibly make the difference between red and not red. But it sometimes must, or a slippery slope argument forces us to extend redness even to green things. You might see this "question" on *Jeopardy*: *The number of its moons is considered unlucky*. The "answer" is *What is Neptune?* The number of Neptune's moons (it's thirteen) would be considered by most contestants a no-brainer. How can it be a no-brainer that the number is thirteen, when the number's very existence is debatable?

Philosophy is shot through with this sort of conundrum. I want to explore a new style of response, based on the examples we started with. The statements seem clearly correct, because the part we care about and fasten on is clearly correct. The number of Neptune's moons is indisputably thirteen, because we see past the numerical bit to what it says about Neptune and its moons. Subliminal color differences seem irrelevant to whether a thing is red, because we see through to the part about

[12] What above we called how matters stand overall.
[13] This section contains material repeated from the introduction.

observational red; this by its nature is a matter that can't be affected by undetectable color shifts. And so on.

I must admit at this point to fudging something. A falsehood, I keep saying, can be true in what it says about m. The part about m can be true when the whole is mistaken. These two notions—what A says about m, and the part of A about m—are not quite the same, and I have been running them somewhat together.[14]

Take first what A says about m. It is subject only to the requirement of being true (false) simpliciter when A is true (false) about m. This tells us nothing about its subject matter, in particular not that its subject matter is included in that of A. The part of A about m is supposed, obviously, to be part of A. But then its subject matter *does* have to be included in that of A. What A says about m differs from the part of A about m just in this one respect. I want to focus for now on the weaker construct: what A says about m.[15] The part of A about m is left to sections **3.4.1** and **3.4.2**.

So, what is the proposition we are speaking of when we speak of "what A says about m"? It's a proposition that is true, we said, just if A is true about m. For A to be true about m means that A, should it be false, is at any rate not false because of how matters stand with respect to m. This admits of a simple test: A is true about m iff one can make A true outright without changing how matters stand where m is concerned.

6 A is true about m in w iff
   A is true simpliciter in a world m-equivalent to w.

That is fine as a definition. But it remains to be seen what kind of compliment we are paying A, when we call it true about m. Does truth about the subject matter under discussion make A "as good as true" for discussion purposes? Does "true about m" function in descriptions of w the way truth simpliciter does? This turns out not to be a simple question.

Truth about m, considered as a modality, is possibility-like: A is true about m in w just if it *could* be true, for all that w's m-condition has to

[14] Thanks here to Yu Gao.
[15] What A says about m has the advantage of always existing. There is not always such a thing as the part of A about m. To see why, consider what its subject matter would be. It will have on the one hand to be included in A's subject matter a; otherwise it's not part of A. It should on the other hand connect up somehow with m; otherwise it's not the part of A *about* m. These conditions pull against each other, if m and a are unrelated.

say about it. The logic of directed truth can to some extent be read off the logic of possibility. A hypothesis and its negation can both, of course, be possible in the same world. Similarly there is nothing to stop them from both being true about m in the same world.[16] Call this the phenomenon of *quasi-contradiction*.

Statements true about m in a world w are supposed to encode genuine information about w; they are supposed to "get something right." That is why we introduced the notion. Isn't it a problem if they contradict each other? Let's see how the problem would go. If a statement is true about m in w, it will be used to describe w, because it gets something right. A and $\neg A$ cannot both get something right, surely. Acceptance of quasi-contradictions thus commits us to claims that are wholly false, claims with nothing right about them.

Rather than picking this reasoning apart, I will present three scenarios, or cases, in which the supposed problem does not arise. (We can then ask where the reasoning goes wrong.) The scenarios have us first quasi-asserting neither statement, then both, then one and not the other.

(*Case 1*) A gets no grip on m. Every m-condition is compatible both with A and its negation. In the terms of section **2.3**, m is orthogonal to whether A. No big surprise if an m that A is not even about fails to decide its truth-value in w. Granted, *Dogs bark* and its negation are both true about the number of cats. But so what? One would not be using them to describe cats in the first place. They have nothing to tell us about cats.

(*Case 2*) A does get a grip on m; not every m-condition is compatible both with A and its negation. Just for this reason, it says something about w that its m-condition leaves A undecided. Why should A and $\neg A$ not be used to convey this something? A conveys that it itself is permitted by the world's m-condition. $\neg A$ conveys that it too is permitted by the world's m-condition. That both are permitted is conveyed by A and $\neg A$ together. Are seventeen-year-olds adults? They are and they aren't. Is Turkey part of Europe? It is and it isn't. *Yes and no* conveys, in these cases, that neither answer is forced on us; both are permitted.[17]

(*Case 3*) *The number of planets > 3* is true about concreta; it's true in existing physical circumstances, supplemented if need be by the

---

[16] That a world's m-condition permits *each* of A and $\neg A$ to be true doesn't mean it permits them both to be true together. Truth about m is not agglomerative.

[17] See Ripley (2011) and Alxatib and Pelletier (2011) on the pragmatics of *Yes and no*.

natural numbers. That, supposedly, is why we quasi-assert it. But then shouldn't we quasi-assert its negation as well? It too is true (isn't it?) in existing physical circumstances, since the numbers can equally be left out.

(*3a*) Maybe *The number of planets > 3* semantically presupposes numbers, in such a way that its negation is *undefined* in numberless worlds. A statement counts as true just if it is true in all worlds m-equivalent to our own *in which it has truth-value*. *The number of planets > 3* counts as true since it is true in our m-cell where evaluable; its negation is false in our m-cell where evaluable.[18]

(*3b*) Maybe *The number of planets > 3* presupposes numbers only in a pragmatic sense. Its negation is *true* in numberless worlds, hence true here about concreta. To count as true, though, is to be true about m "but for *P*," *P* being the presupposition; the statement must hold in all *P*-worlds m-equivalent to our own. *The number of planets > 3* counts as true because it is true but for the possibly absent numbers.[19]

(*3c*) *The number of planets > 3* does not presuppose numbers at all. Its negation is true in numberless worlds, so true here about concreta. To count as true, however, a statement must be true in the "best" worlds m-equivalent to our own— the ones where it reveals its true colors. The best such worlds for a mixed-mathematical statement will contain numbers.[20]

Truth about m may seem like all the truth one could want, when the matter at issue is m. This formula works well enough for most purposes since we instinctively reach for sentences whose best shot at truth is in the intended worlds. Occasionally though, we'll want to check that a statement is true, not only in *some* m-equivalent world, but *all* m-equivalent worlds of the right type.

2.5 WAYS OF BEING

How many ways can it go in a world, where a given subject matter is concerned? Of course, m might not even be defined on *w*. The actual world is not in any particular condition as regards the first Finnish matador. But if *w* is in some m-condition or other, then, Lewis would say, it is in exactly one such condition. Subject matters are, in a word, *exclusive*. There is nothing

---

[18] "True where defined," considered as a modality, is necessity-like. See Dorr (2010).
[19] "True but for *P*" is necessity-like. See again Dorr (2010).
[20] "True in the best m-equivalent worlds" is necessity-like as well.

to stop *different* worlds from being in different m-conditions, as for instance if m = the number of stars and one of the worlds has more stars than the other. Different m-conditions are possible, though, on Lewis's view, only if they are incompatible; we never get two of them in the same world.

Is this right? One way matters stand here at home with regard to the number of Martian moons is, you might think, that Mars has got an *even* number of moons, while another is that Mars has a *prime* number of moons. That is the wrong way to look at it, Lewis would say. That there are evenly many of them, and primely many, are *aspects* of how matters stand in @ where the number of Martian moons is concerned. How they stand in toto is that Mars has an even, prime number of moons, in other words, two moons. Partial m-conditions can hold in the same world. *Full* m-conditions are pairwise incompatible; no world is in more than one.

A similar view is sometimes taken of questions. *Q* may *appear* to have two correct answers in *w*. But that just shows, it is said, that the "answers" are not complete, and so not answers at all, properly speaking. *Evenly many* and *primely many* are two correct *replies*, if you like, to *how many moons does Mars have?* But they cannot be considered *answers*. To answer the question would be to put the number of Martian moons at two. Call this the exclusivity assumption about questions.

About questions, it can seem restrictive. No room is left for "mention-some" questions like *Q = Where can I get an Italian newspaper? Q* is a different question from *Q' = What are all and only the places where I can get an Italian newspapers?* I can answer *Q* but not *Q'* by saying, *At the railway station*, or *At Cafe Roma*. This goes against exclusivity, as there may be Italian newspapers at both places. Again, if Mom asks, *Who wants gum?* then (assuming unlimited supplies of gum), *I do* is a perfectly satisfactory answer.[21] Mom is not expecting you to have in your possession a complete list of gum-wanters. Another satisfactory answer is *Glenda wants gum*, speaking for a child in the next room. This pushes against exclusivity, too, since there is nothing to stop us from both wanting gum at the same time. A case can thus be made for broadening our view of questions so that answers need not be partial to be compatible.[22]

---

[21] As in an age-old Trident commercial (http://www.youtube.com/watch?v=b7-QCG0oDQ).

[22] Some would say the difference here is pragmatic. The "mention some" way of putting it signals that existential answers are *forgivable* or even *desirable*, not that they are complete. I assume *Q* and *Q'* differ semantically, not just in the speech acts performed with them.

Back now to subject matters. The number of stars calls for the *exact* number. But let m be the number of stars give or take ten, and suppose w has a thousand stars exactly. One way matters stand with respect to m is this: There are between 993 and 1,003 stars. Another is: There are between 997 and 1,007 stars. These two m-conditions are no less distinct for being compatible. Or consider the matter of why so and so is qualified for the job, when they are overqualified. Louisa is a doctor *and* a lawyer, when either credential would be enough. That she is qualified both ways at once means the actual world is in both m-conditions. Observational subject matters belong here, too. Suppose w_1 is visually indiscernible from w_2, and w_2 from w_3; but w_1 can be told apart from w_3. Then w_2 is two ways with respect to how things look—the way it has in common with w_1 and the one it has in common with w_3. These are different since w_1 does not look like w_3.[23]

One gets a partition if likeness-where-m-is-concerned is an equivalence relation, and so transitive. Likeness on the score of how things look is famously not transitive. Likeness on the score of the number of stars give or take ten is not transitive, either; if three worlds have respectively 1,000, 1,006, and 1,012 stars, then the first is like the second, and the second is like the third, but the first is not like the third, since the difference is now more than ten. Again, if Louisa is a doctor but not a lawyer in w_1, a doctor and a lawyer in w_2, and a lawyer but not a doctor in w_3, then she is similarly qualified in w_1 and w_2, and in w_2 and w_3. But Louisa's qualifications in w_1 are completely different from her qualifications in w_3.

Here, then, is our second departure from Lewis.[24] Subject-matters will be similarity relations rather than equivalence relations; symmetry is still required, and reflexivity, but not transitivity. Alternatively we can think of them as "divisions" of logical space—divisions being the set-theoretic whatnots standing to similarity-relations as partitions stand to equivalence-relations.[25]

---

[23] This is a particular theme of Williamson (1990).
[24] The first was to allow partial subject matters and extend the definition of part/whole accordingly.
[25] The partition of E corresponding to an equivalence relation $\equiv$ is
$\{C \mid C$ is maximal among subsets D of E such that $x \equiv y \; \forall x, y \in D\}$.

This liberalized conception of subject matter proves its worth with the subject matters of sentences. These, as already suggested, have to do with a sentence's reasons for, or ways of, being true. S can be overqualified for the position of *true description of reality*, much as Louisa was overqualified for the position she was seeking.

Take a simple disjunction $p \lor q$; p is true, if it is, by virtue of p, and q is true by virtue of q. $p \lor q$ is true for a shared reason (p) in $p \& \neg q$-worlds and $p \& q$-worlds, and another shared reason (q) in $p \& q$ and $\neg p \& q$-worlds. But it is true for entirely different reasons in $p \& \neg q$-worlds as $\neg p \& q$-worlds. *True for the same reason*, or *in the same way* is not an equivalence relation. It corresponds to a division of logical space rather than a partition of it.

This confirms us in our decision to let subject matters be made up of incomparable propositions (none entails any other) that are not necessarily incompatible (they may or may not entail others' negations). The definition of subject matter inclusion works just as before. The number of stars give or take five includes The number of stars give or take ten because any way things can be on the first score implies a way they can be on the second, and any way things can be regarding the second is implied by a way they can be regarding the first.[26, 27]

The Cs are called equivalence classes. Likewise the division of E corresponding to a similarity relation $\approx$ is

$\{C \mid C$ is maximal among subsets D of E such that $x \approx y \; \forall x, y \in D\}$.

The Cs are called similarity classes. For discussion see Williamson (1990) and Hazen and Humberstone (2004). Hazen and Humberstone use "decomposition" where we say "division."

[26] That the number lies in the 98–103 range, for instance, puts it between 95 and 105.

[27] I suspect we will want ultimately to depart even further from Lewis. A division is made up of maximal sets of pairwise similar worlds. No maximal set can include another, so the sets are incomparable, making the ways things can be m-wise incomparable too; none entails any other. Consider now The number of stars is between 95 and 105 and The number of stars is between 98 and 103. Both are ways for things to be where the approximate number of stars is concerned, but, or rather so, the approximate number of stars is not a division. More general than divisions are *covers*: assorted subsets of the set that is covered that contain between them all its members. Every cover induces a similarity relation; items are similar if one of the chosen subsets contains both. But the same similarity relation is induced by any number of covers. I have decided for practical reasons to stick with divisions, leaving covers to footnotes, but "really" the whole thing should be redone with them. (Thanks here to Kit Fine.)

2.6 WHOLLY ABOUT

One question is, what are subject matters considered as entities in their own right? A different question is, which of these entities is the subject matter of a particular sentence S? Often one winds up discussing both of these at the same time. But the distinction is still important. Lewis has a well-developed theory of subject matters qua self-standing entities. But all he says about the second question (the "coordination" question) is this:

> 7 S is wholly about m iff S's truth-value supervenes on m, that is, S always evaluates the same in m-equivalent worlds.

He immediately notes a difficulty. An S that supervenes on m cannot help but supervene on any m^+ dividing logical space still more finely; the subject matters S is wholly about are "closed under refinement." A sentence that is wholly about the number of stars, for instance, is also wholly about the number of stars and their combined mass. This is not a particularly happy result. It means, for one thing, that no matter how intuitively unrelated two sentences may be, they have a subject matter in common, namely how matters stand in every respect. This is reminiscent of Hempel's none-too-plausible idea that (almost) any two sentences have content in common, given by their disjunction.

A further problem with (7), given our project here, is this. A sentence has lots of subject matters, on Lewis's definition; there is no such thing as "the" subject matter s of S. But our proposed theory of content-parts requires such an s. A includes B only if a includes b; that is what inclusion adds to implication.

Where has Lewis gone wrong? The "wholly" in "S is wholly about m" can be taken in two ways. One might hear it as focused on the sentence: S is concerned wholly with m; it doesn't care about anything else. But it can also be heard as focused on m: S is concerned with m *in its entirety*; there is nothing in m with which it is not concerned. To see the difference, suppose x is the maximal subject matter, and let S be *Maine is prosperous*. S is wholly about x in the first, Lewisian, sense. It is not about anything else, simply because there isn't anything else to be about. But S is not about x *in its entirety*; there is plenty in how matters stand in every respect with which *Maine is prosperous* is not concerned at all.

Ideally we would like a notion of subject matter that respected both of these "wholly" s. Ideally, S's subject matter would include everything S concerned, *and nothing that S did not concern*. The upward closure point means that Lewis has achieved the first goal but not the second.

If we read aboutness Lewis's way, S winds up being about larger subject matters than we had wanted. How do we knock these out? The strategy that suggests itself is to look for the *least* subject matter which S is (in Lewis's sense) wholly about.

This gives us something far too *small*, however, namely the two-cell subject matter whether or not S. Let's first confirm that S is indeed wholly about whether or not S. A sentence is wholly about m if its truth-value never varies within a cell. The cells in this case are (i) the worlds where S is true, and (ii) the worlds where S is false. Clearly S's truth value never varies between worlds where S is true! Nor does it vary between worlds where S is false. So we have the supervenience of truth-value on m-condition that defines "wholly about." It remains to check that whether or not S is the smallest (the coarsest) subject matter m such that S's truth-value never varies within any m-cell. The only genuinely smaller m is the trivial subject matter that puts all worlds into a single cell. (Whatever, I am tempted to call it.) The minimizing strategy thus delivers an m that is much too small. It is not as bad as whatever, I'll grant you that. But we would like to do better.[28]

2.7 EXACTLY ABOUT

Where do we look for a subject matter that S is "exactly" about? The s we're after has two properties: S is oblivious to matters lying outside of s, and attentive to everything within it. Our idea was to look for the least m satisfying some appropriate condition. The condition we tried in the last section—the one that delivered whether or not S—was too weak; there might be various ways for matters to stand subject-matter-of-S-wise

---

[28] Size is only one problem. Another is that inclusion relations are trivialized; whether or not A cannot include whether or not B except in the trivial case where A and B are true in the same worlds.

whereby S comes out with the same truth-value. A couple of examples where this occurs will help us to figure out how to strengthen it.

The world will end in fire or in ice, Frost writes.[29] One way for things to arrange themselves s-wise is for the world to end in fire; another is for it to end in ice. I take it that matters stand differently with s in fiery-end worlds than icy-end worlds. But both are in the same cell of whether or not *S*: the cell where *S* is true. The second example is from American presidential politics:

> *S = The U.S. president in 2001 is a senator's son.*
>
> in *w*, the president is Dubya, son of former senator George H. W. Bush.
>
> in *w'*, the president is Al Gore, son of former senator Albert Gore, Sr.

S is true either way. All that's changed is the personnel; the president and his father are now different people. This is enough, it seems, to change the state of things where s is concerned. A transworld reporter on the *S* beat could not plausibly claim that there was nothing to report—that it doesn't matter, from a subject matter of *S* perspective, who plays the two key roles.[30]

A change in *personnel* is more newsworthy than a change in the price of cotton. It is pretty clear why. The personnel change is a change in the individuals witnessing *S*'s truth; a change in the witnesses affects *how S* is true; and changes in how a sentence is true cannot be changes in an aspect of reality that *S* is not even about. The explanation in the Frost case is similar. How the world ends makes a difference to the subject matter of *The world will end in fire or in ice* insofar as it toggles the sentence's way of being true. This gives us a new and improved lower bound on the relations qualified to serve as *S*'s subject matter. (Some terminology: *S* is "differently true" in two worlds iff it is true in different ways.[31])

---

[29] *Some say the world will end in fire, some say in ice. From what I've tasted of desire, I hold with those who favor fire. But if it had to perish twice, I think I know enough of hate, To say that for destruction ice Is also great, and would suffice.*

[30] By "changes in, or with respect to, *S*'s subject matter s," I mean *qualitative* changes— changes in how matters stand s-wise—not numerical ones—changes in which subject matter the sentence has. *S*'s subject matter changes qualitatively if the presidency goes to Gore, numerically if *S* comes to mean, say, that the Cretan queen is a minotaur's mom (Pasiphaë supposedly gave birth to a minotaur when queen of Crete).

[31] In entirely different ways, or ways some of which are different? One needn't worry about this just yet, but it's the former.

8 *S* cannot be differently true in two worlds, unless things have changed where its subject matter is concerned.[32]

S must first take *notice* of a phenomenon, the thought is, before variation in that phenomenon can affect how it is true. Sentential subject-matter should be at least as fine-grained as ways of being true.[33]

An upper bound would be nice, too. After all—to state the obvious—not any old way of tweaking a world affects the state of things where *S* is concerned. A lot of the tweaks are going to be off-stage, or beneath *S*'s radar. *Mars has two moons* takes no notice if the presidency goes instead to Gore, or toothpaste comes in more flavors.

Now, the tweaks that do not attract *S*'s attention must presumably have something in common, to distinguish them from the ones that do. Ideally it would be the same *sort* of common element for every sentence; we are operating at that level of generality. This is not an argument, but I ask you: what could these beneath-*S*'s-notice tweaks have in common, if not their irrelevance to how *S* obtains or is true?

9 Something has changed, between one world and another, where *S*'s subject matter is concerned, only if *S* is differently true in the two worlds.[34]

Sentential subject matter should be *at most as* fine-grained as ways of being true.[35] The new upper bound is the same as our previously established lower bound; so we have pinned down sentential subject matter uniquely.

10 the subject matter of *S* = the relation m such that worlds are m-dissimilar iff *S* is differently true in them.[36]

---

[32] Again, we needn't get too precise right now, but "things have changed" means the worlds are not s-similar.

[33] Explicitly: let r be chosen so that worlds are r-dissimilar iff *S* is differently true in them. Then the subject matter of *S* includes r. Our new lower bound on *S*'s subject matter is how *S* is true (the old one was whether *S* is true).

[34] Take again *S* = *The president is a senator's son*. Clearly *S* is not (even slightly) about how many stars there. Why not? (**9**) says: *S* is not about the number of stars, because the number of stars is of no possible relevance to how it is true.

[35] Explicitly: Let r be chosen so that worlds are r-dissimilar just if *S* is differently true in them. Then *S*'s subject matter is included in r.

[36] This also defines "exactly about." *S* is exactly about m iff worlds differ with respect to m just when *S* is differently true in them.

Chapter 2

So far so good, I submit. It seemed earlier that there might be no better candidate for the role of S's subject matter than whether S is true. That worry is now laid to rest. The better candidate is how S is true. One says what S is about by structuring the set of S-worlds according to S's changing ways of being true in them. But, what about the part of logical space in which S is false?

2.8 MATTER AND ANTI-MATTER

Subject matters as explained by (**10**) are not evenhanded as between truth and falsity. They are not even defined unless the sentence is true. This causes three sorts of problem.

(1) Suppose S is false in world w. How do matters stand there where its subject matter is concerned? (**10**) says they don't stand any way. This is hard to believe. S is false for a reason, presumably. That reason is to be found in the goings-on in w to which S addresses itself. To put it the other way around, if there is nothing going on in w to which S is answerable, then it is hard to see why S should be false there.[37]

(2) What a sentence is about is one thing; whether it is *right* about it is something else. One should be able to understand what S is about while remaining ignorant of its truth-value. This is not possible, if s is how S is true. The question presupposes it *is* true; so to determine S's truth-value in w, I need only (according to (**10**)) ask myself whether w is one of the worlds on which s is defined.

(3) Negating a hypothesis should leave its subject matter unchanged. $\neg S$ is about whatever S was about, and vice versa. This is not predicted by (**10**), or even allowed by it. The subject matter s that (**10**) assigns to S is entirely different from the one s̄ that it assigns to $\neg S$. The two are not even defined on the same worlds.

---

[37] *Mount Everest has never been climbed* is false in the actual world @. To go by (**10**), @ is in no particular condition where S's subject matter is concerned. But then why is S false in w? It seems not irrelevant that Everest was climbed by Edmund Hillary and Tenzing Norgay. How could a fact like that not play a role in the (actual) state of things where S's subject matter is concerned?

So—if the subject matter of a sentence is how S is true, we get three very unfortunate results: S has truth-value in worlds where its subject matter draws a blank; learning what S is about tells you its truth-value; negating S changes what it's about. It appears that s = how S is true is only half of the story. The other half is s̄ = how S is false. s̄ can be considered (thanks here to John MacFarlane) the subject *anti*-matter of S. The two together constitute S's *overall* subject matter ŝ (ŝ = {s, s̄}). This addresses the problems we raised above; S's overall subject matter is

(1) defined wherever S has a truth-value
(2) graspable in complete ignorance of S's truth-value
(3) identical to the overall subject matter of $\neg S$

(1) holds because S's overall subject matter includes its subject anti-matter. (3) holds because S's subject pro-matter = the subject anti-matter of its negation.[38] (2) holds because to recover S's truth-value from ŝ = {s, s̄}, you must know which of s, s̄ is the pro-matter and which the anti-matter. One can of course tell from the notation employed that s is meant to be pro- and s̄ is meant to be anti-. But the set itself does not come annotated. Whether S is true is no more determined by the fact that s and s̄ are (in some order) its subject matter and $\neg S$'s than by the fact that "true" and "false" are (in some order) their truth-values.

2.9 SUMMING UP

A few philosophers have tried to think systematically about subject matter. Ryle thought a sentence was about the items mentioned in it. Goodman thought it was about the items mentioned in certain of its consequences. Lewis was the first to consider subject matters as entities in their own right, and the first to link a sentence's subject matter to what it says, as opposed to what it mentions. Lewisian subject matters are equivalence relations on, or partitions of, logical space. A sentence S is wholly about m if its truth-value in a world w is fixed by how matters stand m-wise in w. But he

---

[38] That is, s = $\overline{\neg s}$. Proof that subject matter is preserved under negation: ŝ = {s, s̄} = {$\overline{\neg s}$, ¬s} = {¬s, $\overline{\neg s}$} = $\widehat{\neg s}$.

never identified anything as *the* subject matter of sentence S—the one it is *exactly* about. We define it as the m that distinguishes worlds according to S's changing ways of being true in them. Subject *anti*-matter is defined analogously, and S's *overall* subject matter is the two together. Aboutness comes out independent of truth-value, as we would hope. A sentence is not about anything different from its negation.

- 3 -

Inclusion in Metaphysics and Semantics

3.1 PARTS OF CONTENTS

At this point we know quite a lot. We know for each indicative mood sentence S how to obtain its subject matter—the one it is exactly about. We know what it takes for one subject matter to include another. The larger subject matter has to refine the smaller one. We know, then, what it means for A's subject matter to include that of its consequence B, which is the same as B being part of A. The form of the definition, slightly elaborated from (3) above, is

11   B is part of A just if the argument <u>A, so B</u> is

    1. truth-preserving—A implies B; A's information value includes the information value of B[1]

    2. aboutness-preserving—A's subject matter (anti-matter) includes the subject matter (anti-matter) of B

Aboutness is preserved if worlds where B is true in different ways cannot have A true in the same way. (11) then becomes

12   B is part of A if and only if

    1. A implies B

    2. how B is true cannot change without changes in how A is true[2]

    3. how B is false cannot change without changes in how A is false

Thinking of subject matters as cellular, along the lines of (5), every b-cell should contain an a-cell, which comes to B's ways of being true (false) all

---

[1] A's information value is the set of worlds it rules out.

[2] More precisely: if B is differently true *in two A-worlds*, then A is differently true in those A-worlds. Better yet (as in (12)): every way for B to be true is implied by a way for A to be true. Better yet, though this requires the liberalization mentioned in note 27 of section 2.5: every B-world is B in a way that is implied by some way of being A.

45

being implied by ways for *A* to be true (false). In the obvious notation:

13 *B* is part of *A* if and only if

   1. *A* implies *B*
   2. each *B*↑ is implied by an *A*↑
   3. each *B*↓ is implied by an *A*↓

3.2 PARTS AS SUCH

Are content-parts really *parts*? *Mares eat oats and does eat oats* ought to stand to *Mares eat oats* in a relation not utterly disanalogous to the one bicycles bear to their frames, sets bear to their subsets, and being hot and tired bears to being tired. The problem is that content-inclusion involves subject-matter inclusion. And bicycles, sets, and properties don't *have* subject matters.

Hold that thought for a moment. Our original question was, do content-parts have whatever it is that ties subsets, material parts, and so on, together? There will be time to wonder what bicycles are about when we answer that.

Part/whole is a highly unselective relation. If *x* is somebody's aunt, that tells you *x* is a person. To divide *y* evenly, *x* should probably be a number. If *x* is closer to the North Pole than *y*, then it is *not* a number. Most relations are like that; they obtain only between certain kinds of thing. To learn that *x* is part of *y*, however, tells you nothing about *x* and *y* taken individually. Ontologists have invented, or discovered, some pretty strange entities; but there is nothing so ontologically outré as not to stand in part-whole relations.

One would like to think that part/whole is the same relation, or the same *kind* of relation, in all its incarnations. The leg and the table are carrying on in the same sort of way as Saturday and the weekend, "sky" and "skyscraper," okra and gumbo, Maine and New England, *Martha Quest* and the "Children of Violence" series, and so on. Almost any sort of inclusion is transitive, reflexive, and antisymmetric: a partial order. But this is not saying much, since "most" partial orders have nothing part-whole-y about them.

Consider, for instance, the relation of coming-later-in-the-week-than. Saturday comes later than Friday; why is it not part of Friday? One might look here to mereology's other axioms, beyond those defining a partial order. The one usually mentioned next is *Supplementation*: y is properly part of x, only if a z exists that "makes up the difference" between them.[3] Certainly it is hard to think of a z that counts intuitively as what Friday adds to Saturday. This is not, however, because the axiom *itself* is so demanding. Models are easily devised in which, say, Sunday plays the role of difference maker. The problem is that our sense of what we want in a part goes beyond the axioms.

I do not pretend to know all the reasons that Saturday strikes us as part of the weekend, but not of Friday. One striking difference, though, is the following. What happens on Saturday has immediate ramifications for what happens on the weekend, but not for what happens on Friday. Change the part and you cannot help but change the whole. It's the same with New England and Maine. The play changes when we rewrite the first act.[4] The principle here is

14 *Upward difference transmission*: y is part of x only if y cannot change (in specified respects) while x remains the same (in those respects).

This is highly schematic, of course; one has to specify the "respects" for each particular kind of object. Take first material objects. A bicycle frame y is part of a bicycle x, only if y cannot change intrinsically without x doing so as well. The frame can't be bent or heated up while the bicycle sails on undisturbed.

If x and y are sets, it is membership changes that percolate up. Why is the set of birds not included in the set of flying things?[5] Every new penguin changes the membership of the first with no such effect on the second.[6]

If x and y are pluralities, both sorts of variation—in intrinsic character, and membership—seem like they ought to percolate up. The Crown Jewels are among my possessions only if it reduces my possessions to destroy some of them, and rearranges my possessions to rearrange the Crown Jewels.

---

[3] z makes up the difference if it is disjoint from y and sums with y to form x.

[4] I am as usual stretching the word "change" to cover transworld variation; the number of stars changes between our world and one with additional stars.

[5] Lewis (1991).

[6] Assume for example's sake that sets can survive changes of membership. Alternatively we could speak of one set being *replaced* by another.

When it comes to properties, it's how they're possessed that percolates up. Scalene-hood includes triangularity, because a figure cannot be differently triangular in two worlds, while retaining its manner or way of being scalene. Negative charge includes charge, because a rod cannot lose charge while maintaining its negative charge. Grue is included in grue-and-slithery because a snake that is grue here by being green and examined, there by being blue and not examined, has changed too in its way of being grue-and-slithery.

Changing the part results, in one category after another, in variation in the whole. With material objects, it is changes in intrinsic character that percolate up. With sets, it is changes in membership. With properties, it is changes in manner of possession. A thing's way of being grue affects its way of being grue-and-slithery.

What should we expect to percolate up in the case of content-parts? Ways of being *true*, it must be, for a thing's way of being *P* changes just when *It is P* changes in how it is true. *This is grue and slithery* includes *This is grue* for the same basic reason as *grue-and-slithery* includes *grue*. The difference is only that ways of being grue are replaced by ways for *This is grue* to be true. This gives us another route to the present conception of content-part.

3.3 PART-CONSTRUCTION

Content-part has been explained as a relation on *sentences*.[7] This sits ill with our equation of partial truth with truth of a part. Whether *A* has truth in it ought not to depend on whether the language happens to contain a sentence *B* that captures that truth. The unavailability of such a sentence could be the reason we're using *A* in the first place.

One might think that *A* is partly true if the language *could* contain a *B* like that—a true *B* that was part of *A*. This puts the emphasis in the wrong place, however. Our hypothetical *B* would be part of *A* in virtue of what it *said*: the thick or directed proposition *B* that it expressed. *A*'s real reason for

---

[7] Or perhaps, a binary sentential operator yielding a truth just when *B* is, in the relational sense, part of *A*. The model is C. I. Lewis's fishhook. *A* ⌐3 *B* is true just if *B* is strictly implied by *A*. *A* ≥ *B* is true if *A* strictly implies *B* and *A*'s subject matter includes the subject matter of *B*.

being partly true lies in the relation B establishes between A and B. Shall we say that A is partly true if a sentence that expressed B, if there were one, would be part of A? That may be technically right, but the sentence is doing no work here; one B is as good as another. For A to be partly true is for it to include a *truth*, possibly a propositional truth not expressed by any readily available sentence.

But, how are these propositional truths, which confer partial truth on A, to be identified, in the absence of associated sentences? That is the wrong way to think about it. A's propositional parts don't have to be picked out of a crowd; they are *constructed*. A rule will be given that determines, for each A and Lewisian subject matter m,[8] a proposition that deserves to be called *the part of A about m*, or, more carefully, deserves that title if any proposition does.

Now, A itself already expresses a directed proposition $\mathcal{A}$. $\mathcal{A}$ combines a truth-conditional content A (telling us whether A is true in a world) with a subject matter a (telling us how it is true). Using single uprights for "the truth-conditional content of . . . " and angle brackets for "the subject matter of . . . ,"

15 The directed proposition that A consists of

    1. $|A| = \mathsf{A} = A$'s truth-conditional content, and

    2. $<A> = \mathsf{a} = A$'s subject matter

The part of A about m will similarly involve a truth-conditional content and a subject matter. To maintain the parallel with (**15**), these are seen as attaching to a dummy sentence A_m. Our task is to construct

16 The directed proposition that A_m—consisting of

    1. $|A_m| = A_m$'s truth-conditional content, and

    2. $<A_m> = A_m$'s subject matter

The subtasks here are addressed in the next two sections,

---

[8] A Lewisian subject matter, recall, is an equivalence relation on worlds. That the part of A about m is defined only for Lewisian subject matters m does not mean that *its* subject matter is Lewisian, and indeed it is generally not.

Chapter 3

3.4 THE PART OF *A* ABOUT SUCH AND SUCH

3.4.1 When Is It True?

What should a world be like, for A_m to be true in it? *A* should be true about m in that world. This will be the case if either (i) *A* is true in *w*, or (ii) *A* is false there for reasons unrelated to m—reasons that can be undone without changing how matters stand m-wise. A concept from algebra comes in handy here. Suppose that X is a set and ≡ is an equivalence relation on X.

> 17 X/≡ is the result of expanding X to include everything equivalent to any of its members.

X/≡ is called the quotient set, and the operation taking X to the quotient set is "dividing through by ≡."[9] |*A*| divided through by m is the (thin) proposition that is true in exactly the worlds where *A* is true about m.[10] This is the proposition we want for A_m's truth-conditional content.

> 18 $|A_m| = |A|/m$ = the set of worlds where *A* is true about m.

The truth-conditional content of A_{nos}, for instance, is obtained by dividing the truth-conditional content of *A* through by the number of stars. What do we get if *A* is *There are more stars than planets*? We get the worlds with exactly as many stars as some world whose stars outnumber its planets. A world with any stars at all has that property. Truth-conditionally speaking, what *There are more stars than planets* says about the number of stars is that it is not the case that there are no stars at all.

Another, more fanciful, example. The creation and destruction of macro-objects is, according to Democritus, really just the rearrangement of atoms. The atoms themselves are eternal. One day, let's imagine, Pythagoras convinces Democritus that nothing persists but numbers. He learns from Heraclitus that atoms seem to persist only because new ones are

---

[9] "One way in which the quotient set resembles division is that if X is finite and the equivalence classes are equinumerous, then the number of equivalence classes can be calculated by dividing the number of elements in X by the number of elements in each equivalence class. The quotient set may be thought of as the set X with all the equivalent points identified" (Wikipedia).

[10] Exercise: Show that |*A*| divided by m is *A*'s strongest implication that is, in the sense of definition (7), wholly about m.

constantly rushing in to replace the old. What's really going on, he decides, is that

(D) The *number* of atoms is constant over time.

Then Democritus remembers that he cannot, as a materialist, accept D's implication that there is at least one abstract object. He would like to hold (D) responsible only for its concrete implications. But he is not sure how to arrange this. If both kinds of implication are there, why would D not be evaluated also on the basis of its implications for mathematical ontology?

The proposed answer is that he is not, when he advances D, *talking* about mathematical ontology. He is talking about concreta. D is of interest because of what it says about *that*. The part of D about concreta is a proposition true in w if either (i) w is a Platonist world in which D is true, or (ii) w is a nominalist world in which D is false for irrelevant reasons: reasons that can be fixed while leaving concreta unchanged. One of these scenarios—D is true, or false for irrelevant reasons—obtains, in his view, whenever w is concretely indiscernible from a D-world. If w is Platonistic, then D is true outright. If not, still, numbers are not *prevented* from existing by w's material condition. D holds when they are added back in. Either way, D is true to how matters stand concretely. The concrete world, in Balaguer's phrase, holds up its end of the bargain.

3.4.2 What Is It About?

To be part of A, A_m will need as well a subject matter, and that subject matter will have to be included in the subject matter of A.[11] It will need ways of being true that are implied by A's ways of being true, and ways of being false that are implied by A's ways of being false. Anticipating a bit, allow me to speak of A_m's ways of being true or false as its *truthmakers* and *falsemakers*.

---

[11] What else is the part of A about m going to be about, if not m? A's subject matter is relevant too, however. A_m is about what remains of the subject matter of A when it is forced to treat m-equivalent worlds alike.

What are they going to be? Just as A_m's truth-conditions were obtained by dividing $|A|$ by m, its truthmakers are obtained by dividing A's truthmakers by m. A truthmaker for D might be: |*The number of atoms is always 1*|. To obtain from this a truthmaker for $D_{concreta}$, we divide by concreta. Let us calculate.

|*The # of atoms is always 1*| divided by concreta

$= \{w|$ *The # of atoms is always 1* is true about concreta in $w\}$

$= \{w|$ w is in concrete respects like a $v \in$ |*The # of atoms is always 1*|$\}$

$= \{w|$ there is always a single atom in $w\}$

$=$ the (thin) proposition that there is always a single atom.

Now we look for A_m's ways of being false. Using again the arrow notation from section **3.1**, we are looking for the $A_m\downarrow$s. We know that any $A_m\downarrow$ will have to be implied by an $A\downarrow$—otherwise A_m could not be part of A. If the implication were proper, $A\downarrow$ would be stronger than needed to ensure A's falsity ($A_m\downarrow$ already ensures this, by modus tollens). As a falsemaker, though, it should not be stronger than needed.[12]

Which of A's falsemakers are they? The ones that force A_m to be false, of course. A_m is false where it is not true, that is, where A fails to be true about m. A_m's falsemakers thus emerge as those of A's falsemakers—those of the $A\downarrow$'s—which, in addition to not allowing A to be true outright, do not allow it even to be true about m. Plugging in the definition of truth about m, they are those of A's falsemakers containing no worlds m-equivalent to an A-world.

This completes our construction of the subject matter of A_m, and hence of the part of A that concerns m. Once again, $A\uparrow$ and $A\downarrow$ are to be understood as ranging over A's truthmakers and falsemakers.

---

[12] This by a proportionality requirement elaborated in chapter **4**.

19 The part of A about m is the directed proposition that[13]

1. is true where A is true about m

2. has, for each $A\uparrow$, a truthmaker holding just where $A\uparrow$ is true about m

3. is false where A is not true about m

4. has, for each $A\downarrow$, $A\downarrow$ as a falsemaker just if $A\downarrow$ is not true about m

Take again $D = $ *The # of atoms never changes*. The part of D that concerns concreta is the proposition that is true in worlds with equally many atoms at all times, in virtue of facts like these: There are never any atoms; There is always a single atom; There is always a pair of atoms, ...; and false in worlds whose atoms become more or less plentiful, because of facts like these: There were no atoms, and then one appeared; There was one atom, and then there were none; There was one atom, and then there were two, ...

3.5 SUMMING UP

Parts are subject to a principle of upward difference transmission: tweaking them makes for variation in their containing wholes. The principle is highly schematic; different differences are passed along according to the sort of entity involved. If x and y are material objects, intrinsic variation in x makes for intrinsic variation in y. If they are properties, it is changes in how they're exemplified that percolate up. If they're statements, it is variation in how they're true. This provides a second route to our conception of content-parts as consequences whose ways of being true "change less quickly". Sometimes A and B are given, and we can apply the definition directly. Other times only A is given, and our task is to construct the part of A that concerns the given subject matter.

---

[13] I am fudging here the same thing that was fudged in section **2.4**. The definition purports to deliver, for any A and m, a thing called the part of A about m. But it is doubtful that A always *has* a part about m, for reasons given in that earlier section. The definition does always give us something with the right formal properties. But it may not be an honest to God directed proposition; for $|A\uparrow|/m$ may not be a way for a sentence with $|A|/m$ as its truth-conditions to be true. What we are really getting is a thing that, if its "truthmakers" are rightly so called, is the part of A about m. None of this affects the intended applications, and I propose now to put it aside.

- 4 -

A Semantic Conception of Truthmaking

4.1 ARISTOTLE, TARSKI, ARMSTRONG, . . .

I have been speaking of ways of being true, and sometimes of reasons for truth. The usual term, which I'll use too, is *truthmakers*. I will not be trying to tell you "what truthmakers are," because we can afford to be flexible; it is only their behavior that matters. I allow sentences to be truthmakers. I allow truthmakers that are defined only in particular regions of logical space. I allow truthmaker-makers—reasons, not for *A* to be true, but for something to be in a position to make it true. I allow truthmakers *for* truthmakers. The idea is to present some options, and provide some tools. Truthmakers are as truthmakers do, and they do all kinds of things.

I cannot leave the interpretation of "truthmaker" *entirely* to your imagination, however. Gerry Cohen is supposed to have said, in some tight argumentative corner: "I would like at this point to make a distinction. But I can't think of one." I am in roughly the opposite position. I would like *not* to make a distinction. Truthmaking is a can of worms that I would rather not have to open. Unfortunately, I *can* think of one. So the can will have to be opened, just a bit.

The distinction I am after is like one that Tarski makes in "The Semantic Conception of Truth" (Tarski 1944). To conceive truth *semantically*, Tarski says, is to seek an understanding whereby it can play a foundational role in semantics. He contrasts this with

> the classical Aristotelian conception of truth—which find[s] expression in the well-known words of Aristotle's *Metaphysics*: *To say of what is that it is not, or of what is not that it is, is false, while to say of what is that it is, or of what is not that it is not, is true.* If we wished to adapt ourselves to modern philosophical terminology, we could perhaps express this conception by means of the familiar formula: *The truth of a sentence consists in its agreement with (or correspondence to) reality.* (342–343)

The classical conception is metaphysical. Correspondence is a theory of the *nature* of truth, in the same game as the coherence theory, the identity theory of truth, pragmatism, minimalism, and so on. Tarski would like if possible to "do justice to the intuitions which adhere to the classical conception," as he develops his preferred semantic alternative.

> Consider the sentence "snow is white." . . . If we base ourselves on the classical conception of truth, we shall say that the sentence is true if snow is white, and that it is false if snow is not white. Thus, if the definition of truth is to conform to our conception, it must imply the following equivalence: The sentence "snow is white" is true if, and only if, snow is white. (343)

Truthmaking, like truth, has usually been conceived in metaphysical terms. The Aristotle of truthmakers is David Armstrong:

> The idea of a truthmaker for a particular truth is. . . just some existent, some portion of reality, in virtue of which that truth is true. The relation, I think, is a cross-categorial one, one term being an entity or entities in the world, the other being a truth . . . The "making" here is not the causal sense of "making.". . . The relation is necessitation, absolute necessitation. . . (Armstrong 2004, 5)

Truthmaking is depicted here as a

(m_1) a vertical relation,

(m_2) between "entities in the world" τ and truths φ, whereby

(m_3) φ's truth is metaphysically necessitated by the existence of τ.

The metaphysical conception—defined by these three conditions—will not do for our purposes. We come to truthmakers by way of subject matter, a notion more at home in semantics than metaphysics. Semantic truthmaking is, or can be, a horizontal relation, which holds if the world is φ by being τ (as a cocktail napkin is rectangular by being square). Let's leave the compare and contrast for later, though. Now is the time for wind-tunnel models of the relation. I will be suggesting two.

Chapter 4

4.2 RECURSIVE TRUTHMAKERS

Tarski gave us the semantic conception of truth. Might there be room in his system also for semantic truthmakers? Davidson considers this question in "True to the Facts" (Davidson 1969). He maintains that there is not only room for truthmakers in Tarski, they are in some sense already there. Tarski defines truth, recall, in terms of satisfaction. Sentences are true because of what they are true *of*: certain sequences of objects. Making sentences true, though, is the job description of facts. Sequences are thus what facts become, according to Davidson. Satisfaction is all that remains of correspondence.

Davidson's idea here is puzzling, for sequences are not discerning; a sentence is satisfied by all sequences or by none. Sentences do differ, though, Davidson notes, in how they come by these satisfaction properties.

> [T]ruth is reached, in the semantic approach, by different routes for different sentences. All true sentences end up in the same place, but there are different stories about how they got there; a semantic theory of truth tells the story for a particular sentence by running through the steps of the recursive account of satisfaction appropriate to the sentence. (Davidson 1969, 759).

Something made everything is true because *x made everything* is satisfied by at least one sequence σ; *x made everything* is satisfied by σ because *x made y* is satisfied by all sequences σ' that agree with σ except possibly on *y*. Other truths will have their own derivational history.

The problem is not entirely solved, however, for distinct truths may agree too in their derivational history. Take for instance two universal generalizations, $\forall x\ Fx$ and $\forall x\ Gx$, understood both to be true, and where the predicates are atomic. *Fx* and *Gx* are both satisfied by all sequences, and there is no more to the story than that. This is the wrong result; true generalizations are not all true for the same reason.[1] The idea that suggests

---

[1] *Everything ages*, supposing it to be true, has a different truthmaker from *Everything is extended*, supposing it to be true.

itself is to

> include in the entity to which a true sentence corresponds not only
> the objects the sentence is "about" . . . but also whatever it is that the
> sentence says about them. (759)

The urge is understandable, but in Davidson's view misguided. Scrambling the objects S is "about" need have no effect on its truth-conditions, if compensating changes are made in what it is understood to say about them (this was briefly discussed in section (**1.4**)). The fact making S true is responsible only to S's truth-conditions, in his view; if they are unchanged, so is the "entity to which S corresponds." The fact therefore does not include, or reflect, the things S is about, or what it says about them.

This cuts no ice against a view like ours, as our truthmakers are precisely *not* responsible only to truth-conditions. They are meant to capture an aspect of meaning that floats potentially free of truth-conditions. Of course, it is one thing to rebut an objection to Tarski-style truthmakers, another to say what in a Tarskian setting truthmakers would be. Bas van Fraassen makes a proposal about this in the same volume of *Journal of Philosophy* as Davidson's paper (van Fraassen 1969).

He begins where Tarski does, with an interpreted first-order language L. *Rab* corresponds to the fact that a bears R to b; ¬*Rab* corresponds to a's bearing $\bar{R}$ to b; a conjunction corresponds to the combined truthmakers of its conjuncts; universal generalizations correspond to the product of truthmakers for their instances; and so on.

Some of these complexities are best left for later. Let's focus on the propositional sublanguage obtained by suppressing quantifiers and putting sentence letters for atomic predications *Rab*. Each p has associated with it a positive atomic fact {p}, and a negative atomic fact {$\bar{p}$}.[2] It doesn't matter what p and $\bar{p}$ "really are," metaphysically speaking. One could think of p ($\bar{p}$) as the set of valuations verifying p (falsifying it), or the ordered pair $\langle p, t \rangle$ ($\langle p, f \rangle$), or indeed as the sentence p ($\neg p$) itself. What matters is how the truthmakers of complex sentences bubble up from their components.

---

[2] This is for clutter avoidance. Everything goes through the same if atomic sentences have multiple and/or complex truthmakers.

20 τ is a recursive truthmaker/falsemaker for φ iff

    1. φ is an atomic sentence p and
      (t) $\tau = \{p\}$
      (f) $\tau = \{\bar{p}\}$
    2. φ is $\neg\psi$ and
      (t) τ makes ψ false
      (f) τ makes ψ true
    3. φ is $\psi \vee \chi$ and
      (t) either τ makes ψ true or it makes χ true
      (f) τ is the union of falsemakers for ψ and χ
    4. φ is $\psi \& \chi$ and
      (t) τ is the union of truthmakers for ψ and χ
      (f) either τ makes ψ false or it makes χ false[3]

Davidson's idea that truthmakers ought to supervene on truth-conditions is obviously not respected here. $p \vee \neg p$ has $\{p\}$ and $\{\bar{p}\}$ for its truthmakers, while $q \vee \neg q$ is made true by $\{q\}$ and by $\{\bar{q}\}$. If $p \& \neg p$ were to be true, that would be because of the fact that $\{p, \bar{p}\}$. A different fact, $\{q, \bar{q}\}$, makes, or would make, $q \& \neg q$ true. (It is because these facts can't obtain that the sentences can't be true.) It's the same with "contingent" claims like $p \vee (p \& q)$ and $p \& (q \vee \neg q)$: the first is made true by $\{p\}$ but not $\{p, \bar{q}\}$, the second by $\{p, \bar{q}\}$ but not $\{p\}$, though both are true just when p is true.

Now, van Fraassen is interested in truthmakers, not for their own sake, but for the account they enable of "tautological entailment" (Anderson and Belnap 1962), a kind of relevant entailment.

21 φ tautologically entails ψ iff
    each of φ's truthmakers contains (as a subset) a truthmaker for ψ.

This is intriguing, because (i) we ourselves use truthmakers to define a type of relevant entailment—the entailment of part by whole—and (ii) tautological entailment too is supposed to satisfy the "dogma that for φ

---

[3] So, for instance, $p \vee q$ is made true by $\{p\}$ and by $\{q\}$, and false by $\{\bar{p}, \bar{q}\}$, while $p \& q$ is made false by $\{\bar{p}\}$ and by $\{\bar{q}\}$, and true by $\{p, q\}$.

to entail ψ, ψ must be "contained" in ϕ" (12). So, for instance, $p\&\neg p$ tautologically entails p but not q, since {q} is not a subset of {p, $\bar{p}$}. Which is what the dogma leads us to expect: q is not "already there" in $p\&\neg p$, the way that p appears to be already there.

Do we have in tautological entailment a bona fide inclusion relation? I would say not. A prime example of noninclusive entailment, for us, is $p \Rightarrow p\vee q$, and yet $p\vee q$ is tautologically entailed by p.[4] (Anderson and Belnap are aware of this; they grant that containment *can* be understood so that $p\vee q$ is not contained in p.[5]) The problem can be addressed simply by flipping the quantifiers in the definition just given:

22 φ inclusively entails ψ iff

>   *1.* each of φ's truthmakers contains (as a subset) one for ψ, and
>   2. each of ψ's truthmakers is contained in a truthmaker for φ

For $p\vee q$ to be inclusively entailed by p, its truthmakers, {p} and {q}, would need to each be contained in a truthmaker for p, which {q} clearly is not. Nor does p entail $p\&(q\vee\neg q)$ inclusively, or $p\vee(p\&q)$, though each is logically equivalent to p. Inclusive entailment is a pretty demanding business.[6]

4.3 REDUCTIVE TRUTHMAKERS

In an ideal language, simple sentences would be true for simple reasons, and complex sentences for complex reasons. In English, simple sentences can be true for complex reasons. The recursive approach allows this, but offers no guidance as to what those reasons might be. The recursive approach is thus *incomplete*; it needs to be supplemented with principles

---

[4] p's only truthmaker is {p}, and {p} has as a subset a truthmaker (itself) for $p\vee q$. Thus each of p's truthmakers includes a truthmaker for $p\vee q$.

[5] Some "understand the matter in such a way that for A to 'contain' B, A must be analytically relevant to B," meaning essentially that B contains no new nonlogical vocabulary. The reference is to William Parry's system of analytic implication. But, "there is surely a sense in which A$\vee$B is 'contained' in A" (Anderson and Belnap 1962, 23). See also Fine (1986), Fine (2013).

[6] More demanding than Parry's analytic implication. Parry has $p\&q$ entailing $\neg p\vee q$, for instance, but we do not. A truthmaker for $\neg p\vee q$ that targets $\neg p$ is not included in any truthmaker for $p\&q$. See Gemes (1994).

determining the truthmakers of simple sentences. Then too, complex sentences can be true for simple reasons, not always guessable from their logical form. The recursive approach does not even allow this. It is "over-complete," then, or unduly restrictive. I will focus in this section on the restrictiveness problem, but our results will be relevant to both.

A disjunction is true, according to (20), because of a fact that verifies one disjunct, or a fact that verifies the other. This does not seem to exhaust the options. Why not a fact that ensures that one disjunct or the other is true, without taking sides? That mares eat oats ensures, for instance, the truth in one way or another of *Mares eat oats or does eat oats, or else mares eat oats and does do not eat oats.* That everyone distinct from Sandy is at the reservoir ensures the truth, in one way or another, of *Either Sandy is not at the reservoir, or everyone is at the reservoir.*

Consider next a conditional $p\&q \to p\&q\&r$. It owes its truth, on the recursive conception, either to a fact that falsifies p, or a fact that falsifies q, or a fact that verifies $p\&q\&r$. Why not a fact that blocks the *combination* of $p\&q$ true, $p\&q\&r$ false, without pronouncing on the components taken separately? *If you two are ready, that makes three of us* is true, it would seem, if and because I am ready. The only recursive truthmaker in the neighborhood is the fact that we're all ready. That we are all ready seems like overkill, however, when my readiness suffices.

I do not say that unneeded extra detail is always disqualifying. Maybe my readiness *sometimes should* be supplemented with yours, in a truthmaker for the conditional. Maybe my readiness *always can* be supplemented with yours, in a truthmaker for the conditional. All I am balking at is the idea that my readiness *always must* be supplemented with facts about you. It is one thing to tolerate unneeded extras, another to insist on them. It's the insistence that bothers me.

Suppose that {r} is rejected as a truthmaker for $p\&q \to p\&q\&r$, while {p, q, r} is retained. The sentence will then be true for completely different reasons in $p\&q\&r$-worlds and $\neg p\&\neg q\&r$-worlds. The fact that r does not count as a shared reason, though it holds in both worlds and determines the result in both. Again, *politician(x) → woman-politician(x)* holds of Angela Merkel because she satisfies the consequent, and of Angelina Jolie because she falsifies the antecedent. There is also surely a reason they have in common, though: both are women. This is what the recursive approach is missing.

The quick and easy solution would be to let truthmakers for ψ count also as making φ true, when ψ is logically equivalent to φ. ψ in the present instance would be $p\&q\rightarrow r$. It's a two-way street, however; $\{p, q, r\}$ now becomes (?!) a truthmaker for p, by virtue of making $(p\&q\&r)\vee(p\&\neg(q\&r))$ true. One could tighten the rule so that φ does not inherit those of ψ's truthmakers that are stronger than needed to ensure truth. But ψ in that case drops out as irrelevant; we can apply the nonexcessiveness requirement directly to truthmakers for φ.

Nonexcessive truthmakers were studied long ago by Quine, as part of a project on squeezing redundancy out of truth-functional representations (Quine 1955). Negated and unnegated sentence-letters are *basic* sentences; a conjunction of basic sentences primely implies φ if it implies φ, and its proper subconjunctions do not; φ is represented as the disjunction of its prime implicants.[7] Prime implicants correspond in an obvious way to minimal models—partial valuations of the language that verify φ and none of whose proper subvaluations verify φ. Minimal models can be construed, if we like, as van Fraassen–style facts: $\{p, \overline{q}\}$ is the valuation that assigns truth to p and falsity to q.

> 23 φ's reductive truthmakers (falsemakers) are its minimal models
> (countermodels), or the associated facts.

Reductive truthmaking is both-ways independent of recursive, note: $p\rightarrow(p\&q)$ is recursively verified by $\{p,q\}$ but not $\{q\}$, and reductively verified by $\{q\}$ but not $\{p,q\}$.

4.4 QUANTIFIERS, ETC.

Two pictures of semantic truthmaking have been sketched: the recursive, and the reductive. I call them pictures, rather than theories, for a bunch of reasons. They are defined only for the simplest sort of artificial language. They don't always "scale up" so well to richer languages.[8] Neither gives a

---

[7] The Quine-McCluskey algorithm for identifying prime implicants is still used today.

[8] What would a minimal truthmaker be for *Infinitely many objects exist* or *Everest is over four miles high*?

full account even of simple languages, since nothing useful is said about atomic sentences.[9] And they are apt to come into conflict.

Where does this leave us? The models represent *tendencies* in truth-maker assignment that pull at times in different directions. Reductive truthmaking is, in a propositional setting, intensional, since truth-table equivalents—

(a) p,

(b) $p \lor (p \& q)$, and

(c) $p \& (q \lor \neg q)$,

for instance—hold in the same valuations; all of the sentences have {p} as their sole minimal truthmaker. Recursive truthmaking is hyperintensional:

(1) p has one truthmaker: {p},

(2) $p \lor (p \& q)$ has two: {p} and {p,q}, and

(3) $p \& (q \lor \neg q)$ has a different two: {p,q}, and {p,q̄}

The recursive approach succeeds in distinguishing these sentences only by countenancing truthmakers like {p,q} and {p,q̄} that are stronger than needed to ensure their truth.

Hyperintensionality and minimality may seem intrinsically at odds, but this turns out not to be so. Some degree of rapprochement is possible in, to take the obvious next step, quantificational languages. The following are truth-conditionally equivalent:

(a) No frogs are ungulates

(b) No ungulates are frogs

(c) Nothing is both a frog and an ungulate

The candidate truthmakers, intuitively speaking, are

(1) a certain bunch of things—the *F*s—are none of them *G*s

(2) a certain bunch of things—the *G*s—are none of them *F*s

(3) a certain bunch of things—all of them—are not *F*-and-*G*

Each of (1) to (3) guarantees the truth of each of (a)-(c). Are the truthmaking relations similarly indiscriminate? Clearly not; (1) goes with

---

[9] To assign a single dedicated p to each p only evades the issue.

(a), (2) with (b), and (3) with (c). Adding new *frogs* to a world affects how it is true that no frogs are ungulates. Adding new *horses* does not. What the new horses bear on is how it is true that no ungulates are frogs. How to rationalize it, I am not sure, but the judgment is clearly there.[10] There is no conflict with minimality in this, for (1) to (3) are *all* minimal. None is puffed up with irrelevant extras. Where structure can be respected at no cost to minimality, that is surely the way to go.

I make the point with *No Fs are Gs* because the "restrictor" clause in a binary generalization is generally agreed to function differently from the "scope." The notation $(\forall x: Fx)\neg Gx$ is in this respect less misleading. A similar point holds, however, for unary quantifiers. Take "Nothing Even Matters," which you may recognize as the title of a Lauryn Hill song. Let's assume the title is true: Hugo Chávez doesn't matter, the wide Sargasso Sea doesn't matter, Jupiter's moons do not matter, and so on. That various particular things do not matter has a role to play, obviously, in how it is true that nothing matters. There are things, indeed, such that their not mattering *is* the way it is true that nothing matters. I am speaking, of course, of all the things.

Now, to be sure they have this power only because they *are* everything. Their not mattering ensures the generalization's truth only given the totality fact. But what does this mean, exactly? How does the totality fact contribute? It is usually slotted into the truthmaker alongside the instances.

> $\forall x\, Fx$ is made true, not simply by Fa, Fb, Fc, etc, but by them *combined* with the fact that a, b, c, ... are everything

This seems, however, to confuse the issue of what the truthmaker is, with the issue of how it acquires that status. (Analogy from the causation literature: Suppose you duck to avoid a bullet. The ducking explains your survival; that explanatory relation is explained in turn by the bullet. But the bullet is no part of why you survived.) Better would be

> $\forall x\, Fx$ is made true simply by Fa, Fb, Fc, etc.; they suffice for this purpose because a, b, c,... are everything.

[10] The judgment is based on more than just a syntactic reflex, triggered by the "frog"-term in subject position; for it follows the topic of conversation, not the subject term, when the two come apart. ("Let me tell you about the ungulates. No frogs are ungulates. Check the ungulates in this room, for instance; you'll find that none of them are frogs.")

Keeping the totality fact—the fact that a, b, c, ... are everything—out of the truthmaker (putting it into the truthmaker-*maker*, as it were) is tempting in much the way that we are tempted to think of *No frogs are ungulates* as true simply because certain things, namely the frogs, are not ungulates; that these things *are* the frogs explains how they do it, which puts it into the truthmaker-maker.

This sacrifices, however, a defining feature of truthmakers: they should force the truth-bearer to be true. One could retreat to the weaker claim that S is forced to be true by its truthmaker *and whatever further facts confer on it that status*. But, although that may be right in the end, it's too big a job to be taking on now. Let me propose instead a simple expedient. $\forall x\ Fx$ is necessitated, and made true, by Fa, Fb, Fc, ... "*qua* complete list of instances," or "insofar as a, b,... are everything," or simply "*qua* everything."

> 24 Fa, Fb,... qua everything is like Fa & Fb & .... except in being undefined—rather than failing—in worlds whose population extends beyond a, b,....

This turns the totality fact into something akin to a presupposition. Fa, Fb,... qua everything incorporates the fact that *a* is *F*, because it fails if Fa does. It does not by this measure incorporate the totality fact, for it does not fail (it is guaranteed *not* to fail) in worlds with objects other than a, b,...

One fact *turns on* another, let us say, if the second must obtain for the first to obtain, and also for the first to fail. That Jupiter is bigger than Venus turns on the two planets' existing. That certain things, qua everything, have a certain feature, likewise turns on their being all the things that there are. A fact's truthmaking powers depends not only on where it obtains, but what it turns on. Suppose with Goodman that *Everything ages*. Why is this true? It owes its truth to an exhaustive group's aging, not an aging group being exhaustive.

Some notation from the presupposition literature is helpful here: $P\&\partial Q$ takes its truth-value from P when Q is true, but is undefined when Q is false. $P\&\partial Q$ will be likewise be a fact that obtains (fails) just if P does, in worlds where Q obtains, but is undefined, rather than failing, in worlds where Q fails. The proposal, writing T for the totality fact, and k for an arbitrary non-F, is this:

25   $\forall x\, Fx$ is made true by Fa & Fb & .... & ∂T

     $\forall x\ Fx$ is made false by $\bar{F}k$[11]

Note, P&∂Q implies whatever P&Q does, as they obtain in the same worlds. $\forall x\ Fx$ was necessitated by Fa & Fb & .... & T—its instances plus the fact of their exhaustiveness—so it is necessitated by Fa & Fb &. . . & ∂T—the instances qua exhaustive.

4.5 A NEW CONDITIONAL

All ravens are black owes its truth to what goes on with the ravens. That a raven-shaped white thing turns out to be made of plaster may be evidentially relevant, but it's nothing to do with how or why the generalization is true. The point goes back at least to Belnap (1970).

> Almost everyone, I suppose, has considered from time to time that "All ravens are black" might profitably be read ... as saying not that being a raven implies being black [$\forall x(Rx \to Bx)$], but rather something more like "Consider the ravens: each one is black." (Belnap (1970), 7)

Belnap tries to achieve this result with a device of conditional assertion. Writing (Q/P) for the assertion of P, conditional on the truth of Q, he says that

> If Q is true, then what (Q/P) asserts is what P asserts.
> If Q is false, then (Q/P) is nonassertive. (Belnap (1970), 3)

Committing to (Rx/Bx) is asserting (but only if x is a raven) that x is black.[12] This seems like a step in the right direction, but a *large* step, and somewhat into the unknown.[13] How to quantify into regular conditionals

---

[11] Fa and $\bar{F}k$ stand in here for whatever it is that makes *Fa* true and *Fk* false, which doesn't necessarily involve F. $\forall x\, Red(x)$ might be true because of Scarlet(a), Crimson(b),.... or false on account of Green(k).

[12] Compare a conditional bet: if Gonzaga makes it to the Final Four, I bet they take the whole thing. It's as though I hadn't spoken, if they don't.

[13] Stalnaker (2004) is a good recent discussion.

Chapter 4

we know, but how does one quantify into a conditional speech act? A story will be needed about embedded conditionals, such as *If we have ham, then if we have eggs, we have ham and eggs.* Does this condition a conditional speech act on our having ham? Contraposition is threatened: asserting Q, conditional on P, seems like a different undertaking from asserting $\neg P$, conditional on $\neg Q$; the one does not commit us to the other. But, calling something black if a raven would seem to commit me to its not being a non-black raven. That puts at least some pressure on me to assert that it's not a raven, supposing it not to be black.

A depragmaticized analogue of Belnap's conditional appears to avoid these issues. I write it $Q\!\nearrow\!P$. Where (Q/P) asserts that P, should Q be true, and is otherwise nonassertive, the new conditional takes on P's truth-value and subject matter, should Q be true, and is otherwise nonsubstantive.

26 If Q is true, then $Q\!\nearrow\!P$ is true (false) for the same reason(s) as P.

If Q is false, $Q\!\nearrow\!P$ is vacuously true—true without a truthmaker.

The word "vacuous" is meant to call vacuous generalizations to mind. A statement like *All perpetual motion machines are in Kazakhstan* is true, not because its demands are met, but because it does not make any demands. This is why the standard reading feels wrong; $\forall x(\mathrm{PPM}(x)\rightarrow\mathrm{KAZ}(x))$ is true for the highly *non*trivial reason that perpetual motion machines don't exist. $\forall x(\mathrm{PPM}(x)\!\nearrow\!\mathrm{KAZ}(x))$ is true for no reason; the reason for *that* is that perpetual motion machines don't exist.

The "suppose" conditional $\nearrow$ requires no departure from standard practice; it is truth-conditionally identical to the material conditional. *Rudy is a raven $\nearrow$ Rudy is black* is, like its material counterpart, true when Rudy is black or not a raven, and otherwise false. Only the reasons differ. One is true either because Rudy is not a raven, or because Rudy is black. The other is true, should Rudy be a raven, because Rudy is black, and otherwise for no reason at all. There is again a level-distinction at work here. Reasons for a statement to be true are one thing; reasons why it doesn't need a reason to be true are another.

From here on we follow Belnap. *All ravens are black* is syntactically speaking a regular old universally quantified conditional. The traditional syntax notwithstanding, it winds up with a binary, restricted quantifier type of meaning. If a, b, c,. . . are w's ravens, then $\forall x\ (Rx \nearrow Bx)$ is

27 $\begin{cases} \text{true in } w \text{ if and because each of a, b, c,\dots\ is black in } w \\ \text{false in } w \text{ if and because one of a, b, c,\dots\ is not black in } w \end{cases}$

Let me indicate how one gets this result, given what was said about unary quantifiers and the "suppose" conditional. $\forall x(Rx \nearrow Bx)$ is *true* in w when, and because, certain things (psst, w's inhabitants) are *raven $\nearrow$ black* in w (by (25)). These things, w's inhabitants, divide into w's nonravens and its ravens. Its nonravens are *raven $\nearrow$ black* for no reason (by (26)). Its ravens (a, b, c,. . .) are *raven $\nearrow$ black* by being black (by (26)). The two together, then, are *raven $\nearrow$ black* because a, b, c,. . . are black.

That gets us the first line of (27): $\forall x(Rx \nearrow Bx)$ is true when, and because, as for the ravens, they are black. Now the second. Universal generalizations are false when and because an instance—something of the form $Rk \nearrow Bk$ in this case—is false (by (25)). $Rk \nearrow Bk$ is capable of falsity only if k is a raven; its reason for being false is that k is not black. As it says on the second line of (27), then, $\forall x(Rx \nearrow Bx)$ is false because a certain thing k, assumed to be a raven, is not black.

4.6 TRADEOFFS

Recursion and reduction are natural, sometimes opposing, tendencies in the assignment of truthmakers. Both have much to be said for them. If one can be honored without disrespecting the other, that is the way to go. Otherwise we need to think instrumentally. The recursive approach takes the lead in some applications, the reductive in others; sometimes a compromise has to be struck. Let me run quickly through a few problem areas to illustrate the possibilities: logical omniscience, scalar implicature, confirmation, partial truth, and logical subtraction.

If two statements—$p\ \&\ (q \to p)$ and $\neg(p \to q) \vee (p\ \&\ q)$, say—carve out the same region of logical space, how can the thinker fail to notice this? A region is not so easily reidentified, when plotted in a different coordinate system, or marked out on a different logical grid (Yalcin 2011). The grid is set by the subject matter, which groups worlds on the basis of how a statement is true. $p\ \&\ (q \to p)$ and $\neg(p \to q) \vee (p\ \&\ q)$ need to differ in their truthmakers, for this sort of explanation to work. Their reductive truthmakers are the same—both are true because of {p}—so it is recursive truthmakers we need for this application.[14]

I'll bring cake or pie, you say, thereby indicating that you will not bring cake *and* pie. The implicature vanishes if you say, what is logically equivalent to bringing cake or pie, that you will bring cake or pie or both. Why does $p \lor q \lor (p \& q)$ implicate less than $p \lor q$? Because it "says more," in the sense not of ruling out additional worlds, but bringing in additional truthmakers.[15] For A to implicate $\neg K$, it is not enough that K be a salient, stronger alternative to A. K should be stronger also than A's truthmakers.[16] Again, it is the recursive approach that posits a new truthmaker for each new disjunct, however truth-conditionally irrelevant.

If the issue is probability, recursive truthmakers cut too fine. Statements true in the same worlds are going to be equally likely, since probability is a measure on sets of worlds (though see Windschitl and Wells (1998) and Yalcin (2010)). Insofar as confirmation is a probabilistic notion, confirmation theory ought, you might think, to avoid recursive truthmakers too. But this is not so clear. What is the point of Hempel's paradox, if not to bring out confirmational differences between hypotheses true in the same worlds? The recursive approach helps us to make sense of this, by putting the truth-value of contrapositives (*All ravens are black, All nonblack things are nonravens*) under the control of different facts. The explanation is admittedly not terribly discerning, since *All ravens are black* differs in its recursive truthmakers from all kinds of hypotheses, including some, like *All ravens are black ravens*, from which it is confirmationally indistinguishable. The explanation is also puzzling; if a black raven is evidence for *All ravens are black* and not its contrapositive, it ought to drive their probabilities apart, which by hypothesis it doesn't.[17] More on this later. The point for now is that we need sometimes to have a foot in both camps.

---

[14] Recursive truthmakers track sentential structure only so far. $\neg\neg A$ has the same truthmakers as A, and $A \& B$ the same as $B \& A$. (This echoes Frege on the sense-preservingness of double negation. Whether reversing conjuncts can affect sense for Frege, I don't know.)

[15] I get the example from Kit Fine. See also Sauerland 2012, sections 3 and 4.

[16] In further support of this, $p \lor q$ does not implicate $\neg p$ or $\neg q$. (A good thing, or its implicatures would refute it.) See, among many other papers, Geurts (2009). Thanks here to Danny Fox.

[17] John Hawthorne and Frank Arntzenius made this point.

A falsehood does not get to be partly true just by having among its consequences some that are true. Otherwise every p is partly true, by virtue of implying $p \vee q$; q can be any truth that you like. Only certain consequences reflect favorably back on a falsehood, namely the truths contained in it. This, one of the key motivations for content-part, is largely undone if truthmakers are conceived recursively. For $p \vee q$ is part of, if not p, something equivalent to p, namely $p \vee pq$.[18] To suppose that every falsehood is *equivalent* to a partial truth is only slightly less outrageous than the idea that every falsehood is itself partly true. The reductive model is preferable when we are assessing statements for partial truth.

A tempting approach to logical subtraction says that $A{-}B$ is true in worlds where $B \rightarrow A$ is true "not because B is false," that is, where $B \rightarrow A$ is true for a B-compatible reason or in a B-compatible way. So, for instance, the truth of $p \rightarrow (p \mathrel{\&} q)$ is ensured both by p's falsity and q's truth. The first guarantor is not p-compatible, so we are left with the second. The recursive model doesn't admit the fact that q as a truthmaker for $p \rightarrow (p \mathrel{\&} q)(= \neg p \vee (p \mathrel{\&} q))$, however. A disjunction's truthmakers are inherited from its disjuncts; synergistic relations, if any, between them are ignored. Subtraction lives off these relations, so subtractive truthmakers had better be minimal truthmakers.

I wish I had more to say about how the two models interact. One obvious thought is that sentential structure creates a *presumption* in favor of certain truthmakers. *Some Fs are G* is true, normally, because the *Fs* are some of them *G*. But presumptions can be defeated. *The poisonous ones don't look like that*, A1 says, as a snake family approaches. *Some of them do too look like that*, Betty insists. She is not saying of poisonous snakes in general that some of them look like these here; she is saying of these snakes here that they look poisonous. Again, biconditionals are true, normally, either because both sides hold or because both sides fail. But not always. Why is it true that *There are renates in Bosnia iff there are cordates there, and there are renates in my closet iff there are cordates there, and . . . .* ? Is it because there are renates and cordates in Bosnia, there are no renates or cordates in my closet, and so on? This is what the recursive

---

[18] $p \vee q$'s truthmaker {q}, while not implied by any truthmaker for p, is implied by {p,q}, which is (on the recursive model) a truthmaker for $p \vee pq$.

approach tells us. A better, anyway shorter, answer is that the renates are the cordates.

Alternatively there could be a presumption, also defeasible, in favor of "uncomplicated" truthmakers like the renates being the cordates. Suppose that *A* implies *B*, so that *A* and *A&B* are equivalent. *A&B* could just take its truth- and falsity-makers over from *A*, and should, given our presumption, if *A*'s are particularly simple. So, *Alice is upset and someone is upset* is true/false for the same reasons as *Alice is upset*. The presumption is defeated if *B* raises tricky new issues, for instance if it has falsemakers that are not so easily ruled out as *A*'s falsemakers. *I am sitting by the fire and not a brain in a vat* could in principle be assigned the same falsemakers as *I am sitting by the fire*: I am standing, for instance, or lying down, or etc. This would be the least complicated option. But in practice we would throw in the *B*-relevant possibility that I am a brain in a vat. I will for the most part be assuming minimal truthmakers, rather than recursive truthmakers. But, and this is important, structure will be respected where the assumption allows it, and the assumption is defeasible. One needs a *reason* to go nonminimal. But, one often has a reason.

4.7 TRUTHMAKERS IN CONTEXT

Truthmaking is a two-place relation; let's think about the relata. We have τ, the maker, and φ, the beneficiary. What sort of entity is φ? If truthmakers were generated compositionally, as on the recursive model, the logical choice would be sentences. The recursive model is problematic, though, precisely because of its excessive devotion to sentential structure. The sentence is important but so are stress patterns, salient events, shared agendas, and the like. I see no difference of principle here, and so prefer to treat the sentence employed as one more feature of context, influential but not all-powerful.

Now, even if *S* functions "actively" as an element of context to steer us toward certain truthmakers, that doesn't prevent it from serving also "passively" as the beneficiary of these efforts. There is precedent for such a view in Lewis's theory of de re modal attribution. Consider *Goliath* in *Goliath could not have been pear-shaped*. It contributes, Lewis thinks, in three ways: semantically, by supplying a referent; pragmatically, by raising a certain statue-ish counterpart relation to salience; and metaphysically, by helping to constitute the item that is up for evaluation.[19] One might think the same of S: it contributes semantically, by way of the coarse-grained proposition it expresses; pragmatically, by raising certain truthmakers/falsemakers to salience; and metaphysically, as the item made true. I don't object to this, but want to suggest another candidate for the role. Making a sentence true is "really," underlyingly, making the coarse-grained proposition true, in a context where the vehicle is that sentence; S in a given context gets its truthmakers from S, though the features of context whereby *they* are S's truthmakers may include that the sentence employed was S.

I have been talking about "tendencies" in truthmaker assignment, but it is only in the context of propositional logic that the recursive/reductive distinction is really clear. An advantage of the propositional setting is that precise, model-theoretic definitions are possible. But propositional languages are crude, and they let us off the hook in various ways, witness the lazy, mechanical treatment of atomic truthmakers as made in the image of atomic sentences. Model theory has served us well as a crutch, but at some point we have to confront natural language in all its glory. I will for various reasons be using tools from the reductionist's toolkit, more than recursive tools. One is that reductionism is easier; the recursive approach requires a new semantic insight for each new grammatical construction. Also it is more adaptable. Minimal models are like compact, nondisjunctive, guarantors of truth, which is a notion we know how to work with even where grammar is silent or unrevealing. If you are asked how it comes about that an emerald is grue, you will not answer (as you should, on the recursive model) that it is grue by being grue. An emerald is grue either by being examined and green, or unexamined and blue. A figure is polygonal by being rectangular, or triangular, or etc. Your understanding of the word tells you that it applies in different ways.

[19] Lewis (1971). Crimmins and Perry have a similar idea except that it is modes of presentation that a name makes salient (Crimmins and Perry 1989).

Chapter 4

4.8 NECESSITATION

Now I want to point out some respects in which metaphysical truthmakers are unsuited to the role of semantic truthmaker.[20] Metaphysical truthmaking, you recall, is

(m_1) a vertical relation,

(m_2) between "things in the world" τ and truths φ, whereby

(m_3) φ's truth is metaphysically necessitated by the existence of τ.

Semantic truthmaking, as I will be understanding it, is

(s_1) a horizontal—anyway not inherently vertical—relation

(s_2) between "ways things can be" τ and truths φ, whereby

(s_3) φ is logically necessitated—implied—and explained by τ.

Start with (m_3). Armstrong asks τ only to guarantee φ's truth; it needn't tell us how φ is true, or why. This is a problem if truthmakers are to line up with subject matter. Suppose that φ is necessarily equivalent to φ'. Then the same τs necessitate them, whence they agree in their Armstrongian truthmakers. Necessary equivalents may well not agree, however, we have seen, in what they are about. *All ravens are black* describes the world's ravens as black, while *All nonblack things are nonravens* says of the world's nonblack things that they are not ravens (**4.4**). Requiring τ to explain φ is meant to address this. *All ravens are black* is true because each of $r_1, \ldots, r_j$ (the world's ravens) is black. *All nonblack things are nonravens* is true because $n_1, \ldots, n_k$ (the world's nonblack things) are not ravens.

Staying with (m_3), Armstrong holds that "the necessitation cannot be any form of entailment" (Armstrong 2004, 5).[21] Entailment relations are judged from the armchair, whereas truthmaking (for "scientific realists" like Armstrong) is a matter for empirical inquiry. Given our project here, however, this consideration actually cuts the other way.

---

[20] I will be slighting the recursive aspects of semantic truthmaking, as already mentioned. Allowing them only strengthens the case.

[21] One reason he gives is that "[the] terms of an entailment relation must be propositions, but the truthmaking term of a truthmaking relation is a portion of reality" (Armstrong 2004, 6). This assumes (m_2)—that truthmaking is a vertical relation between worldly items and representers—so it will be left for the next section.

Imagine we are researching a hypothesis φ whose truthmakers are as yet unknown. To understand φ, we should have some idea what it's about. Should we put the project on hold to examine the suggestions ψ that have been made (by chemists, say, or meteorologists) about φ's truthmakers? The problem may arise again with ψ, and with our hypotheses χ about *its* truthmakers, and so on down the line, so that we never manage to work out what we are talking about. Can it really be that new research projects are required before we can understand what was at issue in old ones? There may be some deep truth in the neighborhood of that idea, but it prima facie gets things backwards. It should be possible to know what we're asking before marching off in search of the answer. Logical necessitation (implication) is a better choice for our purposes than metaphysical.

4.9 VERTICALITY

Truthmaking is a cross-categorial relation, according to (m_2). A truthmaker is an element of reality: an object, maybe, or trope, or event, or situation. A truth is a *representation* of reality: a sentence, one assumes, or proposition. There is no possibility, on this view, of truthmakers having truthmakers of their own, for τ must be a "thing" to play the truthmaking role with respect to φ, but a representation, to be made true in turn.

This is unfortunate from a subject-matter perspective, because it obliterates an important distinction: between what a sentence is directly about and what it is indirectly, or ultimately, about. Truthmaker chains are needed to see the difference. What, for instance, are A and B about?

(A) Nobody has a married great aunt.
(B) Grandparents with sisters and in-laws have only sisters-in-law.

Sentence A concerns the family relations of one group of people, a group which includes me. It says that my great aunts, if any, are single. B is about the family relations of a different group, which does not include me. The family relations in A reach back several generations, while those in B are on the face of it intragenerational. My great aunt's marital status figures in why A is false, but not B. My grandmother's brother-in-law falsifies B more directly than A. (A and B are truth-conditionally equivalent, I hope.)

Ah, but I have a married great aunt because my grandmother Masha had a sister Helen. Helen being her sister is relevant also to how Masha wound up with a brother-in-law. We have, then, two truthmaker *chains* with the same endpoint: Someone has a married great aunt because I do, which is owing to Helen's relations to Morris (her husband) and to Masha. Some grandparent has a brother-in-law in part because my grandmother does, which again is owing to Helen's relations to Masha and Morris.

This cannot work if truthmaking is cross-categorial. The middle term would have to be a world-element, to make *Nobody has a married great aunt* false, but also a world-representation, to be made true in part by Masha having a married sister. For claims with the same ultimate truthmakers to differ in subject matter is an intriguing phenomenon, that we need proximal truthmakers to explain.

A truth holds in *w* because of how matters stand there. How matters stand in *w*—that Sparky barks, for instance—is an aspect or property of *w* rather than a part of it. If we follow Lewis in identifying properties with their possible instances, then Sparky's barking is the set of worlds where that is what Sparky does. The fact of Sparky's barking is a truthmaker for the proposition that something barks. If we assume, again following Lewis, that a proposition too is a set of worlds, then truthmakers are of the same category as at least *some* of what they make true, namely other propositions. `Masha has a sister` is true because of this fact: `Helen is a sister to Masha`. Both parties to this relation—the fact and the proposition—are sets of worlds. Semantic truthmaking is vertical insofar as `Helen is a sister to Masha` makes *Masha has a sister* true. It does *that*, though, by making the expressed proposition true. Semantic truthmaking is derivatively vertical, I am suggesting, but at bottom horizontal.[22]

4.10 EXPLAINING TRUTH

Look again at (s_3): φ is necessitated *and explained* by τ. Can necessitators explain? Armstrong wonders about this himself. Truths hold "in virtue of"

---

[22] Why would we want the relation to be horizontal? Truthmaking is something like the dual of inclusion. A paradigm of inclusion is $p \& q \geq p$. A paradigm of truthmaking is $p \Vdash p \vee q$. A paradigm of *non*inclusion is $p \ngeq p \vee q$, while a paradigm of *non*truthmaking is $p \& q \nVdash p$. Inclusion is horizontal, so truthmaking should be too.

truthmakers, he says, which *sounds* explanatory. But there are passages like the following:

> Suppose *p* to be a truth and T to be a truthmaker for *p*. There may well exist, often there does exist, a T′ that is contained by T, and a T″ that contains T, with T′ and T″ *also* truthmakers for *p*. . . . The more embracing the truthmaker, the less discerning it is. For every truth, the least discerning of all truthmakers is the world itself, the totality of being. The world makes every truth true. (Armstrong 2004, 17–18)

He does then go on to discuss *p*'s "minimal truthmakers" as a special case, but without backing off the claim just stated: *p* holds true in virtue of arbitrarily inclusive *p*-necessitators. I find this puzzling. If T is sufficient for *p*'s truth, doesn't that cast doubt on the idea that *p* holds true in virtue of T-conjoined-with-U? Armstrong is surely right that "the 'making' here is not the causal sense of 'making'" (Armstrong 2004, 5). But he wouldn't have to say this, if there were not some sort of analogy. Truthmakers, like causes, should not be overladen with extra detail. (This relates to our idea above of truthmakers as *minimal* guarantors of truth.)

Suppose I shout at my cat, telling it to get off the couch. What causes the cat's departure? My shouting, *Get off the couch*? No, it would have run whatever I had shouted. A better candidate for the role of cause is my (simply) shouting. *Proportionality* says that a cause should not involve irrelevant extras without which the effect would still have ensued. Causes are expected on the whole to be proportional to their effects (Yablo 1992, Yablo 2003).

But of course, the shouting was not strictly required either; the cat would also have taken off, if I'd fired a gun at it. Is the cause my shouting-or-shooting-at the cat? This is where the second constraint comes in: naturalness, and especially nondisjunctiveness. My shouting-or-shooting at the cat is just too disjunctive.[23]

C is not a cause of E if you can improve it on the score of proportionality without making it much less natural. There is a similar tradeoff with truthmakers. They should on the one hand not incorporate irrelevant extras, in whose absence we'd still have a guarantee of truth. What makes it true that there are dogs? Proportionality favors the fact that Sparky is a dog

---

[23] See, however, Sartorio(2005) and Weslake (unpublished).

over the fact that Sparky is a black-and-white cockapoo; the extra detail is unneeded. Now we switch to the other hand. Isn't the fact that Sparky *or Shadow* is a dog still better, from a proportionality perspective?

It is better, from *that* perspective. But again, a candidate truthmaker is not disqualified by more proportional competitors if those competitors are much less natural. For τ to make φ true in world w is something in the neighborhood of τ being an explanatory φ-implier that obtains in w. And τ is not explanatory if it has competitors in w effecting a better tradeoff between naturalness and proportionality.[24]

4.11 SUMMING UP

Truth for Aristotle was a metaphysical notion. Tarski showed how to conceive truth semantically, that is, in such a way that it could play a foundational role in semantics. Armstrong, the Aristotle of truthmaking, conceives it metaphysically, as the a posteriori necessitation of truths by "things in the world." We in a Tarskian spirit seek a semantic conception of truthmakers. Two formal models were suggested, the recursive and the reductive. They represent tendencies in truthmaker assignment that pull, at times, in different directions. Where one can be indulged at no cost to the other, as in the case of quantifiers, that is the way to go. Otherwise a compromise has to be struck. How the tendencies trade off depends on the application. To a first approximation, though, semantic truthmakers are facts that imply truths and proportionally explain them.

[24] Truthmaking owes at least some of its hyperintensionality to the hyperintensionality of explanation. *Some Fs are Gs* has the same thin content as *Some Gs are Fs*. But this content will seem true for different reasons depending on which of the two sentential guises is salient. An event's causal relations can similarly seem to depend on the "features we hit on for describing [it]" (Davidson (1967)). My alerting the burglar is due in part to the burglar's being there to be alerted. Not so my flipping the switch. My flipping the switch caused the light to come on, but my alerting the burglar didn't; the light coming on played, on the contrary, a role in my alerting the burglar. Yet the flipping and alerting are, according to Davidson, same thin (coarse-grained) event.

- 5 -

The Truth and Something But the Truth

5.1 WHY LIE?

Now that we know, more or less, what partial truth *is*, the question becomes why bother with it? Why make false statements with true bits in them, rather than asserting just the true bits? William James suggests a reason in his debate with Clifford:

> a rule of thinking which would absolutely prevent me from acknowledging certain kinds of truth if those kinds of truth were really there, would be an irrational rule. (James 1979, 31–32).

This is usually heard, I assume rightly, as a plea for *epistemic* boldness. If "acknowledging certain truths" carries a risk of acknowledging the odd falsehood, well, that may be a price worth paying. But one can also hear it as a plea for *semantic* boldness. It might be that certain truths are not accessible except as scattered parts of larger falsehoods (or larger hypotheses that might for all we know be false).[1] If access were limited in this way, then dallying with the larger falsehoods could be on balance a good policy. The difference with James is that it's not the falsity of one statement tolerated for the sake of another's truth, but the falsity of a statement tolerated for the sake of the truth of, or in, *that very same statement*—for the sake of the truth it contains.[2]

This apology for partial truth is only as good as the premise that certain truths are only, or best, accessed as part of larger falsehoods. One sees how the premise *could* be true. The construction in section **3.4.2** of the part of *A* about m yielded a (potentially) true *proposition*, but not a sentence expressing it. The only *sentence* available is *A*, which we're supposing is

---

[1] This way of putting it comes from Quine: "The conceptual scheme of physical objects is [likewise] a convenient myth, simpler than the literal truth and yet containing that literal truth as a scattered part" (Quine 1948, 37).

[2] A logic of partial truth is developed in Humberstone (2003).

false. One can *specify* the intended proposition and *endorse* it, but there is no obvious way to *assert* it.

What other option have we, in this situation, than to assert the sentence, or make as if to assert it? Our plea to the charge of misrepresentation is "guilty with an excuse." *Part* of what we said was true; it's not obvious how to assert just that part; and we did our best to clue you in to which part it was—it's the part about such and such a subject matter.

So we see how there *could* be a Jamesian justification, or excuse, for speaking "the truth and something but the truth"—for what might be thought of as a kind of generalized hyperbole. It would be nice to have some actual examples, and I am not sure I do. Here, though, are some possible ones, which may or may not turn out on closer consideration to work. They are meant to illustrate a *kind* of approach that is not on the standard menu of options.[3]

5.2 LOOSE TALK

I am 5 feet 9 inches tall. That is what I say, at any rate, when someone asks me my height, or I have to enter it on a form. Being 5 foot 9 makes me the same height as Carla Sarkozy.

I say these things, but they are not true. I am closer to $5'\,8\frac{3}{4}''$ than to $5'\,9''$, which makes me less than $5'\,9''$; you can't be less than $5'\,9''$ tall and $5'\,9''$ tall at the same time. Similarly for being the same height as Carla Sarkozy. She is a bit over $5'\,9''$, which makes her taller than me rather than the same height.[4]

---

[3] Fictionalism, error theory, figuralism, deflationism, etc. I will not undertake a point by point comparison. But see the last few chapters.

[4] Peter Lasersohn's example: "Suppose I tell John that Mary arrived at 3 o'clock. If John finds out later that Mary didn't arrive at 3 but at fifteen seconds after 3, it would be unreasonable of him to complain 'You said she came at 3!' ... [but] we have to concede that he is, strictly speaking, RIGHT; when I told him Mary arrived at 3, I said something that was literally false, not true" (Lasersohn 1999, 522). See also Sperber and Wilson: "Suppose Marie lives in Issy-les-Moulineaux, a block away from the city limits of Paris. At a party in London, she meets Peter. He asks her where she lives, and she answers: I live in Paris. Marie's answer is literally false, but in ordinary circumstances it is not misleading. ... Peter would be misled by Marie's answer only if he were to conclude from it that she lives within the city limits of Paris rather than in a suburb" (Sperber and Wilson 1985).

These statements sound right, because they are true about height in inches, which is all we normally care about. Worlds are height in inches–equivalent when they agree, for all individuals I, on the number n of inches that is closest to I's actual height. *I am 5' 9"* is true about height in inches (see the definition in section **2.4**) if it can be made true, *period*, by adjusting heights in a way that preserves the n in question. And it can, by "normalizing" everyone to their height in inches. This means topping off people like myself, who are slightly less than their height in inches, and cutting back people like Carla Sarkozy, who are slightly more. *I am the same height as Carla Sarkozy* is true in a normalized world as well. *France is hexagonal* is true about approximate shape, because it can be made true simpliciter while preserving the standard shapes closest to true shapes. *You never take me to Friendly's* is true about what happens birthdays aside, because its truth simpliciter requires only a tweak in what happens on birthdays.

Why proceed in this roundabout fashion? I could have said that 5' 9" is the height in inches closest to my height; that the number of inches closest to Carla Sarkozy's height is the number of inches closest to mine; that *hexagonal* is the standard shape minimizing the area of nonoverlap with France; and so on. But this way of talking is ugly and inconvenient. It requires explicitness about something that ought to be backgrounded—something off the main point and anyway perfectly well understood. Better to stick with the original statement and let the part presented as true track the issue under discussion.

That issue may change as the discussion proceeds. Deb is $6' 1\frac{1}{4}''$, you tell me. Why not call her 6' 1"? Because the simpler statement is false, I assume, about the subject matter you mean to be addressing; it is false about height to the nearest quarter inch. I will not call myself 5'9" any longer, as this too is false about the subject matter now under discussion.

OK, but why can I not reshrink the issue as easily as you expanded it?[5] Why does *I am 5'9"*, since it is false about height to the nearest quarter inch, not return us to height in inches?

[5] "For some reason, the boundary readily shifts outward if what is said requires it, but does not so readily shift inward if what is said requires that. Because of this asymmetry, we may think that what is true with respect to the outward-shifted boundary must be somehow more true" (Lewis 1979, 355).

Chapter 5

To shift the subject matter from m to m', one needs to say something unambiguously directed at m'. This is much more possible if m' is the larger of the two than if it is the smaller. *Deb is 6' 1¼"* looks to be addressing itself to height to the nearest quarter inch rather than height in inches; why otherwise stick in that extra fraction? *I am 5' 9"* could be directed at either issue. I might try to noodge you back some other way: "Nevertheless, as far as I'm concerned, Deb is 6' 1"." This is bad form, however. Speaking to a larger subject matter, you signal the intention not to keep on ignoring some of what our statements were already about. The party proposing *not* to ignore a falsifier has the semantic high ground.

5.3 APPLIED MATH

Imagine we have a strange, kabbalistic reading of Genesis. Go forth and multiply, God commanded. The "multiply" means, we believe, that the animals should proliferate at a constant rate; each year's population was to be n times larger than the year before's. The value of n revealed itself when "forth" turned out to be a mistranscription of "fourth." The command was issued on day 5, and we believe on other grounds that the number of animals at that time was three. According to us, then,

(NA) The number of animals on the nth day $= 3 \times 4^{(n-5)}$.

Unfortunately for this way of putting it, our reading of Genesis *also* tells us that God never got around to creating numbers. So we can't in consistency regard our hypothesis as true.[6] How much should this bother us? Well, how much should it bother Lupoli that Falstaff's testimony

---

[6] Isn't there something odd about wheeling in worlds, sets, propositions, and the like to show how one can avoid commitment to numbers? I confess to not being much concerned about this. The following points seem relevant. First, this book is not just for nominalists. Second, even those who believe in abstract objects may not feel they are committed to them by their acceptance of mixed mathematical laws. Third, the semantic theorist's commitments are not to be visited on ordinary speakers. Fourth, the semantic theorist has the same need for abstract machinery as any other scientist. Fifth, the semantic theorist may have hopes of kicking away the ladder; once you see what the machinery is doing for us, its work is done. Sixth, you should blame me of all people, the one trying to understand how the machinery works.

was not true? It's enough for him that the testimony is true about his client. Similarly it's enough for us if *The number of animals on the nth day is $3 \times 4^{(n-5)}$* is true about the animals, or more generally the physical world. "Why don't you use a sentence whose full content is what the animal multiplication formula says about the physical world?" Maybe we can't think of such a sentence. Also though, even if a nominalistic paraphrase were available, it is not clear what the motivation would be for using it, other than paranoid-schizoid horror at the mixing of truth with falsehood.

Our construction of the physical part of the animal numeration formula runs through worlds that are partly *non*physical—worlds with mathematical objects in them. It's a proposition that is true in w if *The number of animals on the nth day $= 3 \times 4^{(n-5)}$* is true in Platonistically enhanced concrete duplicates of w. If we are nominalists, however, we might question whether these enhanced concrete duplicates are really possible.[7] Platonists will likewise question the possibility of nominalistic worlds. Numbers have traditionally been seen as existing in all worlds or none.[8]

Now, for what it is worth, insistence on the modally extreme character of mathematical objects has been waning of late.[9] Also it is not clear why the same expressive work could not be done by schmumbers, understood to be just like numbers except for the requirement of existing in all worlds or none (Yablo 2002). Suppose though that schmumbers are not available and that the traditional view of numbers' modal status is correct. Still, if they are necessary, this is not because they are demanded by concreta, and if they're impossible, it is not because concreta preclude them. Both hypotheses, the Platonistic and nominalistic, are possible where physical things are concerned, just as the existence of {Socrates} is not decided by Socrates.[10] See the appendix for more on impossible worlds which are, nevertheless, relatively possible.

---

[7] To borrow a phrase from Crispin Wright, it is hard to think what conditions more favorable to the emergence of mathematical objects would be.

[8] "Impure" mathematical objects like $\{x \mid x = Socrates\}$ are another matter.

[9] Field (1993), Hellman (1989), Wright and Hale (1992), Tennant (1997), Colyvan (2000), Colyvan (2003), and Rosen (2006).

[10] Fine (1994).

Chapter 5

5.4 INTENTIONAL IDENTITY

Consider a puzzle sentence of Geach's: "Hob believes that a witch burned down his barn, and Nob believes that she blighted his mare." Given that the barn burned down for natural reasons (a cow kicked over the lantern), not supernatural, there is nothing, it seems, for the sentence to be about; and yet it appears, in the circumstances Geach describes, to be true. The problem as it is usually conceived takes this appearance for granted. It is because the sentence is true that we need a regimentation that carries no commitment to witches. But, how without witches are we to understand the binding relations between "a witch" and "she"? One might see the pronoun as standing in for a description, say, "the witch that burned down Hob's barn." But Nob may never have heard of Hob. No single description can work, because there is no limit to the ways in which Hob and Nob's mental states can acquire what Geach calls a "common focus." Nob may have been told about the supposed witch by Bob; the story may have been written up in the newspaper with Hob's name omitted; it could be common "knowledge" in the community that exactly one witch turns up every year to cause mischief.

These problems arise only if the sentence is true. Is it? Maybe it strikes us that way because it is true about the topic under discussion. That topic is limited, I assume, to events that really occurred. The witch's setting fire to the barn did not occur; it is a figment of Hob's imagination. What is real is the fire itself, and events subsequent to the fire. Let us imagine, then, that the sentence is evaluated on the basis of what it says about f = the fire and everything after. It is true about that if there is nothing in events *since* the fire to preclude its being true full stop. And indeed there is not. One can twist our world into one where Hob and Nob are in every sense thinking about the same witch without laying a hand on events since the fire, simply by putting that witch in Hob's barn, with a torch, a few moments before.

5.5 NARROW CONTENT

Putnam showed in the 1970s that belief, desire, and so on are not "narrow" or "internal" states, as had previously been supposed. States like belief are widely individuated; they depend for their instantiation on events outside the subject's head.

A common reaction was to concede the point about belief proper, while attempting to carve out a narrow analogue of belief that answered to the naive conception. I won't go into all the motivations for this, but they were interesting and initially convincing. There was more at work than nostalgia for the old standards of individuation. "Narrow" or "solipsistic" attitudes were to be, in Dennett's phrase (Dennett 1982), the "organismic contribution" to wide attitudes. They were to be obtained by bleaching out, or abstracting away from, those aspects of externalistic belief that pertain to the external world, in order to focus on what remains: the goings-on in someone's head that enable him or her to believe (plopped down in the right environment) that such and such.

This sounds like a job for subject matter. Sam's narrow belief that salt is plentiful is the part of *Sam believes that salt is plentiful* that concerns goings-on in Sam's head, or, in Stalnaker's phrase, the internal world.[11]

So, what does it say about goings-on in Sam's head in w, that Sam believes in w that salt is plentiful? Less than one might have imagined. Sam narrowly believes salt is plentiful in w if he believes of just about anything—dirt, as it might be—that it is plentiful. For let w' be a world just like w where Sam's head is concerned, but with salt supplanting dirt as the predominant cause of his "dirt"-tokenings. Sam believes in w' that salt is plentiful, and w' is just like w where Sam's head is concerned; that is enough, on the stated proposal, for him to narrowly believe in w that salt is plentiful. This seems like the wrong result. Believing that dirt is plentiful falls far short, intuitively speaking, of narrowly believing that salt is plentiful. That I would rather put salt on my food than pepper should not confer on me a narrow dietary preference for dirt over pepper.

Here is a possible way out. Central, paradigmatic instances of a concept can be distinguished from marginal or peripheral instances. Yard birds are stereotypical, penguins less so. Soup pots are stereotypical, but not chamber or flower pots. This was noticed by Beckett and made into a semantic

[11] One might want to go further, bleaching out also lower-level physical details like blood flow and glucose delivery. Nothing I say will depend on the fine details.

theory by Eleanor Rosch.[12] Whatever one thinks of Rosch's larger view, the distinction between marginal cases and central ones seems very real.

A similar distinction obtains at the sentential level. *Tweety is a bird* is centrally true, said of a sparrow; it is peripherally true, said of a penguin. Here we are still talking essentially about central instances of a concept—the concept of a bird—but we can go further. *She ran to the edge and jumped* is stereotypically true if she jumps off the edge, peripherally true if she jumps in place there, for exercise.[13] *I live with a philosopher* is stereotypically true if there's a philosopher at home other than me, marginally true if the philosopher is myself.

Consider now *Sam believes that salt is plentiful*. I cannot tell you in so many words what it takes for this to be stereotypically true. But one knows the type of situation that people would normally think of—the type of which one could say, *Sam believes that salt is plentiful*, and be comforted. And it certainly does not include the situation where the substance controlling dirt-appearances is in fact salt.

Could it be that the narrow content theorist chose the wrong sort of belief-attribution to cut down to size? *Sam narrowly believes that salt is plentiful* is the inside-the-head part, not of *Sam believes that salt is plentiful*, but *Sam stereotypically believes that salt is plentiful*.[14] Sam narrowly believes that *P* if he stereotypically believes that *P*, in a scenario that is just like ours where the internal world is concerned.[15]

5.6 LAWS AND MODELS

Galileo is supposed to have discovered that distance fallen grows with the square of the time elapsed. This is puzzling, because the "discovery" is, owing to various complications (friction, e.g.), not really true. A familiar reply: "Laws are not meant to be true *in reality*. They hold in *models* where the complications do not arise."

---

[12] "It resembled a pot, it was almost a pot, but it was not a pot of which one could say, pot, pot, and be comforted" (Beckett 1959, 64)

[13] Saul (2012).

[14] The suggestion about Hob-Nob sentences in the last section should probably be stereotypicalized as well.

[15] See Crimmins (1989).

If law-statements are not true in reality, they shouldn't be silent about it, either. It ought to say something about the world as it is that the law holds in worlds *w* corresponding to the model. Translation schemes have been suggested by which actual-world truths $S_@$ are to be read off truths S about *w*. $S_@$ might be to the effect that

1. *S*-worlds are somehow *embeddable* in the actual world, or
2. the actual world in certain respects *resembles* an *S*-world, or
3. the actual world is such as to make S true in a certain story.

Consider a simple-minded alternative

28 *S*'s truth in *w* testifies

> not to the total truth, in @, of $S_@$,
> but the partial truth, in @, of S itself.

That Galileo's Law holds, in a world without other forces, testifies to its truth here about motion due to gravity.

What is that, however? There would appear to be no such separate item as the component of an object's progress that is due specifically to gravity. The fall of an apple does not harbor within it a second, faster, fall, unencumbered by friction. What does it mean, then, for Galileo's Law to hold of motion due to gravity?

Recall the distinction above between observables, like my hand and the Sun, and observation, the subject matter. A theory of observables should have something to say about nuclear fusion. A theory true of observation can fill the Sun with pop rocks, if it likes, as long as it preserves appearances. Gravitational motion must similarly be distinguished from the matter of motion due to gravity. Motion due to gravity is a relation on worlds; it lumps slow-fall frictional scenarios together with their fast-fall frictionless counterparts. For Galileo's Law to hold of motion due to gravity, is for it to be true, period, in a counterpart world with the same gravitational forces as here.[16]

---

[16] Really we need the box-like notion here (section **2.4**) it should be true in all such worlds free of countervailing forces. Otherwise, *Distance fallen is proportional to the square root of the time elapsed* is true about gravitational motion, too, since gravity is offset in some worlds by levitational forces.

This view of component motions has an analog for component forces. The total force on an apple is not really, we might think, the resultant of various sub-forces, all somehow duking it out. Rather we have a subject matter of force exerted by BLAH. Coulomb's Law is true about force exerted by slow-moving charges, on account of being wholly true in worlds with no relevant other forces. Newton's Law of Gravity is true about force exerted by massive objects.

Surely there is something, though, to the idea of total force being resolvable into components? The resolution occurs at the level of subject matter. The truth about total force is obtainable from the truth about force exerted by slow-moving charges of Coulomb's Law, the truth about force exerted by massive bodies of the Law of Gravitation, and so on.[17] We take the electrostatic vector from w and sum it with the gravitational one from w'. One thinks of this as "combining forces." But it might better be understood as combining the states of things with respect to single-force subject matters to obtain the state of things with respect to total force.

Total force is a complicated matter, but the truth about it can be recovered from truths about simpler matters. One might see in this a model for scientific understanding in general. Here is a way of framing the issue, suggested by the work of Nancy Cartwright.[18] By total nomological circumstances ($= n$), let's mean the rule, however complicated, that constrains instantaneous states of the universe and determines evolution from one to the next. The decomposition of forces model seems to suggest that n should be resolvable into a bunch of (presumably orthogonal) n_ks, each governed by a particular sort of law. But it's just that, a suggestion. There is no reason to think this sort of factorization must always be possible.[19]

---

[17] Lange (2009).

[18] Cartwright (1983).

[19] Similar questions arise elsewhere in philosophy. "The value of a whole must not be assumed to be the same as the sum of the values of its parts" (Moore 1903, 79). "For most factors, their role in determining the overall moral status of an act cannot be adequately captured in terms of separate and independent contributions that merely need to be added in" (Kagan 1988, 21).

5.7 NEGATIVE SINGULAR EXISTENTIALS

I believe that, as I'm tempted to put it, *Pegasus does not exist.*[20] But I am not a Meinongian. Pegasus does not subsist either; it has no kind of being whatsoever.[21] "Pegasus" is an entirely empty name. This puts me in a bit of a bind, since sentences with empty names in them are not true. Why do we treat them as true? "What gives us," as Kripke says, "the right to talk this way?"

I want to start with a simpler question. Any difficulty that arises for *Pegasus does not exist* arises also for *Pegasus is not in this room*. Why does *it* seem true? There are two places to look for the answer—Pegasus, and the room—and we are not going to get any help from Pegasus. The truth of, or in, *Pegasus is not in the room*, will have to be found in the room. The first point that needs to be made is that, although *Pegasus is not in the room* is untrue—I will treat it as gappy—this is not because of how matters stand where the room is concerned. There is nothing going on in here to prevent Pegasus from existing out in the hall, in which case *Pegasus is not in the room* is true outright. *Pegasus is not in the room* is true about the room and its contents, or better, the room and its contents.

Is that enough to make it assertible? Not necessarily, for reasons discussed in section **2.4**. *Pegasus is not in the room* can be true, compatibly with goings-on in the room, but who is to say it cannot also be false? The second point is that the room and its contents do seem to preclude this, that is, *Pegasus is in the room* cannot be true compatibly with goings on in the room. Kripke is making, I think, a similar point when he says,

> Without being sure of whether Sherlock Holmes was a person,
> or whether we can speak of hypothetical situations under which
> "Sherlock Holmes did such and such" correctly describes the situation,

---

[20] *Pegasus does not exist* has a paradoxical, self-undermining, flavor. On the one hand, the empty name makes it untrue. But now, why is the name empty? Because Pegasus does not exist. *Pegasus does not exist* is untrue because Pegasus does not exist. The pattern here—*S* is untrue, if it is, because *S*—is not unfamiliar. *This sentence is untrue* is true, if it is, because it is not true. *The number of numbers = 0* is untrue, for the nominalist, because the number of numbers is 0.

[21] "Meinong" here is the popular Meinong, who takes nonexistent objects to have a lesser sort of being.

we can say "none of the people in this room is Sherlock Holmes, for all are born too late, and so on"; or "whatever bandersnatches may be, certainly there are none in Dubuque." (Kripke 2011b, 71)

Pegasus is not in this room can be true, compatibly with how matters stand in the room, but not false, under the same constraint. Of the notions of fidelity to a subject matter introduced earlier (section **2.4**), to be true in some m-equivalents of the actual world, and false in none of them, was the strongest. *Pegasus is not in this room* counts as true, the suggestion is, because it is true, and only true, about the room and its contents.

None of us here is qualified to be Pegasus; that is why *Pegasus is here in the room* is not true about the room and its contents. The reasons are different in different cases. I take it, though, that every x in the room has features Q_x such that, *even allowing that Pegasus, Holmes, and so on could have turned out to exist*, they could not have turned out to be Q_x, or, if you prefer, a Q_x could not have turned out to be Holmes. Kripke speaks of being born too late, for instance. I doubt that this is disqualifying by itself. A devoted spiritualist, Doyle might have had a premonition of one of us and intended the stories as a kind of anticipatory homage. But at some point, as the details are piled on—Doyle never had thoughts about you, there was no ghostwriter involved, and so on—we reach a point of no return. The story cannot be continued so that if things had turned out like *that*, you would have turned out to be Holmes.[22]

The same applies to *Pegasus is nowhere in the solar system, . . . the Milky Way*, and so on. Eventually we get to *Pegasus is nowhere at all*, or *Pegasus is not one of us*, where "us" takes in everything in existence. And now we can try the same strategy as before. *Pegasus is not in the room* counts as true because it is true, and not false, about the room and its contents, *Pegasus is not one of us* counts as true because it is true about a certain subject matter, call it us, while its negatum, *Pegasus is one of us*, lacks this feature.[23]

---

[22] But, you might say, "qualifications" have nothing to do with it, for names lack descriptive content. That none of us is "qualified" is not a reason for *Pegasus is here in the room* to be false. I agree and have said it is *not* false. It doesn't have to be, to be false about m, nor does the name need descriptive content. "Could have turned out" conditionals are sensitive as well to metasemantic features of the sort Kripke tried to capture with reference-fixing descriptions.

[23] "The topic is US?!" The name in *N is P* is topical if the implied question is, *What about N?*, focal if it is *What is P?* "[T]o what question is . . . *John exists* a felicitous answer? I think it is *Who/What exists? . . .*) [Not, *What about John?*] The topic is: what exists. . . ." Note, *John exists*

What goes into the subject matter I have called us? It had better not be *too* comprehensive, or room will not be left for Pegasus to be tacked on as a further item; any such addition will disrupt the state of things where we are concerned. It should be comprehensive enough, though, to stop Pegasus from being smuggled in. We have already seen how to arrange this. Take any individual that you like—you, me, the fencepost, the wide Sargasso Sea, ... , it will have properties such that, granting Pegasus could have turned out to exist, it could not have turned out like *that*. If we import these properties into us, then the state of things where we are concerned blocks any attempt by Pegasus to blend into the existing population.

That explains, maybe, why it counts as true that *Pegasus is not one of us.* What about *Pegasus does not exist?* Why does *it* seem true, notwithstanding the empty name? It makes no sense, on the face of it, to understand *Pegasus does not exist* on the model of *Pegasus is not in this room.* That would be to reckon *Pegasus does not exist* true, *period*, in a world where the existing things are just what they are here, and Pegasus is not among them. How can there be a world *w* that is just like the actual world with regard to what exists, yet *Pegasus* is not in *w* an empty name? There is, of course a tradition, the Meinongian tradition, that treats these two issues as separate; I have already said, however, that I am not a Meinongian.

But so what? I have also already said I am not a Platonist. That didn't get in the way of using Platonic language instrumentally to say something about a non-Platonic subject matter. It suffices for expressive purposes to know what the Platonic doctrine involves, and what it would be for it to hold in a concrete duplicate of actuality. Similarly the fact that I am not a Meinongian should not stop me from using *Pegasus* as though it referred, given that I am not representing the Meinongian implications as true. It is enough for expressive purposes to know what the doctrine involves. I take it we are not utterly baffled by the hypothesis of Pegasus being "there" in a world that is just like ours with regard to what exists in it. One might try to argue that tacking on *abstract* objects, over and above the concrete ones, is easier than tacking on *subsistent* objects under and below the existent ones. But I find it hard to see an in-principle difference here. The

---

and so does Harriett is better than *John exists and writes poetry. John* is a better candidate for focal stress in *John exists* than *exists. John EXISTS* sounds quite unnatural (Atlas 1988, Gundel 1985).

add-ons are in neither case metaphysically possible, perhaps. But, abstract objects are *relatively* possible; they are possible where concrete things are concerned. Subsistent objects are relatively possible, too; they are possible where existing things are concerned.

Here then is my Jamesian excuse for saying *Pegasus fails to exist*, even if it is not true. All I care about is its import for existing things, and I have no other way to articulate that than to say that *Pegasus fails to exist*, on the understanding that I am advocating only for what it says about them. It may seem unfortunate that the construction runs essentially through Meinong worlds, worlds where Pegasus subsists without existing. But it's no worse than the use made of Plato worlds in the explanation of what *The number of planets* = 8 says about the physical. Meinong was wrong, let's agree. But the idea of nonexistent objects nevertheless available to serve as referents is not absurd in itself. *Pegasus doesn't exist* fails to be true *only* because this coherent idea is false.

5.8 PURE MATH

I am a non-Platonist, let's suppose this time a *nominalist*. I think it is *false* that *There are primes over 10*. Like anyone else, though, I want to be able to say it. Why? Well, if we're to continue along the tracks laid down above, it's because the statement has a *part* that I do believe, a part that is interestingly true in my view, and remains so even if numbers do not exist.

This time, though, it is harder to see what the true part might be. Doesn't it follow from the denial of numbers that, as Hartry Field once suggested (Field (1980)), true-seeming existential claims (like *There are primes over 10*) are trivially false, and false-seeming universal claims (like *Primes over 10 are even*) are trivially true? That would seem to leave little room for interestingly true parts to larger numerical falsehoods.

Well, but should we agree that *Primes over 10 are even* is (in the absence of numbers) every bit as true as *Primes over 10 are odd*? To the extent this seems plausible, it is because we take ourselves to be dealing with *enumerative* generalizations about whatever numbers there happen to be. I don't know why we would assume this, any more than we would assume that *Objects suffering zero net force maintain their velocity* is an enumerative generalization about whatever physical objects there happen to be or *Steve advises transfer students from Antarctica* is an enumerative generalization about transfer students from Antarctica, if any. *Objects with no impinging forces explode* sounds false, *even if there are no such objects*, simply because exploding is physically unlawful behavior for "them." It's the same with *Primes over 10 are even*; it sounds false, whether there are primes over 10 or not, because this is mathematically unlawful behavior for "them."[24]

How are we to explain the intuitive falsity of generalizations with no counterexamples? They have a generic part stating how objects of the relevant sort behave *qua objects of that sort*,[25] and an existential part to the effect that the relevant objects are there. *There are infinitely many primes* says in part that *Numbers are of a type to include infinitely many primes*, in part that the type is instantiated. Nominalists, when they say *There are infinitely many primes*, are putting the first part forward as true but not the second. Alternatively we could say they are putting the full statement forward as true about a certain subject matter, that subject matter being the Sosein of numbers rather than their Sein.

5.9 SUMMING UP

"A rule of thinking which would prevent me from acknowledging certain kinds of truth would be an irrational rule" (William James). Truth-puritanism, the policy of accepting only full truths, is irrational in this sense. The difference with James is that, rather than a falsehood here tolerated for the sake of a truth there, a statement's falsity is tolerated for the sake of the truth of, or in, that very statement. Who might stand in need of a Jamesian excuse? The non-Platonist who wants to say, *The rate of star formation is decreasing*, because it is true about the stars. The loose talker who wants to say, *I am 5′ 9″*, because it is true about height to the nearest inch. The non-Meinongian who wants to say that *Pegasus does not exist*, because it is true about what does exist. And, looking ahead a bit, the

---

[24] Lewis takes this one step further. He suggests there might be generalizations *G* about so and so's when, not only are so-and-so's absent, they are absent because of *G*. *Brakeless trains are dangerous* is his example. Another might be *The universal set contains everything, including its own power-set.*

[25] See Correia (2006). Numerical generalizations satisfy standard tests of genericity.

nonskeptic who wants to say that she is sitting by the fire, because it is true, and known to be, about her posture and proximity to the fire.

APPENDIX: IMPOSSIBILITY

Hypotheses are impossible for a reason; there is something that rules them out. These ruler-outs are the "constraints." Let the set of them be Ω.

29 φ is impossible if $\Omega \vdash \neg\varphi$; otherwise φ is possible.

Possible worlds are, or correspond to, maximal possibilities: φs which are logically consistent with Ω but cannot be strengthened so as to remain consistent with it.

The constraints might be general metaphysical principles like *Material objects are spatially extended*.[26] They might take the form of identities (*To be water is to be H_2O*) and semi-identities (*To be water is in part to contain hydrogen*).[27] The best known proposal along these lines is Kit Fine's.[28] The constraints in his system are Aristotelian real definitions, for instance, {*Socrates*} $=_{df}$ *the set whose only member is Socrates, Goliath $=_{df}$ the statue made in such and such a way from such and such materials.*

A scenario is possible, full stop, if there is nothing to rule it out. But we can also consider *relatively* possible scenarios—scenarios that, while perhaps impossible *all* things considered, are possible *some* things considered. φ is possible relative to Γ (a proper subset of Ω) if it is possible when constraints not in Γ are ignored, or possible on the assumption that Γ contains all the constraints there are.

30 φ is impossible$_\Gamma$ if $\Gamma \vdash \neg\varphi$; otherwise it is possible$_\Gamma$.

Possible$_\Gamma$ worlds are, or correspond to, maximal Γ-possibilities: φs such that (i) $\Gamma \nvdash \neg\varphi$, but (ii) $\Gamma \vdash \neg\psi$ for all ψ strictly implying φ.

Clearly more is possible where *some* constraints are concerned than is possible where *all* constraints are concerned. A world that is Γ-possible for some specified $\Gamma \subsetneq \Omega$, but not Ω-possible, is strictly speaking impossible.

---

[26] Peacocke (2002), Sider (2002).
[27] Rayo (2013).
[28] Fine (1994).

But there is nothing contradictory about it; it is just a maximal φ consistent with the given constraints.

For Socrates to exist without {Socrates} is absolutely impossible, Fine would say; it happens in no possible worlds. But there is nothing *in the nature of Socrates* to prevent it. One can know all there is to know about who or what Socrates is without having the slightest idea of his belonging to certain sets. Socrates-without-{Socrates} is an example of an absolutely impossible scenario that is nevertheless relatively possible—possible where Γ is concerned, for some $\Gamma \subsetneq \Omega$.

This bears on a problem raised earlier (section **5.3**) about the modally extreme character of mathematical objects. Just as there is nothing in the nature of Socrates to decide whether {Socrates} exists, there is nothing in the nature of the concrete world generally to decide the existence of mathematical objects generally. It is at peace both with their existing and their not existing; there are relatively possible worlds of both types. *The rate of star formation has been exponentially decreasing* is true about the concrete world iff it is completely true about a world just like this one in concrete respects; that that world is (according to some nominalists) only relatively possible is neither here nor there.

Room has been made for metaphysical impossibilities, and even perhaps mathematical impossibilities. (Cauchy sequences don't necessarily converge, bracketing the real numbers' least upper bound property.) But it may be useful for some purposes to allow in *logical* impossibilities. (**30**) does not allow this. If ψ is a logical falsehood, then it is not Γ-possible for any Γ, since $\neg\psi$ is logically entailed even by the empty set. That being said, the idea of construing relative possibilities as hypotheses that are not refutable *in certain particular ways* may still have something to offer us.

When a scenario is impossible, that is because hypotheses "witnessing" the scenario are ruled out by the constraints. One sort of relative possibility is obtained by weakening the constraints. The kind we are after now is obtained by weakening the conditions on witnesses. Ω gathered together the conditions with which φ had to be consistent, if φ was to be possible. Let Θ be an equivalence relation on formulas such that Ω has to be consistent with all hypotheses Θ-equivalent to φ, for φ to be possible. (Θ can be identity, or logical equivalence, for instance.)

31 φ is impossible iff $\vdash \neg\psi$ for all $\psi \equiv_\Theta \varphi$; otherwise φ is possible.

This is regular old logical impossibility. For the relative notion, we substitute a relation Δ that is weaker than Θ. φ is possible relative to Δ if anything Δ-equivalent to φ is (simply) possible.

32 φ is impossible$_\Delta$ iff $\vdash \neg\psi$ for all $\psi \equiv_\Delta \varphi$; otherwise φ is possible$_\Delta$.

So, for instance, let φ be $\neg(p \supset (q \supset p))$, and let ψ be Δ-equivalent to φ iff ψ is (like φ) the negation of a conditional whose consequent's consequent is identical to its antecedent. φ is impossible$_\Delta$, because no formula of that type is self-consistent. Now we weaken Δ so that ψ is Δ-equivalent to φ iff it is (like φ) the negation of a conditional whose antecedent is repeated in its consequent; we leave out, this time, that the antecedent and final consequent are one and the same. φ now becomes relatively possible, by virtue of being Δ-equivalent to $\neg(p \supset (p \supset q))$, which is self-consistent. A logically impossible world is one that is able to look favorably on a formula like φ, despite its logical falsity, by its not quite laserlike focus on the structural features that prevent φ from being true.

- 6 -

Confirmation and Verisimilitude

Inquiry aims at the truth. What is it for one belief state to be closer to the truth than another? There are two dimensions to this. One relates to the kind of attitude we adopt. If *A* is true, our attitude toward it should be as close as possible to full belief. The other is to do with the attitude's content. If the *content* of our belief is *A*, then *A* should be as truthlike or verisimilar as possible. Confirmation theory is directed at the first goal. The theory of verisimilitude is directed at the other.

6.1 SURPLUS CONTENT

Imagine that we are investigating a hypothesis *H*, when we learn that a certain consequence *E* of *H* is true. *E* rules out certain ways *H* might be false: the ones that require *E* too to be false. Eliminating opportunities for falsity is confirmation *of a sort*. Suppose we are flipping a fair coin; *E* is *The coin just came up heads* and *H* is *It always comes up heads*. *E* confirms—makes it likelier that—*The coin always comes up heads*, by eliminating a possible counterexample.[1] What it does not provide is evidence for the rest of *H*— for, let us say, *H*–*E*. Positive instances make a generalization likelier even if they are irrelevant to, even in fact if they count *against*, the rest of the generalization. To come at it from the other direction: no matter how much *E* counts against *X*, *E* counts in *favor* of a hypothesis that entails *X*, namely *X*&*E*.

Call that basic or simple confirmation. A second and more demanding notion is obtained by asking *E* to bear favorably also on the rest of *H*—its *surplus content* relative to *E*. *The coin came up heads* does not in the more demanding sense confirm *It always comes up heads*, for it says nothing about other tosses. Still less does *No one has ever run a three-minute mile* confirm *Today will be the first three-minute mile ever*, though it makes that hypothesis overall likelier.

[1] If *H* entails *E*, $0 < \text{pr}(E)$ and $\text{pr}(H) < 1$, then $\text{pr}(H|E)$ exceeds $\text{pr}(H)$.

The distinction between "mere content cutting" (Gemes (1994)) and, let's call it, *inductive* confirmation goes back at least to Goodman, who used it to characterize lawlike, as opposed to accidental, generalizations. *All Fs are Gs* is lawlike, Goodman suggested, if it is inductively confirmed by its instances. *All ravens are black* is lawlike to the extent that a raven observed to be black counts in favor of other ravens' being black; the tested part of the hypothesis reflects favorably on the untested. Nothing like that occurs with *Everyone was born on a Thursday*; the generalization is thus accidental. But, where Goodman focuses on generalizations, our notion of inductive confirmation is meant to be completely general: to inductively confirm *H*, *E* should bear favorably on *H*'s surplus content relative to *E*, whatever form that surplus content might take. So, for instance, that the planets have roughly elliptical orbits should count in favor of each of Newton's three laws of motion and the law of gravitation along with the auxiliary hypotheses needed to derive it from those laws.

Inductive confirmation is tied up with *surplus content*; so views about what *H*'s surplus content with respect to *E* is will guide one's thinking about when inductive confirmation occurs. Popper and Miller claim, in a 1983 letter to *Nature*, that it never occurs. *H* is likelier given *E* than without it, we assume; *E* basically confirms *H*. To test for inductive confirmation, we need to isolate *H*'s surplus content. When this is done, they say, we find that *E* *lowers* its probability:

1. *H* is logically equivalent to $(H \vee E)\&(H \vee \neg E)$
2. The first conjunct $H \vee E$ simplifies to *E*, since *E* is entailed by *H*
3. The surplus content over *E* of $E\&(H \vee \neg E)$ is $H \vee \neg E = E \rightarrow H$
4. *E* makes $E \rightarrow H$ *less* likely: $p(H \vee \neg E | E) < p(H \vee \neg E)^2$
5. *E* does not inductively confirm H[3]

Line 3 says that the surplus content over *E* of $E\&(H \vee \neg E)$ is $H \vee \neg E$. What is the argument for this? Popper and Miller seem to be conceiving logical remainders on the model of numerical remainders. To find $m - n$,

---

[2] Provided $p(H|E) \neq 1 \neq p(E)$.

[3] Popper and Miller could have made an even stronger objection to inductivism. *H* entails *E*, so $H \vee \neg E$ is equivalent to $\neg E$. *E* not only fails to confirm the surplus content $H \vee \neg E$, it positively contradicts it! Something is wrong with your theory if what *H* adds to *E* is coming out to be $\neg E$.

one looks for a y such that $m = n + y$; $m - n$ is that y. To find H–E, we are to look, apparently, for a Y such that H is equivalent to $E \& Y$.

But the cases are not really analogous. The equation $m = n + y$ determines a unique y for each m and n, while the "equation" $H \Leftrightarrow E \& Y$ does not. *It's wet* ought surely to be a candidate for what *It's cold and wet* adds to *It's cold*. Popper and Miller don't allow this, however. They think that $C \& W$ adds $C \to C \& W$ to C, and more generally that H–$E = E \to H$.[4] Line 3 assumes that the surplus content is one, relatively complex, thing when it could just as easily be another, much simpler thing. The analogue of line 4 for the simpler thing is quite likely false, and in cases of interest, the opposite of the truth. E will indeed make H–E likelier if H adds a conjunct to E, and E is positively relevant to that conjunct.

Granted that it is not the only solution to $H \Leftrightarrow E \& Y$, could $E \to H$ be the best solution? Hempel seems to be backing it when he says that $E \to H$ "has no content in common with E since its disjunction with E is a logical truth" (Hempel 1960, 465). He relies here on an idea already considered (section **1.3**), namely that A and B both say inter alia that $A \lor B$, giving them nontrivial common content unless A and B subcontraries. We'll be reviewing this at length in chapter **8**, but two points can be made now. The first is that *Snow is white* does not in any sense whatsoever share content with *Charlemagne was Holy Roman Emperor*. Second, the idea that H–E is $E \to H$ overreacts to the (correct) point that H–E should not be *false* just because E is false, by making it *true* when E is false. E should really be as far as possible *independent* of H–E.[5]

6.2 CONDITIONS ON CONFIRMATION

The golden age of confirmation theory began with Hempel's enunciation (in Hempel 1943, 1945a, 1945b) of four conditions on

---

[4] This was a not uncommon view at the time. "Th[e] 'new' information contained in H is expressed by the sentence $H \lor \neg E$. (For H is equivalent to $(H \lor E) \& (H \lor \neg E))$" (Hempel 1960, 465). "The purely scientific utility of adding H to E is ... $m(H \lor \neg E)/m(E)$" (Bar-Hillel and Carnap 1953, 150).

[5] See Gemes (1994, 1997). A good many of the ideas in this chapter are due to Gemes.

evidential support: ENTAILMENT, CONSISTENCY, SPECIAL CONSEQUENCE, and CONVERSE CONSEQUENCE.

> EN *E* confirms any *H* that it entails.
> CO If *E* confirms *H*, *E* does not confirm anything contradicting *H*.
> SC If *E* confirms *H*, it confirms whatever *H* entails.
> CC If *E* confirms *H*, it confirms whatever entails *H*.

A fifth principle, mentioned in passing, is

> CE *E* confirms any *H* that entails it.

He accepts the first three conditions, but not the two CONVERSES. His objection to CONVERSE CONSEQUENCE is that it trivializes the confirmation relation, given ENTAILMENT and SPECIAL CONSEQUENCE. To see why, let *E* and *H* be any statements you like.

> 1. *E* confirms *E* (ENTAILMENT)
> 2. *E* confirms *E*&*H* ((1), CONVERSE CONSEQUENCE)
> 3. *E* confirms *H* ((2), SPECIAL CONSEQUENCE)

This objection has been found puzzling. Why put the blame on CON-VERSE CONSEQUENCE? Its contribution is only to get us to (2): *E* confirms *E*&*H*. But (2) may seem plausible in its own right. Also (2) follows directly from CONVERSE ENTAILMENT, which seems on solider ground than CON-VERSE CONSEQUENCE. (If *H* entails *E*, then ¬*E* precludes *H*. *E* removes the threat that ¬*E* poses to the truth of *H*.) CONVERSE ENTAILMENT is backed, too, by the Bayesian analysis of confirmation: pr(*H*|*E*) almost always exceeds pr(*H*) if *H* entails *E*. SPECIAL CONSEQUENCE, on the other hand, is from a Bayesian perspective completely untenable. Evidence making *H* likelier *cannot* make all its consequences likelier; there are consequences like *E*→*H* whose probability is bound to go down.

Why is Hempel so attached to SPECIAL CONSEQUENCE, when the problems nowadays seem obvious? Carnap thought that Hempel might have been mixing up two notions of confirmation. Let c(*H*, *E*&*K*), a real number between 0 and 1, be *H*'s likelihood given *E*, relative to some body *K* of background information. *E* confirms *H* incrementally, relative to *K*, if $c(H, E\&K) > c(H, K)$. It confirms H absolutely if $c(H, E\&K)$ exceeds $1-\epsilon$ for some suitable ϵ.

Absolute and incremental confirmation should definitely not be confused, but is Hempel confusing them? One would expect Carnap to argue that some of Hempel's conditions hold only for the absolute notion, others only for the incremental notion. But all of Hempel's conditions hold for the absolute notion! It is CONVERSE CONSEQUENCE and CONVERSE CONSEQUENCE, which he rejects, that fail to hold absolutely.

The problem is that his rhetoric and his examples, which tend to involve generalizations and their instances, suggest the incremental notion. A black raven makes it likelier, not absolutely likely, that all ravens are black. The incremental notion is naturally understood as positive probabilistic relevance, or probabilification. And probabilification satisfies neither of Hempel's two principal conditions. Contra CONSISTENCY, *Rudy is a raven* is positively relevant both to *Rudy is a happy raven* and *Rudy is an unhappy raven*. Contra SPECIAL CONSEQUENCE, *Rudy is a black raven* incrementally confirms *Rudy is a black raven and all other ravens are white* despite being negatively relevant to *All other ravens are white*.

6.3 A THIRD WAY

Hempel doesn't have a leg to stand on, it seems. His conditions hold for absolute confirmation, but that is not what he means to be talking about. Incremental confirmation, which is something like probabilification, does not meet his conditions. This does not entirely settle the matter, however, for a reason noted by Earman:

> ... There may be some third probabilistic [notion of] confirmation that allows Hempel ... to pass between the horns of this dilemma. But it is up to the defender of Hempel's instance-confirmation to produce the *tertium quid*. (Earman 1992, 67)

Hempel left, in fact, a number of clues suggesting what the third probabilistic notion might be. Here he is introducing the stronger condition of which SPECIAL CONSEQUENCE is meant to be a corollary Hempel (1945b, 103 emphasis added):

> an observation report which confirms certain hypotheses would invariably be qualified as confirming any consequence of those hypotheses. Indeed: *any such consequence is but an assertion of all or part of the combined content of the original hypotheses* and has therefore to be regarded as confirmed by any evidence which confirms the original hypotheses. This suggests the following condition of adequacy:
>
> GENERAL CONSEQUENCE: If an observation report E confirms every one of a class P of sentences, then it also confirms any sentence $[Q]$ which is a logical consequence of P.

Hempel's reasoning here is interesting. Any consequence Q of P—let P be, for simplicity, $\{P_1, P_2\}$— "is but an assertion of all or part of the combined content" of P_1 and P_2 (103). Q "has therefore to be regarded as confirmed by any evidence which confirms" P_1 and P_2. The implicit assumption is that E's support for P must be regarded as carrying through to its parts.

The support carries through, if E confirms "every one" of the sentences in P. Why does Hempel want E to confirm both of P_1, P_2, as opposed to either of them, or their conjunction? If one says *either*, then E confirms any F that you like, by virtue of confirming a member (the first) of $\{E, F\}$. Similar difficulties arise if it's the conjunction we focus on; E might confirm $E\&F$ entirely by way of its first conjunct. Hempel asks E to confirm each of P's members separately because otherwise GENERAL CONSEQUENCE would not be plausible.

But now, having insisted in GENERAL CONSEQUENCE on "wholly" confirming evidence—evidence confirming *both* of P_1, P_2—should he not also require wholly confirming evidence in SPECIAL CONSEQUENCE? Any reason there might be for wanting E to confirm both members of $\{P_1, P_2\}$ is a reason for wanting it to confirm both conjuncts of $P_1\&P_2$. SPECIAL CONSEQUENCE as we read it today imposes no such requirement. This could be an oversight on Hempel's part. Or, it could be that the requirement *is* imposed by SPECIAL CONSEQUENCE as he understands it.

Consider another objection he makes to CONVERSE CONSEQUENCE; it has *Rudy is black* confirming *All ravens are black & force = mass × acceleration*. This is puzzling on the standard interpretation, since Rudy's blackness *does* "basically" confirm the conjunction; it does make it likelier. The objection has got to be that Rudy doesn't confirm *all* of the conjunction, because it's irrelevant to whether $F = ma$. To fully confirm a conjunction, Hempel is thinking, E must confirm both conjuncts. In Bayesian terms, E must probabilify the conjuncts—or, to avoid syntacticizing the notion, the parts—together *and separately*.

(FC) E fully confirms H iff E probabilifies H and its parts.[6]

E must pervasively probabilify H, the thought is, to fully confirm it.

Now we return to a problem noted in the last section. Hempel has three conditions on confirmation: ENTAILMENT, CONSISTENCY, and SPECIAL CONSEQUENCE. Two of the three fail for the kind of confirmation that he is supposedly talking about. How could he have missed this? Let me list the conditions again, first as traditionally understood, and then in modified form, with full confirmation (confirmation$_F$) put in for basic confirmation.

ENTAILMENT

(B) If E entails H, then E basically confirms H.
(F) If E entails H, then E fully confirms H.

ENTAILMENT holds, we know, in its basic form, but full entailment is stronger. To see that it too is correct, suppose that E entails H, and let X be part of H. E entails X by transitivity of entailment, so $\text{pr}(X|E) = 1$. But then $\text{pr}(X|E) > \text{pr}(X)$ unless $\text{pr}(X) = 1$. This is what it means for E to fully confirm H.

CONSISTENCY

(B) If H contradicts Y, then E does not basically confirm both.
(F) If H contradicts Y, then E does not fully confirm both.

Here is a typical counterexample to CONSISTENCY in its original version. E basically confirms $H = E\&F$ and $Y = E\&\neg F$, since both entail E and a statement's consequences make it more probable. Are both fully confirmed

---

[6] Strictly, those of its parts that are not already certain. $\text{pr}(X|E) > \text{pr}(X)$ for each $X \leq H$ such that $\text{pr}(X) \neq 1$.

101

by E, that is, does E enhance the likelihood of H and Y and their parts? Certainly not, for it would then have to probabilify both F and $\neg F$.[7]

SPECIAL CONSEQUENCE

(B) If E basically confirms H, it basically confirms H's consequences.

(F) If E fully confirms H, then it fully confirms H's parts.

Suppose that E fully confirms, or pervasively probabilifies, H. Then it probabilifies H's parts, and hence (by transitivity of inclusion) the parts of its parts—which is the same as pervasively probabilifying the parts. If this is how Hempel understands SPECIAL CONSEQUENCE, then one sees why he finds it obvious. That an E confirming H and its parts confirms, too, *their* parts, is virtually a logical truth.

A word finally about Hempel's positive theory of evidential support, which is related to the hypothetico-deductive model of confirmation, and also to the CONVERSE ENTAILMENT condition, which he rejects. A hypothesis is not always confirmed by its entailments, Hempel thinks, but a certain *kind* of hypothesis—a generalization—is, it seems, confirmed by a certain kind of entailment, what he calls its "development" for a particular class of individuals.

Now, G's development for I *sounds* like it should be the part of G that concerns the relevant individuals. Hempel's positive theory would then be that a generalization is confirmed by certain of its parts. But the definition he gives is this:

G's development for I

$= G$ with its quantifiers restricted to the individuals in I.

This way of doing it *sometimes* delivers a part. *All ravens are black*, with its quantifiers restricted to birds in the backyard, is *All ravens in the yard are black*. But not always. G's development for I is not always even a consequence of G, much less included in it.

Let pluralism be the theory that for all x, there exists a y that is not identical to x. Pluralism is true, let's suppose. But its development for one-element domains is false; there is indeed just one thing, leaving aside all

---

[7] I assume that F and its negation are parts (not only conjuncts) of H and Y.

the other things. Pluralism's development for one-element domains is not even a consequence, then, of the theory itself. *G*'s development for *I* may not support *G* even if *G* entails it. Let monism be the denial of pluralism: every *x* is identical to every *y*. Monism's development for {Chicago} says that everything identical to Chicago is identical to everything else with that property. This is a truth entailed by monism. But it hardly sounds like a point in favor of monism that Chicago is only one thing.[8]

6.4 BAYES AND HYPOTHETICO-DEDUCTIVISM

Hempel thought that qualitative confirmation theory should be developed first, followed by comparative confirmation—*E* favors *H* over *H'*—and then quantitative. That is certainly not the view today; quantitative confirmation has stolen the spotlight. Bayesians are sometimes willing to *share* the spotlight with Hempel and company, if only for motivational purposes. A typical textbook begins by isolating the grain of Bayesian truth in, say, the hypothetico-deductive model of confirmation, or inference to the best explanation. Not everything can be saved, but that itself is instructive. The feeling seems to be that what was right in the qualitative tradition is explained by Bayes, and what was wrong is refuted by Bayes.

One tests a hypothesis, according to the hypothetic-deductive model, by seeing whether its consequences check out. False consequences count definitively against *H*; true consequences confirm it.

> (HD) *E* confirms *H* if *H* entails *E*; it confirms *H* relative to background
> information *K* if *H*&*K* entails *E*, and *K* alone does not.[9]

Bayesianism seems to vindicate the HD model, since if *H* entails *E*, then $p(H|E) \geq p(H)$. This may not be entirely to its credit, however, for hypothetico-deductivism has some surprising implications.[10] Our focus will be on the so-called 'tacking paradoxes.'

---

[8] Insofar as developments were intended by Hempel to be parts, our objection is only this: the part of *G* that concerns a population-based subject matter cannot always be obtained by restricting *G*'s quantifiers to the relevant population.

[9] Christensen (1997) goes into some of the complications.

[10] There is a huge literature on these paradoxes: I'm drawing particularly on Gemes (1990), Gemes (2005), Grimes (1990), Schurz (1994), Moretti (2006), and Sprenger (2011).

TACKING BY DISJUNCTION If H entails E, then it entails $E \vee E'$ as well. The class of *confirmers* of a given hypothesis is thus closed under the operation of tacking on a random disjunct. *All emeralds are green*, if confirmed by *This emerald is green*, is confirmed also by *Either this emerald is green, or no emeralds are green*.[11]

TACKING BY CONJUNCTION If H entails E, then E is entailed also by $H \& H'$. The hypotheses confirmed by a given piece of evidence are closed, then, under the operation of tacking on random conjuncts. A green emerald comes out confirming *All emeralds are red, apart from this green one*.[12]

Surely there is something right, though, about the idea that a theory is to be judged by its consequences. Not *all* its consequences, perhaps, given the tacking by disjunction problem; not *all* theories with the given consequences, given the tacking by conjunction problem. But if E is the right *kind* of consequence, and H the right kind of implier, then, it seems, the relation should hold (Gemes 1998).

Fine, but what is the right kind of consequence? That H with a random disjunct tacked on is the wrong kind suggests that, of its consequences, H is better, or more reliably, confirmed by those that are parts.[13] And what is the right kind of E-implier? That H with a random conjunct tacked on is the wrong kind suggests that, of its parts, H is better confirmed by those that probabilify its *other* parts.

6.5 BAYES AND INSTANCE CONFIRMATION

Hempel's paradox of the ravens has four elements:[14] three plausible-looking premises and a nutty-looking apparent consequence of those premises.

---

[11] Bayesianism backs the HD model up on this; it too has *This emerald is green or no emeralds are green* confirming *All emeralds are green*.

[12] Bayesianism backs the HD model up on this; it too has *This emerald is green* confirming *All emeralds are red apart from this green one*.

[13] Alternatively, by those of $H\&K$'s parts that are not included in K alone.

[14] Hempel (1945a,b).

Nicod's Criterion: *All Fs are Gs* is confirmed by its instances.
Equivalence Condition: Logical equivalents are confirmationally alike.
Equivalence Fact: *All Fs are Gs* is equivalent to *All non-Gs are non-Fs*.
Paradoxical Result: *Ravens are black* is confirmed by nonblack nonravens.

If there is a standard response to this, it's to embrace the paradoxical result. A nonblack nonraven *does* confirm that all ravens are black. But, it confirms it just the teeniest little bit—not as much as a black raven does. The idea was apparently first suggested by the Polish logician Janina Hosiasson-Lindenbaum (1940). A randomly chosen item is likelier nonblack than a raven, hence we sample a larger portion of the space of possible counterexamples by looking at ravens. Hempel in his response to Hosiasson-Lindenbaum asked an obvious question, which has never been addressed to my knowledge: "[I]s this last numerical assumption [that non-black things greatly outnumber ravens] warranted in the present case and analogously in all other 'paradoxical' cases?" He is worried that the paradox could still arise if a randomly chosen item were just as likely a raven as nonblack.

This is hard to imagine, so consider a different, silly, made-up example. *H* says that *Charged particles lack spin*—they are, to have a positive term for spinlessness, "poised."[15] The numerical assumption is, a randomly chosen particle is likelier neutral than poised.

Well, but it's our example; we can stipulate that the assumption is false, that there are exactly as many charged particles as spinny ones. Doesn't it *still* seem that a charged, poised particle confirms *Charged particles are poised* more, or better, than a spinny neutral one? One can even imagine that *Charged particles are poised* and *Spinny particles are neutral* are distinct laws, each with its own physical underpinnings. The first is like *Cheaters never prosper*, on the theory that there is something about cheaters that prevents prosperity—they are found out and ostracized, say. The second is like *The prosperous never cheat*, on the theory that there is something

---

[15] "[The] claim that 'All nonblack things are nonravens' is not projectible needs a closer look. ... Even granting that the predicates here are ill entrenched, this seems to illustrate no general principle. Surely 'nonmetallic,' 'noncombustible,' 'invisible,' 'colorless,' and many other privative predicates are well entrenched. Furthermore, it should be noted that a privative predicate will be as entrenched as any of its coextensive predicates" (Scheffler and Goodman 1972, 83).

(else) about prosperers that keeps them honest—they have no motive for cheating, maybe, on account of their prosperity.

If the paradox still arises when a generalization's contrapositive is statistically indiscernible from it, and just as lawlike, then we need an approach that does not require us to pick winners. Hempel mentions one briefly:

> Perhaps the impression of the paradoxical character of [these cases] may be said to grow out of the feeling that the hypothesis that *All ravens are black* is about ravens, and not about non-black things, nor about all things. (Hempel 1945a, 17).

One generalization is about *charged* particles. How is an uncharged particle supposed to tell us about them? The most it can accomplish is to take itself out of the running for the role of counterinstance; counterinstances have to be charged. The other is about spinny particles. A poised particle can serve, again, only as a thwarted potential counterexample: *it* at least, does not witness the possibility of a spinny particle that is charged.

How these subtleties could matter to confirmation is not obvious. Confirmation is to do with probability, and statements true in the same circumstances are equiprobable. The answer is that the statements' *parts* may not be true in the same circumstances, and inductive evidence has got to probabilify parts. *No Fs are Gs* and *No Gs are Fs* differ inductively, by differing mereologically; they differ mereologically, by differing in what they're about.

6.6 PARTS AND INSTANCES

Rudy supposedly confers likelihood on the parts of *Ravens are black*, but not the parts of *Nonblack things are not ravens*. If the parts are distinct, and have their likelihood controlled by different factors, it is hard to see how the wholes can remain equiprobable—as they must given their logical equivalence. This puts pressure on *Ravens are black* to share its parts with its contrapositive—which destroys the proposed explanation of confirmational differences in terms of mereological differences. I reply that the two generalizations have *matched* parts, agreeing in probability but not inductive significance[16].

---

[16] I rely here on the treatment of quantifiers in section **4.4**

What is said by *All ravens are black*? One could treat it as the first-order generalization $\forall x(Rx \rightarrow Bx)$, equivalently, $\neg \exists x(Rx \& \neg Bx)$. But that confuses the role played by something's non-raven-hood in the truth of *All ravens are black* with that played by Rudy's blackness. Nonravens help to determine what it *takes* for all the world's ravens to be black. They bear on the *content* of the demands made by a sentence that attributes blackness only to ravens. Black ones are relevant not to the content of the demands but how far the world goes toward meeting them.

A semantic analogue of Belnap's conditional assertion operator was sketched in section **4.5**. *Bx supposing that Rx*, written $Rx \nearrow Bx$, is true in the same worlds as $Rx \rightarrow Bx$. But the reasons differ. One is true either because x is not a raven or because x is black. The other is true, should x be a raven, because x is black. Otherwise it is *vacuously* true—true not because its demands are met, but because it doesn't make any demands. Explicitly, $Rx \nearrow Bx$ is

$$
\begin{cases}
\text{true for the reason(s) } Bx \text{ is true, should } Rx \text{ and } Bx \text{ be true} \\
\text{false for the reason(s) } Bx \text{ is false, should } Rx \text{ be true and } Bx \text{ false} \\
\text{true for no reason at all, should } Rx \text{ be false}
\end{cases}
$$

Corresponding to the two ways for $Rx \nearrow Bx$ to be true, there are two ways it might gain in probability. One kind of evidence lowers pr(Rx), thus boosting the chances of $Rx \nearrow Bx$ being vacuously true. Another kind leaves pr(Rx) unchanged while lowering that of pr($Rx \& \neg Bx$), thus boosting the chances of $Rx \nearrow Bx$ being *substantively* true. There is a corresponding distinction at the level of generalizations. White socks increase pr($\forall x(Rx \nearrow Bx)$) by making more of its content trivial—by cutting into what it (nontrivially) says. A black raven does it by making the substantive part(s) more probable.

The problem was this: *Ravens are black* needs, on the one hand, to have different parts than *Nonblack things aren't ravens*. Otherwise we can't explain their inductive differences in the way proposed. They should on the other hand have the same parts, lest their probabilities be driven apart by evidence bearing on the parts only of, say, *Ravens are black*.

With virtual parts distinguished from real ones, we can understand the situation as follows. $Rx \nearrow Bx$ (for a given x) has a counterpart $\neg Bx \nearrow \neg Rx$ that (i) agrees with it in probability, but (ii) with substantive and trivial likelihood interchanged. As the chances rise of Rudy being (substantively) black if a raven, they rise as well of his being (trivially) a nonraven if nonblack. As the chances rise of Betty being (substantively) not a raven if not black, they rise of her being (trivially) black if a raven. Rudy's effects on the *probabilities* of $\forall x(Rx \nearrow Bx)$ and its contrapositive are the same. Its the mechanism that is different. Rudy confirms what $\forall x(Rx \nearrow Bx)$ says, while (in a manner of speaking) changing what $\forall x(\neg Bx \nearrow \neg Rx)$ says.[17]

6.7 VERISIMILITUDE

Confirmation is tied up with the aims of science; we want our beliefs to be as close as possible to the truth, and believing confirmed hypotheses is supposed to help us achieve this. But proximity to the truth has another aspect that confirmation theory is blind to. We want to maximize the *amount* of truth we believe and minimize the amount of falsehood.

Popper was famously pessimistic about the first aim; he emphasized the second.[18] Science progresses, not when our theories are better confirmed, but when they achieve greater verisimilitude. His initial definition, with X and Y ranging over theories, and X's truth-content X^T (false-content X^F) defined as the set of its true (false) consequences, is this.

X is at least as truthlike as Y iff

$Y^T \subseteq X^T$: any truth implied by Y is implied also by X, and

$X^F \subseteq Y^F$: any falsehood implied by X is implied also by Y

X is more truthlike than Y if in addition Y is not as truthlike as X, that is, one of the above-mentioned inclusions is strict.

[17] Zsa Zsa Gabor is supposed to have found a way to keep "her husband" young and healthy: remarrying every few years (Hare 2007). No individual is made younger by this process, rather "her husband" acquires younger referents. Betty's way of making "the hypothesis that ravens are black" likelier is similar: "the hypothesis" becomes likelier by acquiring a likelier referent.
[18] "I intend to show that while we cannot ever have sufficiently good arguments in the empirical sciences for claiming that we have actually reached the truth, we can have strong and reasonably good arguments for claiming that we may have made progress toward the truth" (Popper 1972, 58).

Popper's definition has some desirable features. Among true theories, verisimilitude goes with logical strength. A false theory can never be as close to the truth as its truth-content.[19] But it has as well some truly horrible features.

Suppose that X and Y are false and that neither implies the other. Then each has truth-content the other lacks; X alone implies $Y^T \to X^T$, and Y alone implies $X^T \to Y^T$ (Tichý 1974, Miller 1974). False theories are thus left completely unranked by Popper's proposal. They are not in most cases even ranked lower than their negations, which are true. (Proof: Let N be the negation of X. Suppose that N is true, and let Z be a truth that it does not imply. N does not imply $N \to Z$ either, but N's negation does imply it, by virtue of contradicting the antecedent. $N \to Z$ is thus a truth implied by the falsehood $\neg X$ but not the truth X.[20])

Attention has turned in recent years from *content*-oriented theories, like Popper's, to the *likeness* approach: X has greater verisimilitude than Y to the extent that it holds in worlds closer to actuality. But now, what does it mean for the X-worlds to be closer to actuality than the Y-worlds? There are any number of ways to combine the distances of individual worlds from ours into a measure of how far the set of them is from our world (Niiniluoto 1987). If one thinks of the worlds as each casting a vote, it becomes an aggregation of judgment problem and limitative theorems from voting theory suggest there may be no fully satisfactory way of doing it (Zwart and Franssen 2007).

A second look at the content approach seems in order. Popper went wrong, in identifying X's truth-content with its true *consequences* (Gemes 2007a). Suppose we define it rather as the sum of X's true *parts*. His definition then becomes

X is at least as truthlike as Y iff

Y's true parts are all implied by true parts of X, and

X's false parts are all implied by false parts of Y

---

[19] If Y is false, it is further from the truth than Y^T. Proof: Y's truth-content is included in that of Y^T, because it *is* Y^T. Y's false-content strictly includes that of Y^T, for Y^T's false-content is empty; truths don't imply falsehoods.

[20] Gemes (2007a).

This doesn't quite work, however. Suppose $X = P \& Q$ and $Y = Q$, where P is true and Q is false. X should come out ahead since it adds a true conjunct. But it has a false part not implied by Y, Gemes observes, namely itself. This seems a merely technical problem. What's false about $P\&Q$ is Q, and Q *is* part of Y. A theory's false-content should be seen as made up of its *wholly* false parts—the ones with no nontrivial true parts buried within. (True parts are wholly true automatically.) The proper definition is

> X is at least as truthlike as Y iff
>
> Y's wholly true parts are implied by wholly true parts of X, and
>
> X's wholly false parts are implied by wholly false parts of Y

A kind of verisimilitude that this perhaps misses involves differences in accuracy. *Light travels at a hundred miles per hour* is further from the truth than *Light travels at a million miles per hour*. Does the second underestimate of light's speed have a true part not implied by the first underestimate? *Light travels at no less than a million miles per hour* has the right sort of flavor; but it may be doubted whether traveling at least n miles per hour is included in traveling exactly n miles per hour. (This is in fact the tip of a scary iceberg that I would rather avoid just now.)

Another interesting feature of our account is that logically equivalent hypotheses can be at different distances from the truth. *All men are mortal* has plenty of truth in it. It contains, for instance, the truth that *Socrates is mortal, supposing him to be a man*. *Immortals are never men* has very little truth in it. Certainly it does not contain anything to imply the aforementioned truth about Socrates. *All men are mortal* is thus apparently more truthlike than *Immortals are never men*, though the two hold in the same worlds. I am not sure if this is the right result.

6.8 SUMMING UP

Logical subtraction has a role to play in confirmation theory, via the notion of surplus content. Subject matter does, too, via the notion of content-part. Content-part lets us define a new type of evidential relation; E pervasively probabilifies H if it probabilifies "all of it," meaning H and its parts. This helps with the tacking and raven paradoxes. Equivalent generalizations can be about different things, which affects their evidential relations. Inductive skeptics don't care about confirmation, but they derive some benefit too, for they care about verisimilitude—one theory having more truth in it than another—and the truth in a theory is made up of its wholly true parts.

- 7 -

Knowing That and Knowing About

7.1 INTIMATIONS OF OPENNESS

If one statement or claim implies another, and the first is clearly true, then one would expect the second to be clearly true, too. Controversy should not erupt between the premises and the conclusion of a valid one-premise argument. And yet sometimes the weaker statement does seem, if not controversial, then at least harder to know than the stronger one. Examples:

> (Frege) The number of Fs = the number of Gs. So there are numbers.
>
> (Moore) I have a hand. There are physical objects
>
> (Nozick) I am sitting by the fire. I am not a bodiless BIV.
>
> (Dretske) That is a zebra. So it is not a cleverly disguised mule.
>
> (Kripke) I turned off the stove. Evidence I didn't is thus misleading.
>
> (Cohen) That is a red wall. So, it is not a white wall bathed in red light.
>
> (Vogel) I will teach logic next year. Lightning won't kill me this year.[1]

To throw my own example into the mix, Alma watches Usain Bolt win the gold on TV, and reads about it the next day in the newspaper. The evidence she gets from these sources does not address the issue of what will become of Bolt's refrigerated blood sample. If tests reveal that he had been using a banned substance, he will be retroactively disqualified. Alma does know that Bolt is the winner, it seems. But does she know that tests won't be devised in 2018 which disqualify him?

These look like counterexamples to closure, the principle that a known proposition's consequences must themselves be known or anyway, no less

---

[1] These are in argument form only for rhetorical effect. The issue is not supposed to be knowability on such and such a basis. The existence of numbers strikes us as a harder question than whether the number of Martian moons is prime, quite apart from any inferences we might be tempted to undertake. I am much clearer that I turned the stove off than that contrary evidence is misleading, even if the entailment never occurs to me.

knowable. Never mind, for now, whether the examples are genuine. What there does seem to genuinely be is a phenomenon of *apparent* closure violation. Either we feel the pull ourselves, or can tell when it is apt to be felt by others. There is something here that tempts us to *think* that closure is violated, whether we give in to the temptation or not. Part of it is that the transitions seem *ampliative*. Q goes beyond P, not in the stringency of its requirements (P implies Q, after all), but the aspects of reality to which those requirements are addressed.

Kripke in *Naming and Necessity* had a notion of appearances, or intuitions, of possibility—IPOs. An IPO is less trustworthy, he reasoned, if we can explain how it arises without supposing it to be accurate. I want to speak in a similar spirit of intuitions, or intimations, of openness—IONs.[2]

A few philosophers have taken IONs at face value; Nozick and Dretske are the people usually mentioned. You know that P, in Nozick's view, only if your belief that P is sensitive to whether P is true; had P been false, you would not have believed it.[3] You would have noticed, for instance, if you were standing rather than sitting. You would not have noticed, if you were a brain in the right kind of vat. You would have noticed, if the number of Martian moons had been different, but not if there was no such entity as the number of Martian moons. You would not expect to be teaching logic next year, if you were going to be on leave; teaching assignments are settled far in advance. The course that lightning takes is more of a last minute thing. You would not have seen it coming.

This sort of view has fallen so far out of fashion that we may forget its advantages. Alma believes, quite rightly, that she is not going to win the lottery. She has plenty of evidence on the matter. Why does she fail to know? She would have believed the same thing, even if she were going to win. Smith rightly believes that someone in his office owns a Ford, on the basis of seeing Nogot driving around in a rented Ford; the real Ford-owner is Havit. Smith's belief does not constitute knowledge, because it would still have been there if Havit had sold the Ford, or taken a different job. The skeptic is unanswerable because he is right; the bizarre-seeming hypotheses that he floats are not known to be false. How in light of that

---

[2] Knowledge is open if it is not closed.
[3] For Dretske it is your evidence that should be sensitive to whether P, rather than your belief.

can we go about our daily business? Our daily business turns on the truth of lightweight propositions like *I am sitting*, which we do know. Part of what makes the antiskeptical consequences *heavy* is that we are not as sensitive to their possible falsity as to that of their lightweight impliers.

7.2 THE UNDENIABILITY (?) OF CLOSURE

The current view, maintained by just about everyone, is that IONs pose no real threat to the closure principle. The proper reaction is not to question closure, but to look for an explanation of how it can *seem* to fail in some cases. Even if Q is known, there are lots of reasons why it might seem more precarious than P. Maybe

1. Q is not known *on the basis* of P; it had to be known beforehand
2. Q is not KNOWN, this being the relation "knows" *comes* to express
3. we don't *know* that Q is known
4. the knowledge is *unearned*; we have no real evidence for Q
5. epistemic anxiety prevents us from fully *believing* that Q

Whatever the merits of this or that attempt to explain IONs away, some such explanation has got to work, it is felt, because there is no good way of denying closure.

What would be a "good way of denying" it? Closure cannot just be thrown under the bus. A good way of denying it would tell us what is right in the principle—call that the defensible core—and explain how the remainder can be done without.

One problem is that we have no idea what the defensible core is supposed to be. All known technologies for containing closure wind up either strangling it in the cradle, or letting too much survive. The best known technology is Nozick's, so let's look again at that. Nozick thinks closure ought to fail when Q is a skeptic-baiting consequence of some evident truth. His theory seems at first to deliver this result: I would not have believed I had hands, had they had simply gone missing, but my beliefs would be in relevant respects unchanged, were I a brain in a high enough quality vat.

But, although this is a case where closure might be expected to fail, the theory also makes for *egregious* violations (Kripke 2011a): one can know that there is a red barn in the field, without knowing there is a barn there. This will be the result if the closest alternative to a red barn is a green one, while the closest alternative to a barn is a convincing fake. The theory makes as well for egregious *non*violations of closure (Hawthorne [2005]). I may not know, on Nozick's view, that I am not a brain in a vat, but I do know that I am breathing and not a brain in a vat, since I would realize it, if I were not breathing, which is how the relevant possibility would come about. This is the sort of heavyweight knowledge that we are not supposed to possess.[4]

A second problem is that the defensible core would have to be extremely weak, for the full principle comes roaring back on modest assumptions (Kripke 2011a, Hawthorne 2004). Two such closure-reinstating assumptions are *Addition* and *Distribution*:

Ad   S knows that P, and properly infers $P \vee Q$ $\Rightarrow$ S knows that $P \vee Q$.
Di   S knows that $P \& Q$ $\Rightarrow$ S knows that P and that Q.

Either of these does the job, given the obvious-seeming *Equivalence* principle:

Eq   S knows that P, P is a priori equivalent to Q $\Rightarrow$ S knows that Q.

To see how it works with *Distribution*, let Z and M be *That animal is a zebra* and *That animal is a cleverly painted mule.*

1. Alma knows that Z [given]
2. Z a priori entails $\neg M$ [given]
3. Z is a priori equivalent to $Z \& \neg M$ [Logic, (2)]
4. Alma knows that $Z \& \neg M$ [Eq, (1,3)]
5. Alma knows that $\neg M$ [Di, (4)]

Closure would have to be severely restricted to avoid this argument. And yet (this is the third problem) to restrict it *at all* has absurd results. If knowing P needn't put me in a position to know that Q, then deduction can lead us astray—taking us from known premises to unknown conclusions—even when properly carried out. Kripke used to bring out the strangeness of

---

[4] Both sorts of egregiousness have the same source: sensitivity to R ensures sensitivity to any $R \& S$ such that R fails in nearer-by worlds than S. In Kripke's example, R is and S are *That is red* and *That is a barn*. In Hawthorne's example, R and S are *I am breathing* and *I am not a brain in a vat*.

this by exclaiming, in the course of some irreproachable line of reasoning, "Oh no, I just committed the fallacy of logical deduction!" Do we really want to add valid reasoning to the list of seductive fallacies? No one can take this seriously.

7.3 IMMANENT CLOSURE

Now we see why the closure debate is found confusing. One side—the losing side, at present—insists on various intuitively vivid anomalies. The other side does not deny the anomalies! They just refuse to be cowed by them. Closure-denial is seen as a hysterical overreaction to one particular sort of data point. A full account of these matters should take note of *all* the data, including, to begin with,

1. closure's intrinsic plausibility
2. the strategies for explaining the counterexamples away
3. the egregious violations point (Kripke's red barn)
4. the egregious nonviolations point (the breathing envatted brain)
5. the knowledge-preservingness of deduction
6. the proof of closure from innocent-seeming assumptions.

A word first about the innocent-seeming assumptions. *Addition* and *Distribution* are about similarly basic transitions: disjunct-adding in the one case, conjunct-dropping in the other. Looking back, however, they are not formulated in quite the same way. *Addition* says that one knows $P \vee R$, on competently inferring it from P. *Distribution* does *not* say that one knows P on competently inferring it from $P \& R$. This is as it should be. To know that snow is cold and white, you should know it is cold *already*, whereas there is no requirement of first knowing that snow is cold *or* white before you count as knowing that snow is cold.

The difference in formulation suggests there might be two forms of closure at issue. Some conclusions are such that you should *already* know them, to know the premise. With others, you are assured of knowing the conclusion only if you engage in some reasoning. The first form might be called *immanent* closure, the second *transeunt*. Let's start with the first. What sort of consequence is it that we know "in" knowing that P, as opposed to being merely in a position to know it?

The idea behind *Distribution* is that Q should be a conjunct of P. But that way of doing it is too narrow, and assuming the *Equivalence* condition, also too broad. Too narrow: To know that there are red barns, you should know that there are barns. But it is hard to think of an R such that *There are red barns* is *There are barns* conjoined with R. Too broad: Not any old consequence of P has to be known "already." But any consequence is a conjunct of something logically equivalent to P, namely, $P\&Q$. Immanent closure thus fails to draw the intended distinction, if we formulate it syntactically in terms of conjunction.

A generalized, desyntacticized analogue of the relation $Q\&R$ bears to Q seems called for here. What about logical inclusion? A logical part is something like a "deep conjunct" of its containing whole. This helps with the first problem, since *There are barns* is included in *There are red barns*. It helps with the second problem as well, if we think of inclusion as "seeing through" a sentence's logical structure to its reasons for being true. The condition we want is

(IC) If S knows that P, and Q is part of P, then S knows that Q.

The principle might equally be called *topical* closure, given how we defined inclusion. If Alma knows that P, she knows those of its implications that do not change the subject.

7.4 SAYING MORE

IONs evidently *do* change the subject. *That animal is a zebra* is not about painted mules. *I am sitting* is not about brains. *I turned off the oven* is not about evidence. *The wall is red* is not about colored light. *Bolt won the gold* is not about blood samples. If one changes the example to eliminate this feature, Q no longer seems harder to know. *Bolt won the gold and Blake the silver, so Blake won the silver* is quite free of the difficulties besetting *Bolt won the gold, so he will not be disqualified*. IONs are *ampliative*, not truth-conditionally, but with respect to their aboutness properties. Q raises additional issues, not contemplated in P. It is Q's claims about these additional issues that make it harder to know.

I grant, of course, that Q is in one respect easier to know. A weaker hypothesis holds in a larger region of logical space, and it is easier to place ourselves in a larger region than a smaller one. But the shape matters, too. The not-a-brain-in-a-vat region is less unified. It has jagged edges, newly exposed flanks . . . you pick the metaphor. An irregular, disunified region is not as defensible as a compact region with smooth boundaries.

This is all very picturesque, but picture thinking takes us only so far. One would like to spell out the mechanism whereby Q's not being part of P makes it additionally vulnerable. Q is a mere, or unincluded, consequence of P, recall, just if it has new ways of being true—"new" meaning, not implied by any way for P to be true—and/or new ways of being false—not among Q's ways of being false.[5] The question is, why would these make Q more epistemically vulnerable? I don't have a worked out answer at present, especially on the truthmaker side, but let me offer the following as proof of concept.

A new way for Q to be true is like a disjunct that is not implied by any disjunct of P. It might just be tacked on beside P's disjuncts, but in cases of interest, *most* of Q's disjuncts are new, perhaps all; they are not extendable into ways for P to be true. So, for instance, what are the ways of not being a painted mule? Being an unpainted mule, or a lion, or a toaster, and so on. Being a lion or toaster is not halfway to being a zebra. How might evidence against the moon landing be misleading? The affidavit was forged, the "confession" was false, and so on. Confessing to faking the moon landing is not a way of landing on the moon, nor are there ways of landing on the moon that necessitate or involve such a confession.

This is relevant to knowledge insofar as each new disjunct is a new opportunity to believe Q for the wrong reasons. You know that you turned the stove off (P), by virtue of remembering the event. What about the dogmatic implication Q that counterevidence is misleading? There were ten witnesses, let's suppose, and the counterevidence is drawn from their reports. *One* way for Q to be true is for the first witness to testify against you. Another way for Q to be true is for the first two witnesses to testify against you. And so on. You have got to suppose that the number is small, since as it grows so does the likelihood you are misremembering. You cannot

---

[5] As already mentioned, falsity-makers for the part are among (not only implied by) falsity-makers for the whole. If the implication were proper, Q's falsity-maker would be stronger than needed to falsify P.

afford to be neutral about how Q is true, since if the story is too fantastic you should not be believing that P. As we know from Gettier, though, mistakes on this score can be knowledge-destroying (Gettier 1963). You are right to regard Q as true, but, if you are sufficiently confused about *how* it is true—about how things stand with respect to its subject matter—then you don't know that Q. Your evident vulnerability to failing to know in this way—through, as George W. Bush might put it, misunderestimating the counterevidence—may inhibit you even from believing Q, which poses a further threat to knowledge.

The threat posed by new ways for Q to be false is more familiar; they are new counterpossibilities for the knower to be on guard against. I will speak generically of being "on top of" a counterpossibility, because the details don't matter. A new way of being false is, as a purely structural matter, one more thing for the knower to be on top of, in whatever sense of "on top of" you like.[6]

Now, to say that Q gives us new battles to fight, if it isn't contained in P, is not to say we don't know it; the battles might be winnable (section **7.8**). The advantage of parts is that they already *have* been won. We showed ourselves to be on top of the counterpossibilities to Q, when we dealt with the counterpossibilities to P.

7.5 HYPERINTENSIONALITY

Immanent closure has got be weaker than (full, regular) closure; otherwise we are just spinning our wheels. It is not clear how it can be weaker, though, given its similarity to a principle—knowledge transmits through

---

[6] Q's ways of being false are, let us say, $\bar{Q}_1, \ldots, \bar{Q}_n$. Alma is on top of $\bar{Q}_k$, on a sensitivity-type theory, if she would have noticed, or had different evidence, had $\bar{Q}_k$ obtained. She is on top of it, on a relevant alternatives theory, if she can rule $\bar{Q}_k$ out, whatever exactly that may involve (Stine 1976, Lewis 1996). A safety-type theory might see the counterpossibilities as each dangerous in its own way. Alma is on top of $\bar{Q}_k$ if she could not easily have been wrong in the way it suggests. She is on top of $\bar{Q}_k$, on a probabilistic theory, if the chance of believing that Q, conditional on $\bar{Q}_k$, is low (Roush 2009). She's on top of $\bar{Q}_k$, on an explanatory theory, if the hypothesis that $\bar{Q}_k$ fails to explain how she could wind up believing Q despite its falsity (Cross 2010).

to conjuncts (*Distribution*)—that was shown to blow up into closure in section **7.2**. Let's look again at the argument:[7]

1. Alma knows that Z [given]
2. Z a priori entails $\neg M$ [given]
3. Z is a priori equivalent to $Z \& \neg M$ [Logic, (2)]
4. Alma knows that $Z \& \neg M$ [Eq, (1,3)]
5. Alma knows that $\neg M$ [Di, (4)]

Distribution is used only once, to assure Alma of knowing that $\neg M$ if she knows that $Z \& \neg M$. Immanent closure provides us the same assurance, however! For it assures us of knowing parts, and $\neg M$ is part of $Z \& \neg M$. Immanent closure thus threatens to be thus every bit as sufficient for (full, regular) closure as *Distribution*.

Now, the fact is that *Distribution* is *not* quite sufficient for full closure— the argument relies as well on *Equivalence*. *Equivalence* is apt, however, to seem obvious. How can Alma know just one of a pair of a priori equivalent propositions? That would be, in the case of interest, to know that Z (the animal is a zebra), without knowing that $Z \& \neg M$ (it's a zebra and not a disguised mule), though Z implies $\neg M$ and is hence equivalent to $Z \& \neg M$.

But, as we know, equivalents are liable to differ in what they're about, which can drive a wedge between them epistemologically. $Z \& \neg M$ says more than Z, their truth-conditional equivalence notwithstanding: it stakes a larger claim aboutness-wise, which makes it more open to question. If this is right, then the Kripke/Hawthorne argument can be answered. Alma knows that Z, but that does not tell her that $\neg M$, since not to be a disguised mule is a mere consequence, not a part, of being a zebra. Not being a disguised mule *is* part of being a zebra and not a disguised mule. Alma *would* by immanent closure know that it was not a disguised mule, if she knew it was the not-a-disguised-mule sort of zebra. She would know that too, if equivalents were equi-knowable. But, the suggestion is, they are not.

Knowledge as we are beginning to conceive it is subject-matter sensitive. This should not strike anyone as outrageous; subject-sensitivity is of a piece with focus- and question-sensitivity, which are well-attested phenomena

---

[7] Z and M are *That animal is a zebra* and *That animal is a cleverly painted mule*.

(Dretske 1972, Beaver and Clark 2009, Schaffer 2007). But it would be good to have some examples.

Students will say, after a first encounter with Descartes's dream argument, that they might, for all they know, be dreaming. They will then often remark, that *their own* dreams are, as a matter of fact, not as lifelike as the experience they are enjoying now. They know that

> My dreams are not this lifelike.

But they admit to doubts about

> Appearances this lifelike are not dreams (of mine).

And yet the two are logically equivalent: *No Ds are L* stands or falls with *No Ls are D*. Pressed for an explanation, we might distinguish the hypotheses as follows. One concerns my dreams and how lifelike they are; the other is about experiences like *this* and how liable they are to be dreams. I feel more attuned to the first issue—the felt quality of particular dreams—than the second—the metaphysical nature of particular appearances. If the dream had been more vivid, I might have noticed. If present appearances, their lifelike qualities held fixed, were a dream, it all would have seemed just the same.

Imagine yourself in fake barn country. All of the many barns are red, and so, let us suppose, are all of the many fake barns. You have seen most if not all of the barns, but are, as a matter of pure dumb luck, yet to lay eyes on a fake. You know, I take it, that all of the barns in this area are red. (Imagine someone questioning this on the ground that you haven't checked any of the nonbarns.) We need only a weaker claim: you know that

> At least one of the barns in this area is red.

Now turn it around. Do you know that

> At least one of the red structures in this area is a barn?

It seems clear that you don't; things would look the same either way. To know that at least one F is G is easier than knowing that at least one G is F, if you are an excellent judge of G-ness but have trouble making out what is F. And yet one of the Fs is G just if one of the Gs is F.

7.6 WAYWARDNESS

Knowledge-attributions care about subject matter, over and above truth-conditions. They take note of how *P* is true or false in various worlds, not only which worlds it is true or false in. Of course, one doesn't want to complicate matters unless it is really necessary. Shouldn't we be trying harder to resist the introduction of "ways" into the semantics of knowledge claims? I am not going to say that resistance is futile. But it comes to seem misguided when we broaden our focus a bit. "Waywardness," as Kit Fine calls it, is a fact of semantic life (Fine 2012).

You will feel better if you eat, the doctor says, and we can assume this is true. Will you feel better, if you eat pie or poisonous mushrooms or dolmades or dirt or rice or rotten fish and so on? Surely not. *You will feel better if you do this or that or the other* carries the implication that you will feel better if you do this, and also if you do that, and also if you do the other.[8] You won't feel better if you eat poison, therefore you won't feel better if you eat pie or poison or some other thing. Now, you can't eat without eating this, that, or the other, and vice versa. (It is not a difference in modal profile we are dealing with, but in semantically operative ways of obtaining.[9]) The truth-value shift occurs because eating *x* is a way for it to be true that you eat *x*, *y*, or *z*, but not, or not without additional stage-setting, a way for it to be true that you eat.[10]

Believing truths is better than avoiding belief in falsehoods, according to William James. Now let's throw one more element into the mix: the *un*truth of what we do *not* believe. Which is better, to believe truths, or that propositions we do not believe are not true? The first seems better. One wants to extend the attitude of belief to propositions already true, not

---

[8] This is nothing special to do with disjunction. *If you had more tinfoil, you'd be happier*, requires that you'd be happier if you had one more piece of tinfoil, and also if you had two, and so on. *If we don't both sign our names, the contract is invalid* implies that it will be invalid if you don't sign, and also if I don't. (See Alonso-Ovalle (2009) for a theory emphasizing disjunction.)

[9] *W* counts in context as a way for *P* to obtain if *Q*, *if P* depends for its truth, in that context, on *Q*, *if W*. This gives us a quick, though not infallible, way of identifying truthmakers.

[10] Imagine we make it a relevant way of eating, by steering you toward a table with rotten fish on it. It then arguably becomes false that you will feel better if you eat.

shrink the set of truths until it contains nothing we don't believe.[11] And yet, believing all true hypotheses is equivalent to hypotheses' not being true if we don't believe them.

Desire-contexts are wayward, too, then, apparently. Wanting all *F*s to be *G* is not the same as wanting non-*G*s not to be *F*, though the one outcome occurs if and only if the other does. President Bush hoped for the day when no child was left behind. He did not hope for the day when no one left behind was a child. He did not hope for a device that turned underperforming children into adults before they could be left behind.

Conditionals and desire attribution are not unconnected.[12] A well-known problem with desiderative verbs is how to arrange for the "backgrounding" of content-elements that are treated as given, rather than part of what is wanted, or hoped, or regretted, or what have you. Wanting to catch a spy is not wanting there to *be* a spy, although it is wanting a thing that cannot occur unless spies exist. Stalnaker and Heim suggest, in this connection, that to desire that *P* is to prefer how things would be if *P* to how they would be if ¬*P*.[13] Preferring the nearest catch-a-spy world to the nearest don't-catch-one world is not to prefer spies' existence, for they exist in both of the worlds just mentioned.[14]

If this is how we understand desiderative verbs, then the waywardness of desire might be seen as tracing back to that of conditionals. I want to find my lost dog. I do not want to find him dead or alive, though finding him is necessarily equivalent to finding him dead or alive. Why this difference? If I found him, that would be better than not finding him. *Find him* occurs here in the antecedent of a conditional, though, where it may not be intersubstitutable with *find him dead or alive*. If I found him dead or alive, would that be preferable to not finding him? No, because it would not be better to find him dead. Finding the dog dead is a way of finding him dead or alive, but not in the relevant sense, a way of finding him. That

[11] The second goal is advanced by destroying what we don't understand.

[12] "[E]motives and more generally causatives select the subjunctive because their lexical semantics involves counterfactual reasoning" (Schlenker 2005, 304). See also Adams (1998).

[13] Heim (1992).

[14] Humberstone develops another way of exempting undesired content in Humberstone (1987). Wanting to catch a spy is believing both that there are spies and that it would be good to catch one. See also Schoubye (2011) and Humberstone (1982).

is why the phrases function differently in conditionals, and hence in desire attributions.

God tells Eve, you may eat as many apples as you like—even infinitely many—apart from this one; this one is from the tree of knowledge of good and evil.[15] God does not permit Eve to eat infinitely many apples, *period*, for she is not to eat the bad apple. As we know, though, the two scenarios are equivalent. One apple cannot make the difference between infinitely many and finitely many. Eve eats infinitely many apples just if she eats infinitely many apples apart from the bad one.

God permits *P*, but not *Q*, though *P* and *Q* hold in the same worlds, differing only in their ways of being true. Eating infinitely many apples, including the bad one, is a way for it to be true that *Eve eats infinitely many apples* but not a way for it to be true that *Eve eats infinitely many apples distinct from the bad one*. This falls out of the wayward nature of conditionals if an act's permissibility is explained as: God won't be angry with you, if you perform it (Anderson 1958).

Consider next evidential verbs: show, testify, establish, and so on. Al testified that Claire stole the diamonds, but not that it was diamonds she stole.[16] The blood test shows that you don't have bronchitis, though it is (let's suppose) sensitive only to the viral kind; bacterial bronchitis is too uncommon to worry about. The test does not show, however, that you don't have viral or bacterial bronchitis. Look now at the corresponding conditionals. It would have come back positive, if you had bronchitis, because you would have had the viral kind. It is not the case that it would have come back positive, if you'd had viral or bacterial bronchitis.

Alma catches sight of a meteor streaking across the sky. True, it could in principle have burned out in the time it took the light to reach her eye. That somehow doesn't bother us much; it doesn't stop her from seeing that that there is a meteor in the sky. But, although the bare, unrealized possibility of its disappearance allows her to see *that*, does it allow her to see that there is a *still existing* meteor in the sky? This is not so clear to me, since things would have looked the same if the meteor had burned out. Substitute a not very distant star if you like, so that it takes the light a few minutes to get

---

[15] This is based on an example of Kit Fine's. Assume that the tree of knowledge produces only a single apple.

[16] Schaffer and Szabó (2013). He has not perjured himself, if it was sapphires.

here. Seeing that there is a star on the horizon does, or may, not suffice for seeing that there is a currently existing star on the horizon, though the one outcome obtains if and only if the other does.

Examples like these are not a million miles from standard epistemology. If all we have go on is Al's testimony, then we don't know it was diamonds Claire stole, for Al did not speak to that issue. You know that you don't have bronchitis, because you have been tested, and that is what the test shows. You cannot claim on the same basis to know that you don't have viral or bacterial bronchitis, since the bacterial sort was never tested for. Knowing that there is a star on the horizon is easier than knowing that there is a still existing star there.

7.7 KNOWLEDGE DESTROYED

If knowledge is subject-matter sensitive, then it is sensitive to whatever the factors are that subject-matter depends on. What are those factors? And do they really have the expected epistemic effects?[17] Let me mention a few possibilities, some of which we have already seen. Imagine we have utterances both of *S knows that P* and *S knows that P'*, where *P'* is necessarily equivalent to *P*, but there is a shift, between the two occasions of utterance, in aboutness properties. This could happen, for instance, because

1. *P'* contains different words than *P*
2. it contains the same words, but differently arranged
3. it is the same sentence, but differently pronounced or uttered
4. it is similarly uttered, but the surrounding conversation is different

An example of the first scenario is where *P'* adds on a new conjunct *Q*, which though logically redundant (*P* implies it) breaks new ground on the subject matter front. *P* is equivalent to *P* & *Q* = *P'*. *I locked the door* is about me and the door; *I locked the door, and any evidence to the contrary is misleading* is about more than that. A redundant adjective will do it as well. A Rolex is a real Rolex and vice versa. But they bring different issues to the forefront. The issue with *It's a Rolex* is Rolex versus Timex; the issue with

[17] More carefully, the expected semantic effect in epistemic contexts.

125

It's a real Rolex is Rolex versus knock-off thereof (Hawthorne 2004). You can see how that might make it harder to know that it's a *real* Rolex than that it's a Rolex.

Next, logically irrelevant changes in word order. Take *No cities are above 9,000 feet*. This says the same as *Nothing that high is a city*, but if you asked me how and why they are false, I would answer differently. The first gets us thinking of well-known cities that are at a remarkably high altitude. It is false that no cities are above 9,000 feet because Quito, the capital of Ecuador, is that high. The second gets us thinking about places at a high altitude that turn out to be cities. It is false that nothing that high is a city because, for instance, the principality of Andorra, famous for its high-altitude skiing, is also, perhaps surprisingly, a city. Insofar as Quito's altitude is better known than Andorra's civic status, *No cities are as high as 9,000 feet* is apt to seem more clearly false than *Nothing that high is a city*.

The third possibility was noted long ago by Dretske (1972). *Clyde gave me the TICKETS* seems somehow to strike a different note than *Clyde GAVE me the tickets*. The first marks off worlds where it is tickets he gave me from worlds where it is chewing gum, or tobacco. The second marks off worlds where he *gave* them to me from worlds where he took them, or sold them to me as the highest bidder. This makes no truth-conditional difference if the sentences are sitting there all by themselves. But it matters when they are embedded in focus-sensitive contents. Clyde gave ME the tickets by mistake—he meant to give them to Bob—but he did not give me the TICKETS by mistake—tickets are what he deals in. I regret that Clyde gave ME the tickets—Abby wanted them more—but not that he gave me the TICKETS. My nonregret here is because I can pass the tickets on to Abby.

Then finally there is discourse context. *No vegetarians play golf* gives us negative information about vegetarians' hobbies. You know the vegetarians? None of them are golfers. But consider it in response to *Golfers are not much for moral crusades. What kind of person plays golf?*. Then it is telling us something *positive* about a different group's eating habits, namely that they eat meat. The subject matter can also be tweaked *retroactively* by developments after the fact: *No vegetarians are golfers, and no fruitarians or pescatarians either. Golfers are carnivores*. To pick up on a case from section 7.5, we are not as confident of *Some barns are red* in a discussion

126

of the red structures—which are real and which fake?—than a discussion of the color of local barns.

7.8 DEDUCTION

Immanent closure applies only when Q is part of P. It says nothing about the case where Q merely *follows* from P. And that case is very important. I may not have to know "already" that Q, if Q ranges thematically outside of P. Still, to know P does presumably put me in a *position* to know that Q. So far we have done nothing to provide for this. Deduction is not supposed to be an epistemically hazardous enterprise. To be told that it is not hazardous, when the conclusion is contained in the premise, does not really provide much comfort. It is not as though anyone ever bothers to *check* that it is part of the premise, before treating the conclusion as known. How could we be so irresponsible? Also, most conclusions are *not* parts. One needs apparently a second closure principle—"transeunt" closure—to deal with knowledge of conclusions drawn from premises that do not contain them.

The principle will have to be carefully formulated, for conclusions of this sort are *not* always known, or even believed. This is a point stressed by Harman. Having reasoned her way to Q from P, Alma faces a choice. One option is to accept Q. Or, if Q is unacceptable, she may prefer to abandon P (Harman 1973). She faces a similar choice when it comes to knowledge claims. Should she find herself appearing to know she is sitting, she can go with Moore in claiming knowledge also of *I am not a brain in a vat*, or with the skeptic in allowing that she might after all not know what her body is doing.

The second approach is more plausible, if falsity-makers hook up in the advertised way with aboutness. Mooreans suppose in effect that *I am not a brain in a vat* loses some of its subject matter, when it is deduced from *I am sitting*. Skeptics have *I am sitting* acquiring new subject matter, as non-postural alternatives to sitting come into view. I am with the skeptic on this. Which is likelier, that *I am not a brain in a vat* loses interest in skeptical counterpossibilities, or that *I am sitting* gains interest in them? Q's subject matter and counterpossibilities are visited back on P, surely. This is why P strikes us as increasingly doubtful when antiskeptical conclusions are drawn. It expresses a bigger proposition; a bigger proposition gives us more to be on top of, which makes P harder to know.[18]

This somewhat addresses the problem of knowledge of unincluded conclusions. The problem obviously does not arise, if the premise ceases to be known. What about the other case, where P continues to known after its subject matter grows to include that of Q? The problem does not arise in that case either, for Q now *becomes* a part. Knowledge of parts is covered already by immanent closure. A "transeunt" closure principle may not be needed, then. Such a principle is valid only when restricted to cases that are covered by the principle that we already have.

7.9 KNOWLEDGE RETAINED

Carnap points out the cognitive switch that is pulled when a heavy duty conclusion like *Numbers exist* is drawn from a humdrum premise, say, *60 has three factors*. The premise, established initially by calculation, grows before our eyes into some kind of metaphysical giant. It is similar with some of the other IONs mentioned. *I have a hand* takes on a bold new aspect when wielded against the skeptic. *I am teaching logic next fall* seems suddenly to be thumbing its nose at death. P appears often, if not always, to blow up into a larger and more formidable hypothesis when it becomes the base camp for an assault on Q.

What is going on in these cases? Some say that P's modal domain expands; the proposition now expressed is defined on more worlds.[19] I am suggesting something different. P has the same truth-values in the same worlds; it expresses the same coarse-granted propositions; it is only the subject matter that changes. The conclusion's ways of being false are taken on by the premise, necessitating a reconsideration of that premise. It's as though a tourist map of Bel Air, indicating where the stars live, were produced in a legal dispute about oil rights and property lines. The map says the same as before—it rules the same way on the same worlds—but is surprised to find itself applied to such a sensitive issue.

---

[18] Again, discourse context is not limited to what takes place before, and during, the utterance whose subject matter is in question. One must look also at what comes after. This includes the uses to which P is put, and in particular the *deductive* uses.

[19] Lewis (1996).

Let's write P^+ for P with the puffed up subject matter. The BIV worlds might, for instance, be marked out as a newly distinguished counterpossibility. P^+ holds in the same scenarios as P, but in additional ways, with the result that it contains Q where P did not.[20] There are two possible outcomes here: either we know P but not P^+, or we know P^+ in addition to P.

Suppose we know that P^+. Then since Q is contained in P^+, we know that Q, by immanent closure. This is the ordinary case, in which knowledge is preserved under deduction. Knowing that I am sitting gives me knowledge that I am sitting or crouching, because I continue to know I am sitting, even when its subject anti-matter is expanded to include neither-sitting-nor-crouching as a distinguished alternative. To put it in sensitivity terms, I would have noticed, had I been standing or lying down, which is what I do when not sitting or crouching.

Imagine alternatively that P is known but P^+ is not. That our P-knowledge is lost when P grows to include Q suggests that Q is contributing counterpossibilities that we are not on top of. To know what *I am sitting* says now, I must be on top of the possibility of being a BIV. Since I am *not* on top of it, I cannot be said any longer to know that I am sitting. I know the thought *I am sitting* did express, but not the thought it expresses now.

In ordinary contexts, I know that I am sitting; in skeptical contexts, I seemingly don't. This cannot not the whole story, though, for lightweight propositions are, even in skeptical contexts, better known than their heavyweight consequences. I still feel in a better position with respect to *I am sitting* than *I am not a bodiless BIV*, when, due to BIV worries, I fail to know that I am sitting. Contextualists who invoke shifting standards have trouble explaining this. Neither proposition is known, judging by higher standards; both are, judging by lower.

The difference is that lightweight propositions retain *even in skeptical contexts* a substantial known part. Let the original, preskeptical subject matter of *I am sitting* be my posture. The alternatives recognized by my posture, are, say, I am standing, I am crouching, I am lying down, I am leaning, I am doing handstands, I am hanging by my heels, and

---

[20] Really it's the same sentence on both occasions—only the directed proposition changes—but the new proposition will be given its own sentence. P^+ says in all contexts what P says when we infer from it that Q.

(as a final catchall category) "other." The part of *I am sitting* that concerns my posture is still kicking around inside, even when the sentence has come to say more.

7.10 SUMMING UP

Seeming closure violations have been met with three main responses: counterfactualism (Nozick), contextualism (Cohen, DeRose, Lewis), and Carnap's idea that *There are numbers* is harder to know because it addresses a trickier sort of question. Our picture has some contextualism in it, since the subject matter of *I am sitting* changes in skeptical contexts, thereby "destroying our knowledge." It has some counterfactualism in it, insofar as being on top a counterpossibility is being such that one would have noticed, had that counterpossibility obtained. It has some Carnap in it, too, for when the doubters come round, one takes refuge in the ordinary, "internal," part of *I am sitting*, the part that concerns its old, nonskeptical, subject matter. The ordinary part we do know. Backgammon can to this extent be played in the seminar room.

- 8 -

Extrapolation and Its Limits

8.1 EINSTEIN'S DOG

Once again, it would be nice if I could explain the topic with examples, but we will have to make do with anecdotes. The first concerns a conversation Einstein is supposed to have had with some puzzled citizen.

> *Citizen*: How does the telegraph system work? I don't see how a message goes down an electric wire.
>
> *Einstein*: What's so difficult? Imagine a dog with its head in Moscow and tail in Leningrad. Pull the tail in one place, and the head barks in the other.
>
> *Citizen*: I'm with you so far, but what about the wireless telegraph? How does *that* work?
>
> *Einstein*: The same way, but without the dog.

My second example comes from the 1980 presidential debates between Ronald Reagan and Walter Mondale. Reagan had been showing some considerable ignorance of world affairs. Asked about Valery Giscard D'Estaing, then the president of France, he said, "I don't believe I have heard that name". The moderator asked Mondale if it bothered him, that there was so much Reagan didn't know. "Not really", Mondale said. "It's not what he doesn't know that bothers me; it's what he knows for sure that just isn't true." (Borrowed from Will Rogers, apparently.)

Is it clear what these stories have in common? In both we've got a hypothesis *A* that implies another one *B*—pulling the dog's tail to get its head to bark implies there's a dog there, and knowing (as Reagan "knew") that food stamps are used by welfare queens to buy vodka implies that that is how food stamps are being used—and the two hypotheses together are supposed to determine a weaker hypothesis that is, as we might put it, *A stripped of its implication that B*. Mondale, for instance, seems to be worried that Reagan only *quasi*-knows a lot of what he takes himself to know, where

131

quasi-knowing that P is something like knowing (or "knowing for sure") that P, stripped of its implication that P.

This kind of implication-stripping, or cutting a content down to size, might be seen as a challenge to analytic philosophy's traditional self-image. Frege and Russell sought to characterize contents of interest "from below," by showing how they could be built up out of weaker contents.[1] They never, as far as I know, took the opposite tack, approaching a content from above by first overshooting the target, and then stripping away unwanted extras. One can certainly imagine reasons for this. Logical *addition* lines up pretty well with conjunction, while logical *subtraction* is somewhat of a mystery. I suspect it's no accident that Wittgenstein, as he began tearing himself free of the analytic paradigm, found himself wondering about logical subtraction. What is left, he asked, if we subtract my arm going up from my *raising* that arm? What is left if you subtract from *It hurts!* the fact that it's you who is hurting?[2]

8.2 LEFTOVERS

Logical subtraction is baffling, but that is not to say we don't sometimes attempt it. Colloquially it is expressed by phrases like "with the possible exception of Joe" and "only maybe not all at once," and "barring an act of God" (von Fintel 1993, Gajewski 2008). Philosophers talk this way all the time. A statement is lawlike, according to Goodman, if it is a law, *except it might not be true*. "We can investigate the world, and man as a part of it, and find out what cues he could have of what goes on around him. Subtracting his cues from his world view, we get man's net contribution as the difference" (Quine 1960, 4). Shoemaker explains quasi-memory in something like the way we explained quasi-knowledge on behalf of Will Rogers.[3] A theory is empirically adequate if it is true, ignoring what it says about theoretical entities. Warrant is whatever "makes the difference between knowledge and mere true belief" (Plantinga 1993, 3).

---

[1] Though Frege saw limits to this approach (Tappenden 1995).

[2] Humberstone (2000), Humberstone (2011), Fuhrmann (1996), and Fuhrmann (1999).

[3] "Someone's claim to remember a past event implies that he himself was aware of the event at the time of its occurrence, but the claim to quasi-remember [it] implies only that someone or other was aware of it" (Shoemaker 1970, 271).

"A judgment = what is left of a belief after any phenomenal quality is subtracted" (Chalmers 1996, 174). The scare quotes sense of a moral term is the regular sense, minus any implication that the act is thereby commendable (deplorable).

But although philosophers do sometimes engage in the *act* of subtraction, they tend not to reflect on what they are doing. They are nervous about it, without knowing exactly why. That is one reason for looking further at logical subtraction. It is a favorite philosophical tool, at the same time as philosophers have doubts about it. The immediate reason is that leftovers bear on the issue of how far content-parts can be considered *parts*.

Here is what we said in section **3.1**: B is part of A iff the inference from A to B is, first, truth-preserving and, second, aboutness-preserving. Aboutness-preservation was explained as subject-matter inclusion, which had to do with A and B's ways of being true or false. Let a *decider* of hypothesis S be a possible truthmaker for S or a possible falsemaker for it. Then

33 $B \leq A$ iff A implies B and each B-decider is implied by an A-decider.[4]

From this, we see that content-part has the core properties of a part/whole relation:

34 reflexivity: $A \leq A$
    antisymmetry: if $B \leq A$ and $A \leq B$, then $A = B$.[5]
    transitivity: *if $A \leq B$ and $B \leq C$, then $A \leq C$.*

How, for instance, do we get transitivity? Each of C's deciders is bound to be implied by one of A's, if it is implied by a decider for B, and all of them are implied by deciders for A.

The core properties make content-part a partial order, but that is not enough to warrant use of the term "part." *Later in the alphabet than* is a partial order on letters; that doesn't make "z" part of "a." The relation sets bear to their subsets is a partial order. But, although the set of elephants and mice has the set of mice as a subset, it is not part of the set of mice.

---

[4] I mean that each B-decider is implied by an A-decider *of the same valence.* Truthmakers are implied by truthmakers, falsemakers by falsemakers.
[5] Here we are treating sentences as identical if they express the same thought. Antisymmetry holds absolutely when framed as a condition on thoughts.

The problem with *later in the alphabet than* is that there isn't anything you can point to as the *rest* of "a": the part or parts whereby it exceeds "z." Likewise there isn't anything you can point to as the extra bit or bits whereby the set of mice exceeds the set of mice and elephants. A relation of parthood should meet the further condition that when x is a part of y falling short of the whole, there is something left over: y has other parts that are disjoint from (share no parts with) x. (Ideally those other parts should get us y back when summed with x.)

Content-parts are properly so called, it seems, only if, in addition to the three conditions above, we have

35 leftover: if $B < A$, there is a $C < A$ that is disjoint from B.[6]

I call this the *leftover principle*, in honor of Wittgenstein's question in the *Philosophical Investigations* (Wittgenstein 1953, §62):

> what is left over if we subtract from the fact that I raise my arm the fact that my arm goes up?

A proper part C of A that is disjoint from B will be called a (logical) leftover. Should it be that there's a distinguished leftover R that makes up the difference between A and B (A should hold, for one thing, in the same worlds as $B\&R$), it will be a candidate for the role of the *remainder* when B is subtracted from A, for short, $A-B$.

The fate of content-parts is thus tied up with the existence of logical leftovers and remainders.[7] This could be trouble, as we have hardly even considered the issue, and there is reason to be concerned.

8.3 RECIPE IDEAS

Given an A that implies B, is there always something that we can point to as what A adds to B? The logician in us wants to look for a recipe that

---

[6] The official name is *Weak Supplementation*. Really we should say that there's a thought $C < A$ that is disjoint from B; there need be no sentence that expresses the thought. I will mostly ignore this and assume a C can be found.

[7] The issue up to now has been subtraction of content-parts. The next section brings in implications that may or may not be parts. Eventually, starting in section **10.4**, we look at subtrahends that may or may not be implications.

delivers a remainder in every case, and by a uniform method. I am going to suggest something like that myself, but what are the proposals that have been made so far? By far the most common is this:

36 A–B is the material conditional $B \rightarrow A$[8]

Call it the *horseshoe* theory, since the material conditional is usually written $B \supset A$ (B-horseshoe-A). An argument in its favor was given by J. L. Hudson in "Logical Subtraction" (Hudson (1975)).[9] He asks us to think first of numerical subtraction. a–b is the number c which, when added to b, gives us back a. Logical subtraction should work, as far as possible, like *that*. A–B should be the C such that $B \& C$ is equivalent to A.

Problem, however: there is no such thing as "the" C that makes that equation true. Any number of Cs are equivalent modulo B to A. So, for instance, A is equivalent modulo B to everything of the form $D \equiv A$, where D is implied by B. And also to everything of the form $B \& D$, for any D intermediate in strength between A and $B \rightarrow A$.

Since the equation is satisfied by lots of Cs, A–B will have to meet some further condition. A–B is a C that is somehow special. This presumably means, it is either the *strongest* statement which combines with B to yield A, or the *weakest* such statement. The strongest is A itself. A is a terrible candidate for the role of A–B! We want a C that picks up where B leaves off, not one that takes us across ground already covered.

That leaves the *weakest* C such that $B \& C$ is equivalent to A. The weakest C with that property is $B \rightarrow A$.[10] So, if A–B is to be a statement *canonically* equivalent modulo B to A, it should be, Hudson says, the material conditional $B \rightarrow A$.

The horseshoe theory has much to be said for it; it wasn't pulled out of a hat. But let's try it out on an example. $(p \& q)$–p, we are told,

---

[8] Subtraction here is a sentential connective, like conjunction.
[9] Other supporters include Hempel, and Carnap and Bar-Hillel. Hempel seeks to identify "that part of the information contained in H which is not contained in E, and which thus goes beyond what has been previously established. This 'new' information contained in H is expressed by the sentence $H \vee \neg E$" (Hempel 1960, 465). Bar-Hillel and Carnap identify "the information conveyed by a statement J in excess to that conveyed by some other statement I" with "the content of $I \rightarrow J$" (Bar-Hillel and Carnap 1953, 150).
[10] Compare set-subtraction. X–Y should be a Z whose union with Y is X. There are many such sets, so we look at the largest and smallest. The biggest is X. But subtracting Y from X should yield a smaller set, not X again. The smallest Z such that $Y \cup Z = X$ is the set of things in X but not Y. This is how set-remainders are in fact defined.

is $p \to (p \& q)$. This is a surprising result. What remains, one would think, when we subtract from $p \& q$ one of its conjuncts, is the *other* conjunct, in this case q. Hudson's candidate, $p \to (p \& q)$, is a great deal weaker than q; it is implied by $\neg p$, for instance, while q and p are independent.

That is an intuitive argument, but we can say something more principled. The point of introducing leftovers was to see how far content-parts could be made to satisfy the usual mereological laws. A–B is helpful in this respect only if it is a *part* of A that is disjoint from B.

Now, maybe the right sort of A–B cannot always be found; that's a question for later. The point right now is that it can *never* be found, on the horseshoe theory, even in the intuitively most favorable cases. Recall that the truth of a part is supposed to confer partial truth on the whole. Does the truth of $p \to (p \& q)$ reflect favorably in that respect on $p \& q$? Not at all, for the conditional might be true because p is false. That a conjunction is half wrong (one of its conjuncts is false) cannot be thought to make it half right![11] $B \to A$ cannot in fact ever be part of A, or A would be partly true thanks to the falsity of one of its implications. The horseshoe theory fails in this respect as badly as it could: it says that the result of subtracting a part is never part of the whole, when it should ideally always be part of the whole.

Of course, some other recipe for constructing remainders might do better. At this point, however, the prospects look bleak. There can be a recipe only if remainders always exist. And there appear to be clear counterexamples to such an idea. What does *Tom is red* add to *Tom is colored*? What does *They danced badly* add to *They danced*? What does, to give a more contemporary example, *Alma knows that water is wet* add to *Water is wet*, or *Alma believes water is wet*, to *Water exists*?[12] It's a strange sort of part that is inextricable from its containing whole.

---

[11] $p \to (p \& q)$ is officially part of $p \& q$ only if each truthmaker for $p \to (p \& q)$ implied by a truthmaker for $p \& q$. One truthmaker for the conditional is $\bar{p}$, the fact that $\neg p$. $\bar{p}$, however, far from being implied by a truthmaker for $p \& q$, is incompatible with all such truthmakers.

[12] A classic formulation of this worry:

> It sometimes seems to be thought that we can sidestep the question of whether "sees" has "success grammar" or "existential import", by arguing as follows: Let us grant that "see" as used in current English licenses inferring "D exists" from "S sees D". But . . . this usage is philosophically inconvenient; hence we should conduct our discussion in terms of "see*", where "see*" means just what "sees" means, except that "S sees* D" does not entail "D exists". There is, however, a fundamental problem with such a procedure. Consider someone writing on

So we are caught in a dilemma. On the one hand, leftovers should *always* exist when *B* is properly part of *A*; otherwise *content-part* is under suspicion of not really being a kind of parthood. On the other hand, *B* may well strike us as inextricable from *A*—dancing can't be pulled out of dancing badly— in which case the remainder is apparently just not there.[13] We come back to this in section **8.5**.

8.4 EXTRAPOLATION OF THE FOURTH KIND

The issue was supposed to be *extrapolation*, not extrication. Extrapolation will be serving, later, as a model for extrication. But I admit that the two strike us initially as quite different.

What the word "extrapolate" initially brings to mind is Hume's puzzle about why the observed part of reality should resemble the unobserved part—why the greenness of *these* emeralds should confirm the hypothesis that other emeralds are green as well. This, the puzzle of *inductive* extrapolation, is not our topic here, obviously.

If I tell you it has more to do with *projection* than confirmation, you will think of Goodman's new riddle of induction. Hume wants to know whether the unobserved part of reality *does* resemble the observed part. A prior question is, in what respects is it even *supposed* to resemble it? These emeralds are as much grue as green; why should it be the greenness that is expected to carry over to other emeralds, rather than their property of being grue? This is the puzzle of *projective* extrapolation: what are the inductively fruitful ways to project from observed cases to new cases? Projective extrapolation is at least as puzzling as inductive, probably more so. But it is not our topic, either.

---

the secondary qualities who observes that "X is red" entails that X is colored, and decides to introduce the term 'red*' to mean precisely what "red" means except that "X is red*" does not entail that X is colored. The question such a procedure obviously raises is whether the deletion of the entailment to "X is colored" leaves anything significant behind. (Jackson 1977, 4–5).

[13] Our solution is hinted at in the last paragraph. A strange sort of part is still a part. A strange sort of remainder is still a remainder.

The kind of extrapolation at issue here has more of a logical flavor—it's more to do with going on in the *same* way than the inductively *fruitful* way. This puts us in mind of Kripkenstein's rule following paradox. Imagine that we have found an answer to Goodman; we know that new emeralds are expected to be *green* rather than blue. There is still the question of where this expectation gets its content.

How does it come about that the property of unexamined objects whereby they are properly conceived as "green" is GREENNESS rather than something else? The samples from which I learned the word have *lots* of chromatic properties. Why should "green" in my mouth not be true of objects resembling the samples in *schmolor* rather than color? This time it is truth- or application-conditions we want to extrapolate—how does the predicate come to be true of just those objects?—so I will speak of *alethic* extrapolation. Alethic extrapolation is in Kripke's view more puzzling even than projective and inductive extrapolation:

> Wittgenstein has invented a new form of skepticism. Personally I am inclined to regard it as the most radical and original skeptical problem that philosophy has seen to date. (Kripke 1982, 60)

The kind of extrapolation I want to talk about has, again, to do with truth-conditions, and is suggested, again, by certain passages in Wittgenstein. Type 4 extrapolation is in some respects more puzzling even than alethic. One reason for this is that type 4 problems remain even if, as Kripke says, we bracket the alethic problem that *Wittgenstein on Rules and Private Language* mainly concerns. Also though, the traditional puzzles are *skeptical* in nature. No one seriously doubts that inductive, projective, and alethic extrapolation "work." Type 4 extrapolation, however, as we'll see, may in some cases not work.

The Kripke book *mainly* concerns type 3 extrapolation, but type 4 comes up in an appendix, on the so-called "conceptual problem of other minds" (Wittgenstein 1953, §300). Type 4 extrapolation rears its head in the following (admittedly enigmatic) passage:

> If one has to imagine someone else's pain on the model of one's own, this is none too easy a thing to do: for I have to imagine pain which I do not feel on the model of the pain which I do feel.

He does not say in so many words why it is difficult—more than, say, imagining next year's fireworks on the model of this year's—but presents an analogy that is meant to evoke the appropriate sense of bewilderment:

[Suppose] I were to say: "You surely know what 'It is 5 o'clock here' means; so you also know what 'It is 5 o'clock on the sun' means. It means simply that it is the same time there as it is here when it is 5 o'clock." (Wittgenstein 1953, §350)

Kripke:

The "5 o'clock on the sun" example seems obviously intended as a case where, without the intervention of any arcane philosophical skepticism about rule-following, there really is a difficulty about extending the old concept—certain presuppositions of our application of this concept are lacking . . . Wittgenstein seems to mean that, waiving his basic and general skeptical problem, there is a special intuitive problem . . . illustrated by the 5 o'clock on the sun example. (Kripke 1982, 118–119)

How is it possible to extend an old concept, or content, to an area where some of its presuppositions, or more generally implications, are lacking? To extend, for instance, the content of *Ouch, it hurts!*, which we understand initially in a first-personal way, to people such that when you put their hands on a hot stove, it doesn't hurt one little bit? To extend the content of *Reagan knows that food stamps are used by welfare queens to buy vodka* to worlds where food stamps are *not* used to buy vodka? How is it possible to extend the content of *Alma thinks water is wet* to worlds where there is no water for Alma to be thinking about?

I hope you see *some* connection between the Wittgensteinian issue of how to extrapolate contents beyond their original field of application, and the earlier, broadly logical, issue of content-subtraction—how to subtract from *A* one of its implications *B*. The proposal is going to be that they are the same operation. Subtracting from *A* an implication *B* (or abstracting away from that implication, or bracketing it—I won't distinguish these) just *is* extrapolating *A* from within the *B*-region of logical space to outside that region—to worlds where *A*'s implication *B* doesn't hold. I might note, to beat a possibly dead horse, that the content-extrapolation problem just mentioned (5 o'clock on the sun) was devised by the man responsible for the best-known subtraction problem. To subtract my arm going up from the fact that I raise it, is to extend the path that fact takes through the arm-up region to the rest of logical space, where my arm stays down. To extrapolate "It's 5 o'clock here in Cambridge" to the sun, one has to subtract the assumption that "here" is a place like Cambridge, far enough from the sun that diurnal time-determinations make sense.

8.5 THE MYSTERIAN AND THE LOGICIAN

"Why should we need a theory of when, and how, subtraction "works"? It's enough if we can tell in particular cases."

But we can't. Our judgments stem as much from philosophical temperament as features of the case. *Logicians* reason as follows: if *A* says more than *B*, there has got to be such a thing as the more that it says; the *engineers* among them believe it ought to be constructible in some uniform way from *A* and *B*. To *mysterians*, subtraction is a leap into the darkness that lands us who know where.

> *The Mysterian Thesis*: You say that there has to be such a thing as the remainder. But there is no must about it. We don't even know what we *mean* by "remainder." The job-description is irremediably unclear.

How much of a mysterian Wittgenstein means to be, I am not sure. But there are certainly mysterian elements in the literature he inspired. Robert Jaeger in "Action and Subtraction"[14] points out a problem already noted:

> The question "What is left over?" . . . presupposes . . . that there is exactly one statement with certain logical properties. [But] whereas there is exactly one number *r* such that $r + 2 = 5$, it is not the case that there is exactly one statement *R* such that *R* & *my arm goes up* is logically equivalent to *I raise my arm* (321, 328)

[14] Jaeger (1973); see also Jaeger (1976).

140

J. L. Hudson responds, as we saw, that

> if there are several different propositions whose conjunction with B is A, then . . . the weakest . . . . of these [viz. $B \to A$] shall be considered the difference between A and B.[15]

Generalizing a bit, we have the

> *The Logician's Antithesis:* The feeling that there *must* be a remainder is quite correct. A–B is the best, most eligible, R such that $B\&R$ is equivalent to A.

The best R in Hudson's view is the weakest one, but other worthy candidates may emerge. The logician need not even have a candidate. She is convinced on general grounds that A adds some definite thing to B, and makes it her job to find it.

8.6 SUMMING UP

If A implies B, is there always something that we can point to as what A adds to B? The logician, or logical engineer, says yes. The mysterian says no. To get a bead on the issue, we distinguished four types of extrapolation: inductive, as in Hume, projective, as in Goodman, alethic, as in Kripkenstein, and type 4, as in Wittgenstein's "conceptual problem of other minds" and his example of 5 o'clock on the sun. Logical subtraction is understood, to begin with, as type 4 extrapolation. A–B is the result of extrapolating A beyond the bounds imposed by B. The question is whether this can always be done.

---

[15] Hudson (1975, 131), with inessential relettering.

- 9 -

Going On in the Same Way

9.1 A FRAMEWORK FOR SUBTRACTION

Who is right about remainders, the mysterian or the logical engineer? The extrapolation model allows a synthesis: A can always be extrapolated, but not always as far as one might like. It helps to view the matter diagrammatically (see Figure 9.1).

The all-enclosing rectangle is logical space. Truth-conditional contents are regions of that space, containing the worlds where a sentence is true.[1] The proposition that B is the column on the left, and the proposition that A is where that column intersects with the horizontal bar. The bar is labeled R to mark it as the remainder when B is subtracted from A. The A-worlds lie within the column because A implies B. They lie within the bar because A implies A–B. The "home" region (the column) is the region A is extrapolated *from*. The rest, marked "away," is the region that A is projected *into*. We have to find the projection rules, the rules telling us how R should behave away, given how it behaves at home. I take it that

37   R extrapolates A beyond B iff
    (i) R's behavior at home is modeled on that of A
    (ii) R's away behavior is modeled on its behavior at home.

Clause (i), like the basis clause in a recursive definition, is to get us started. Clause (ii) is about how to on from there. It says that the line separating R from $\neg R$ in the $\neg B$-region should follow the track laid down in the B-region.

---

[1] Or pairs of regions, for contents that are not defined on all worlds. We confine ourselves to the simple case.

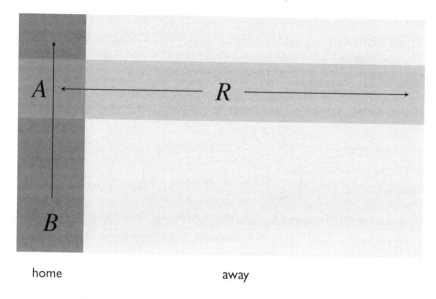

home   away

Figure 9.1 Extrapolating A beyond B to obtain $R = A-B$

9.2 HOME AND AWAY

Let's think first about the *kinds* of condition R should meet. "Home" conditions speak to R's behavior within the B-region. "Away" conditions speak to R's behavior *outside* the B-region. A second distinction, crosscutting the first, is between "classifying" conditions and "rationalizing" conditions. Classifying conditions are to do with *whether* R is true in a given world. Rationalizing conditions are to do with *how and why* R is true in a world, its way of being true there. Conditions will thus be needed of four basic types:

(HC) home-classifying;
(HR) home-rationalizing;
(AC) away-classifying; and
(AR) away-rationalizing.

This way of dividing up the task suggests a certain order of operations. One begins at home, asking in which B-worlds R is to be true and in which false; that's (HC). One looks into the reasons for these truth-value assignments; that's (HR). The factors controlling R's truth-value at home are carried over to the away-region; that's (AR). *R*'s reasons for being true/false in away-worlds will then hopefully offer some guidance as to its truth-value in such worlds; that's (AC).

In which *B*-worlds is *R* true? *R* could hardly count as extending *A* from the *B*-region, if *R* and *A* were not equivalent in that region. Our first requirement is

(HC) *Agreement*

$$R \text{ is } \left\{ \begin{array}{l} \text{true} \\ \text{false} \end{array} \right\} \text{ at home just when } A \text{ is } \left\{ \begin{array}{l} \text{true} \\ \text{false} \end{array} \right\}.$$

Agreement tells us that *R* "does the right thing" at home; it is true in the right *B*-worlds, those where *A* is also true. Now we want it to do the right thing for the right reason What would a good reason be, though, for *R* to hold in a given *B*-world? It might seem that, if *R* is true/false just when *A* is in the *B*-region, so *R* should be true/false for the same *reasons* as *A* in the *B*-region. But that cannot be right. *A*'s reasons for being true obtain only at home; for they imply *A*, which implies *B*. We were looking for reasons that stand a chance of obtaining also away from home. The proposal is this; *R* is true in a *B*-world *w* because *w* has whatever is it that sets *B*&*A*-worlds apart from *B*&¬*A*-worlds—whatever it is that makes *w*, its *B*-ness given, in addition an *A*-world.

(HR) *Rectitude*

$$R \text{ is } \left\{ \begin{array}{l} \text{true} \\ \text{false} \end{array} \right\} \text{ at home for the reasons } A \text{ is } \left\{ \begin{array}{l} \text{true} \\ \text{false} \end{array} \right\} \text{ given B.}$$

The truth-given-*B* of *A* is the truth *simpliciter* of $B \rightarrow A$. We are talking, then, about reasons for $B \rightarrow A$ to be true of the sort that can obtain in *B*-worlds—*B*-compatible truthmakers for $B \rightarrow A$. (Reasons for *A* to be false given *B* are likewise *B*-compatible truthmakers for $B \rightarrow \neg A$.)[2]

Next is to identify *R*'s truthmakers and falsemakers in away-worlds, as a function, presumably, of its truth- and falsity-makers at home. A hypothesis

---

[2] *Rectitude* is spelled out further below. *R*'s truthmakers (falsemakers) in a *B*-world *w* are ultimately defined as $B \rightarrow A$'s ($B \rightarrow \neg A$'s) "targeted" truthmakers in *w*. A truthmaker for $B \rightarrow X$ is targeted if it is *B*-compatible and *B*-efficient. The formulation in the text leaves *B*-efficiency out of it, because it doesn't have much to do at this point. *B*-efficiency begins to bite later, when we drop the requirement that *A* implies *B*.

continuing A into a new region of logical space should not suddenly develop new reasons for being true/false; it should be true/false away for the same reasons as it was true/false at home.

(AR) *Integrity*

$$R \text{ is } \begin{Bmatrix} \text{true} \\ \text{false} \end{Bmatrix} \text{ for the same reasons away as it is } \begin{Bmatrix} \text{true} \\ \text{false} \end{Bmatrix} \text{ at home.}[3]$$

It remains to specify R's truth-value in away-worlds—as a function, presumably, of the *reasons* R has available to it in such worlds for being true or false (see *Integrity*). You might expect R to be true in any away-world where a home-style truthmaker obtains. But what if a home-style falsemaker obtains in the same world? (An example is given in section **9.4**.) R has in that case no more reason for being true than false. The proper rule is

(AC) *Determination*

$$R \text{ is } \begin{Bmatrix} \text{true} \\ \text{false} \end{Bmatrix} \text{ away if it has reason to be } \begin{Bmatrix} \text{true} \\ \text{false} \end{Bmatrix} \text{ and none to be } \begin{Bmatrix} \text{false} \\ \text{true} \end{Bmatrix}$$

Putting the pieces together (including the clarification in note 2), we get the following as R's evaluation rule:

38 R is true (false) in a world w, be it home or away, just if

   (1) $B \rightarrow A$ has, and $B \rightarrow \neg A$ lacks, a home-style truthmaker in w

   (2) $B \rightarrow \neg A$ has, and $B \rightarrow A$ lacks, a home-style truthmaker in w.

A simpler formulation is given below (section **9.4**): R is true if A "adds truth" (and only truth) to B, false if it adds (only) falsity.

---

[3] That is, any reason R might have for being true/false in an away-world is a reason that obtains also in at least one home-world. This is a one-directional inclusion only. We do not assume that R's ways of being true/false at home obtain also in away-worlds.

Chapter 9

9.3 SYNTHESIS

The mysterian about remainders thinks that the notion is ill-defined. The logician, or logical optimist, hopes for a definition. If the stated conditions are correct, there is truth on both sides.

9.3.1 The Truth in Mysterianism

The lesser truth is that $B \to A$ is a bad candidate for the role of $A–B$. A good candidate would be an R whose truth-value was controlled by the same factors outside the B-region as within it. $B \to A$ is true in $\neg B$-worlds because B is false, or because of whatever it is that makes B false. A fact making B false cannot obtain in any B-world. But then, $B \to A$ can be true in away-worlds for a non-home-style reason, which (by **Integrity**) disqualifies it for the $A–B$ role.

The greater truth is that B cannot always be neatly excised from A. To raise my arm, I must (let's agree) will my arm to go up. Is the act of will what my arm's going up adds to my raising it? No, for I could have willed it up (R) without raising it (A), even had my arm gone up (B). (It might have gone up for other reasons.) This is a violation of **Agreement**. *I will my arm up* does not imply *I raise my arm* in the region of logical space where my arm goes up.

What about *I effectively will my arm to go up*? It has the opposite problem; it is too strong. One way for *I effectively will my arm to go up* to be false is that my arm stays down, making the act of will ineffective. But, my arm staying down is not the kind of falsity-maker that can obtain also in home-worlds: worlds where my arm goes up. *I effectively will my arm to go up* picks up new falsity-makers as we pass out of the region where my arm goes up. This a violation of **Integrity**.

9.3.2 The Truth in Logical Optimism

What we are looking for in a remainder is an R that agrees with A in the B-region, and agrees with itself across the $B/\neg B$ border. An R like that always exists, I claim. There is a recipe in the next section.

146

But, don't we know that, in some cases, it cannot exist? That subtraction is not always well defined? Note a subtle equivocation here. It is one thing to say that subtraction is well-defined *as a logical operation*. That means there is always such an item as *A–B*. It is another thing to say the proposition *itself* is well-defined. For the proposition to be well-defined means that, go to any world you like, it is true or false there. Subtraction is well-defined in the first sense, but not the second. This is the proposed synthesis: when *B* is intuitively inextricable from *A*, a proposition *A–B* still exists, just don't try evaluating it at (too many) worlds where *B* fails.

9.4 VALUE ADDED

One objection to the horseshoe theory is that $B \to A$ is not part of *A*, whereas *A–B* sometimes *should* be part of *A*, particularly when *B* is part of *A*.[4] Another, not unrelated, objection is that *A–B* lacks integrity since it takes on new truthmakers when *B* is false.

A third, more directly intuitive, objection is this: the theory makes it too difficult for *A–B* to be false, and too easy for it to be true. Suppose with Hudson that *A–B* is $B \to A$. Then it is false only when *B* is true, and true whenever *B* is false. That was not the idea! The point of subtracting *B* is to arrive at a hypothesis whose truth-value is independent, or as independent as possible, of *B*'s truth-value; we bracket *B* to put ourselves out of its reach truth-value-wise. This means, not only that *B*'s falsity should not force *A–B* to be false; but also that it should not force *A–B* to be true.

Suppose that *F* is Falstaff's total testimony, and let *G* be his testimony about Jones's colleague Green. *F–G* is Falstaff's testimony about Jones. One would not have thought that Falstaff, in order to misrepresent Jones, had to speak the truth about Green! Why should it not be possible to misrepresent both at once? This is disallowed, however, by the horseshoe theory. Falstaff's testimony strictly about Jones, construed as $G \to F$, is automatically true if he lies about Green.

---

[4] Let *A* and *B* be *p&q* and *p*. Why is $p \to (p\&q)$ not part of *p&q*? It has truthmakers, such as $\bar{p}$, which are not implied by truthmakers for *p&q*, and falsemakers, such as p&q̄, that are not implied by falsemakers for *p&q*.

The problem seems to be this. "*A* false, *B* true" is the limiting case of a broader phenomenon of *A* being false in its own right, in a way owing nothing to *B*. *A–B* is false, not only in that limiting case, but when *A*, as I'll put it, "adds falsity" to *B*.

What is this relation of adding falsity, or being additionally false, or being false not just because *B* is false? I want to say that *X* adds falsity to *B*[5] when *B*&*X* is false for a reason that does not trade on *B* being false, as is shown by its being instantiable even when *B* is true. This is the same as *B* → ¬*X* being true for a reason that can obtain even when *B* is true. Reasons like this, that do not trade on *B*'s falsity, are the kind we above called *B*-compatible or *B*-friendly.

So, for instance, *p&q* strikes us as adding falsity to *q*—compounding any offense against truth committed already by *q*—if *p* is false, and truth (its negation adds falsity) if *p* is true. Asked to explain *why p&q* adds falsity to *q* when *p* is false, we point out that it is false for a reason (viz., $\bar{p}$) that can obtain equally well when *q* is true—which is the same as *q* → ¬(*p&q*) being true for such a reason. Asked to explain why ¬(*p&q*) adds falsity to *q* when *p* is true, so that *p* adds truth, we observe that *q* → (*p&q*) is true for a reason (viz., p) that can hold when *q* is true. The principle here is that

39 *A* adds truth (falsity) to *B* in *w* iff

B → *A* (*B* → ¬*A*) is true in *w* for a *B*-friendly reason.[6]

The truth-conditions of *A–B* (**38** above) can now be restated as follows:

40 *A–B* is

    1 false in *w* iff *A* adds falsity, but not truth, to *B* in *w*

    2 true in *w* iff *A* adds truth, but not falsity, to *B* in *w*

    3 otherwise undefined

The qualifiers "but not truth" and "but not falsity" are because a world does not always speak with one tongue; that *A* adds truth in *w* is compatible

---

[5] In particular, when *X* is *A*, or its negation.

[6] Strictly, *A* adds truth (falsity) to *B* iff *B* → *A* (*B* → ¬*A*) has a *targeted* truthmaker. A targeted truthmaker for *B* → *A* is a *B*-compatible truthmaker that "uses as much of *B* as it can," in the sense of minimizing the extent to which *Y* → *A* is also implied, *Y* ranging over *B*'s parts. The new clause gets little traction when the consequent implies the antecedent; proportionality has much the same effect. It becomes important later (section **11.1**), when we drop the implication requirement.

with its adding falsity too. Example: *A* and *B* are *Both of Herb's dogs have fleas* and *Herb has exactly two dogs*; *w* is an away-world where Herb has three dogs, of which two have fleas. *R* has a truthmaker in *w*, since the two aforementioned dogs form a *B*-compatible truthmaker for *Herb has exactly two dogs → Both of Herb's dogs have fleas*. But *R* has a falsemaker there as well, since Herb's third dog is a truthmaker for *Herb has exactly two dogs → It is not the case that both of Herb's dogs have fleas* that is compatible with Herb's having exactly two dogs. *A = Both of his dogs have fleas* adds both truth and falsity to *Herb has exactly two dogs*—truth in that it gets two of his dogs right, falsity in that it misrepresents the other dog.

9.5 PRESUPPOSITION FAILURE

Look again the third clause of our definition of *A–B* ((**40**) above), which specifies when *A–B* is undefined. In added-value terms,

> 41 *A–B* is undefined in *w* iff
>
> > (i) *A* adds neither truth nor falsity to *B* in *w*, or else
> > (ii) *A* adds both truth and falsity to *B* in *w*

An interesting test case arises if *A* presupposes *B*, as, for instance, *The king of France is bald* presupposes *France has a king*.

France has a king→The king of France is bald is true because France lacks a king.[7] Such a truthmaker is not *B*-friendly, though; it forces *B* to be false. The lack of a *B*-friendly truthmaker means that *The king of France is bald* does not add truth to *France has a king*. Neither, for similar reasons, does it add falsity to *France has a king*. By condition (i), then, *The king of France is bald–France has a king* is undefined.

If indeed *The king of France is bald* adds neither truth nor falsity to its presupposition, this may explain why, as Strawson observed, it strikes us as unevaluable. Not every king-of-France statement strikes us that way; *The king of France is in my garage right now* seems false. Intriguingly, the latter sentence *does* add falsity to *France has a king*. *France has a king → The*

---

[7] Not because France lacks a bald king. This by proportionality; the "bald" is an irrelevant extra.

king of France is in my garage is false because my garage is empty, which is compatible with France having a king.

A presupposition fails *catastrophically* if, as with *The king of France is bald*, the question of truth or falsity no longer arises. *The king of France is in my garage right now* is a case of *noncatastrophic presupposition failure*. That we find it easier to evaluate the *A* that "adds something" to its presupposition *P* suggests that *P* fails catastrophically when *A* adds neither truth nor falsity to *P*. This is a *sufficient* condition for catastrophic presupposition failure. Is it also necessary? I am inclined to think not. What if *A* adds truth *and* falsity to *P*, as occurs, apparently, with *A = The author of Principia Mathematica is bald* and *P = Principia Mathematica has exactly one author*. (*A* adds truth on account of Whitehead, falsity on account of Russell.) This too strikes me most days as unevaluable ("the question of truth or falsity does not arise"). Let me then conjecture that

42 *A* suffers from catastrophic presupposition failure iff

  (i) *A* adds *neither* truth nor falsity to *P*, or

  (ii) it adds *both* truth and falsity to *P*.[8]

Equivalently given (**41**), *P* fails noncatastrophically iff *A–P* is defined despite *P*'s falsity. A natural further conjecture is:

43 *A*'s felt truth-value is the real truth-value of *A–P*.[9]

If something like this is correct, then philosophical arguments relying on intuitive truth-value judgments are liable to misfire when *A* has a presupposition whose truth-value is the point at issue. A certain kind of Platonist, for instance, argues like this:

1. *The number of planets ≠ zero* is true.
2. It could not be true unless there were numbers.
3. So there are numbers.

---

[8] See Schoubye (2009) for an interestingly different account of catastrophic presupposition failure.

[9] *A* counts as false, then, if *A* adds just falsity to *P*, that is, $P \rightarrow \neg A$ has a *P*-compatible truthmaker and $P \rightarrow A$ does not. This is meant to improve on the proposal in Yablo (2006b): *A* counts as false if it has, and ¬*A* lacks, implications that are false for *P*-compatible reasons. The difference is that we worry now about one implication only, viz. $P \rightarrow X$; *X* is *A* or ¬*A*, as the case may be.

The challenge is to distinguish this argument from a superficial analogue:

1. *The king of France ≠ zero* is true.
2. It could not be true unless France had a king.
3. So France has a king.

The first premise is open in each case to a similar challenge. "Strictly speaking, the undeniable-seeming sentences are untrue. They strike us as true because we are a semantically forgiving tribe; we try not to hold the falsity of sentences' presuppositions against them. A is evaluated in many cases as though it were A–P. A–P really is true in these cases. But we can't derive an ontological conclusion from it, for the conclusion depends on P; and P has been subtracted away. (Otherwise A might not have struck us as true.)"

9.6 SUBTRACTION, CONJUNCTION, TRUTH-TABLES

Logical subtraction is sometimes introduced via a problem to which it is supposed to be the solution: find the logical operation that stands to conjunction as numerical subtraction stands to numerical addition. Or the problem could simply be: find the inverse of conjunction. The problem is a little unclear since there are two things it could mean for one function or operation to be the inverse of another. It could mean, letting the functions be f and g, that f undoes g's action—$f(g(x)) = x$. It could also mean that g undoes f's action—$g(f(x)) = x$.

These are distinct possibilities, as we see by looking at the case of interest. Subtraction undoes conjunction if $(A\&B)-B \equiv A$; call that *Recovery*. Conjunction undoes contraction if $(A-B)\&B \equiv A$; call that *Return*.

Recovery is a nonstarter. Suppose that A implies B, as it has so far in this book. Then $A\&B \equiv A$, so $(A\&B)-B = A-B$. *Recovery* thus says, in effect, that subtracting B from A always leaves A unchanged. That is absurd.

What about *Return*? It can fail only if $(A-B)\&B$ fails to imply A, or vice versa. The first entailment fails iff there's a scenario where $(A-B)\&B$ is true but A is false. A–B must be true in this scenario, since its conjunction with B is true. So we are looking at a scenario where A–B is true even though B is true and A false. Subtracting a truth from a falsehood should yield

Table 9.1 Quasi-Truth-Table for Subtraction

A	B	A adds truth to B?	A adds falsity to B?	$A-B$ is
t	t	Yes, $B \rightarrow A$ is true for a B-friendly reason.	No, $B \rightarrow \neg A$ is not even true.	t
t	f	Impossible, A implies B.		N/A
f	t	No, $B \rightarrow A$ is not even true.	Yes, $B \rightarrow \neg A$ is true for a B-friendly reason.	f
f	f	Yes.	No.	t
		No.	Yes.	f
		Yes. (Or, No.)	Yes again. (Or, No again.)	n

a falsehood, surely. Imagine conversely a scenario where A is true, but $(A-B) \& B$ is false. $A-B$ must be false, since B is implied by A. So we are looking at a scenario where $A-B$ is false even though A is true. Relieving a truth of one of its implications should yield a truth, surely.

Note that we have just in effect begun a truth-table for $A-B$. It is false, if A is false and B is true, and true, if A and B are true. This gives us the top two lines, and the third line—A true, B false—is not possible, since A implies B. $A-B$'s truth-value is determined by those of A and B, until we get to the last line. It is only when A and B are both false that the truth-value of $A-B$ floats free of the truth-values of its components.

Why "officially" is $A-B$ true in a world w where A and B are both true, as on the first line? $B \rightarrow A$ is true in w and so has a truthmaker there. Any truthmaker is bound to be B-compatible, since it obtains in w and w is a B-world. So A adds truth to B in w. It adds falsity in w iff $B \rightarrow \neg A$ has a B-compatible truthmaker in w. That it can't, because $B \rightarrow \neg A$ is false. A thus adds truth and no falsity.

Why is $A-B$ false in a w where A is false and B is true, as on the third line? A can't add truth in w, for $B \rightarrow A$ is false there. It adds falsity in w iff $B \rightarrow \neg A$ is true there for a B-compatible reason. $B \rightarrow \neg A$ is indeed true in w for such a reason; for it is true there, and its truthmaker is bound to be B-compatible since B too is true in w. A thus adds falsity in w and no truth.

If $A-B$'s truth-value is left open when A and B are false there, that is because their falsity is silent on the question of what A adds to B. Suppose

B is *Barky is good* and that this is false. *Barky is a good dog* adds only truth to *Barky is good*, what with Barky being a dog.[10] *Barky is a good god* adds only falsity, since Barky is not a god. *Barky is known to be good* adds neither truth nor falsity, we may suppose; no one is a state that needs to be supplemented only with Barky's goodness to make for knowledge that Barky is good. *Barky is a good dog—Barky is good* is accordingly true, while *Barky is a good god—Barky is good* is false, and *Barky is known to be good—Barky is good* is neither true nor false. This is the one respect in which A–B is not truth-functional: nothing follows, truth-value-wise, from the assumption that A and B are both false.

9.7 DEGREES OF INEXTRICABILITY

The quasi-truth-table determines for us the one and only coarse-grained proposition expressed by A–B; it is the function taking worlds to truth-values according to the indicated rules. That we get a remainder proposition in every case would seem like a point in favor of the logician's approach. Let's now try to offer something to the mysterian.

The quasi-truth-table shows that A–B is never *entirely* undefined.[11] The worst possible outcome for A–B is to be defined on B-worlds only. This, then, presumably, is the case where B is so securely lodged in A that nothing evaluable remains when we try to extricate it.

> 44 B is perfectly inextricable from A iff A–B is defined only on B-worlds. To say it another way, A does not add only truth, or only falsity, to B except when B is true.

The traditional paradigm is the inextricability of determinables from their determinates.[12] Here is a tomato, Tom. Let $C = $ *Tom is crimson*, and $D = $ *Tom is red*. Perfect inextricability would be the result if *Tom is crimson* did not add truth or falsity to *Tom is red*, unless Tom was red.

---

[10] Assume for example's sake that "good" is an intersective adjective.
[11] I assume the B-region is nonempty.
[12] Determinate/determinable relations are said to differ from species/genus relations on precisely this point (Searle and Körner 1959, Woods 1967, Funkhouser 2006.)

Chapter 9

So, let's go to an away-world *w*—a world where Tom is not red but, say, green. Does *Tom is crimson* add falsity to *Tom is red* in *w*? The definition says that

> *Tom is crimson* adds falsity to *Tom is red* in *w* just if Tom fails to be crimson, in *w*, for a reason that does not trade on the fact that Tom is green—for a red-friendly reason. It adds truth just if Tom fails to be *otherwise* red—a shade other than crimson—in *w*, for a reason compatible with Tom's being red.

Now, both *Tom is a crimson-y red* and *Tom is a noncrimson-y red* do have falsity-makers when Tom is green—the very fact of Tom's greenness, for instance. That is not the problem. The problem is that *all the falsity-makers that come to mind would seem to trade on Tom not being red.*[13] The question before us is whether there is something *else* about green-Tom—something that Tom can keep when he's red—which prevents him from being crimson, or, which prevents him from being some other, noncrimsony, shade of red. ("Prevents" in the sense of being *how* he's not crimson, or that in virtue of which he's not crimson.)

What would this red-friendly feature be? I find myself reaching here for the kind of thing Wittgenstein says in *Remarks on Color* (Wittgenstein 1977): *There can be transparent red, but not transparent white*, for instance, or *A luminous grey is impossible*. Let's imagine that Wittgenstein has discovered somehow that there can't be a dull crimson. Crimson is, of its nature, vibrant and glorious.[14] And let's imagine that Tom is, in *w*, a particularly lackluster sort of green. Then one could try to say that *Tom is crimson* is false, not (or not only) because Tom is green, but due to the lack of vitality of Tom's color *whatever that color may be.*

I cannot say for certain that no one could develop a system along these lines. But on the face of it, it seems silly. The reason Tom is not crimson

---

[13] *He's crimson* adds falsity to *He's red* in *w* iff *Red→¬Crimson* has a *Red*-friendly truthmaker in *w*, which, since *Red→¬Crimson = ¬Crimson*, means that Tom is noncrimson for a reason compatible with his being red. *Crimson* adds truth to *Red* in *w* iff *Red→Crimson* is true—*Red&¬Crimson* is false—for a *Red*-compatible reason. The remainder is unevaluable, when Tom is green, if there is no good (= red-friendly) for green-Tom to be crimson-if-red, and no good reason for green-Tom to be *another*-shade-of-red-if-red.

[14] Locke writes of a "studious blind man" who claimed that he "now understood what scarlet signified. Upon which, his friend demanding, what scarlet was? The blind man answered, It was like the sound of a trumpet" (Locke 1706, book 3, chap. 4, para. 11).

154

is that Tom is green, not that Tom has some special higher order dullness property that red things and green things can in principle share. Likewise the reason that Tom is not some other, noncrimsony, shade of red is that Tom is green; it has nothing to do with some polymorphous property of green-Tom that red things can possess unless they have the misfortune to be crimson. A thing has to be red, it seems, to have a feature that boots red up into a particular shade of red, or into that shade's relative complement within red. (Figure 9.2 lays this out in quasi-truth-table form. A "good" way to be C-if-D means a D-compatible, or D-friendly, way. X is "no way" to be C-if-D just when it is not a good way.)

Tom is crimson–Tom is red looks like a case of perfect inextricability. So does *Tom weighs a pound–Tom weighs over an ounce*; *Tom is red–Something is red*; *I washed half as many tomatoes as you–You washed some tomatoes*. It would be interesting to check these examples against (**44**). But we need to move on to the opposite kind of perfection:

45 B is perfectly extricable from A iff A–B is defined everywhere; go
    to any world you like, A adds falsity to B there, or it adds truth,
    but not both.

To simplify the Genesis example from above, let's say there were a few amoebas to begin with, and the number then grew, slowly at first, then more and more quickly. It is conjectured that #(k)—the number of amoebas after k hours—is an exponential function of k.

(E) $\#(k) = 2^k, k = 0, 1, 2, \ldots$

E is not entirely about amoebas; it implies, or assumes, that there is the number 2, which has various integral powers, themselves given numerically; it assumes, for short, that

(F) Numbers exist.

How far can *Numbers exist* be extricated from *The number of amoebas after k hours is 2 raised to the power of k*? For perfect extricability, we'd need it to hold in every numberless world either that $\#(k) = 2^k$ adds truth to *Numbers exist*, or $\#(k) = 2^k$ adds falsity to *Numbers exist*, but not both.

This would seem to be the case. For let a world w be given. Either it starts out with just a single amoeba, with the population then doubling hourly; or it starts out with several, or no, amoebas, or the population on

Table 9.2 Inextricability of *Tom Is Red* from *Tom Is Crimson*

C	D	C adds truth?	C adds falsity?	C–D
t	t	Yes, crimson is a good way to be crimson-if-red.	No, crimson is no way to be noncrimson-if-red.	t
t	f	Impossible, crimson implies red.		N/A
f	t	No, scarlet is no way to be crimson-if-red.	Yes, scarlet is a good way to be noncrimson-if-red.	f
f	f	No, green is no way to be crimson-if-red.	No, green is no way to be noncrimson-if-red.	n

some occasions more than doubles, or less than doubles. Starting out with a single amoeba, the population then doubling hourly, is (or ensures) a number-friendly truthmaker for

$$\textit{Numbers exist} \rightarrow \#(k) = 2^k \textit{ for all } k \geq 0.$$

and precludes a number-friendly truthmaker for

$$\textit{Numbers exist} \rightarrow \#(k) \neq 2^k \textit{ for some } k \geq 0.$$

Starting out with, say, two amoebas, the number then tripling hourly, is a number-friendly truthmaker for the second conditional, and precludes one for the first. The remainder when *Numbers exist* is subtracted from $\#(k) = 2^k$ is thus a proposition that is true in one kind of numberless world and false in numberless worlds not of that kind.[15] *Numbers exist* would appear to be cleanly extricable from *The number of amoebas after k hours is 2 raised to the power of k.*

Between these two extremes lies a vast unexplored ocean of imperfect extricability. One example we have already seen: that my arm goes up is caught up in my raising it, but not, as it were, glued in place. The action exceeds the bodily movement enough for *I raised my arm* to add falsity in scenarios where I am unconscious, say, or unequivocally opposed to raising it; unconsciousness and unequivocal opposition are up-friendly truthmakers for *It went up → I did not raise it.* Worlds where *I raised it* adds falsity are prima facie worlds where *I raised it—It went up* is false.

Are there worlds where the remainder is true? I struggle to raise my arm, but you have me wrapped in duct tape. Can we find an up-friendly

---

[15] Worlds with the wrong temporal structure belong to the second category.

truthmaker for *My arm goes up → I raise it*? My struggling to raise it seems like a candidate, until we remember that trying to move a limb does not suffice for moving-it-if-it-moves; the trying has to be efficacious, via the right sort of causal chain. What makes the conditional true is simply that my arm stayed down. The remainder appears to be evaluable in away worlds only as false, never true. *P* is partly extricable from bringing it about that *P*, but, it seems, in a one-sided way: *B*[*P*]–*P* is false in every away-world where it is evaluable.[16]

So much for action, let's try knowledge. Is *P* any more extricable from *K*[*P*] than it was from *B*[*P*]? I was initially skeptical, since *P* is causally tied into both, albeit in different directions. Bringing *P* about is, as Searle says, causally mind-to-world, while knowing is causally world-to-mind; it involves, in most cases, believing that *P* because of the fact that *P*. But the connection is not exceptionless in the case of knowledge. Mathematical beliefs do not have to be caused by mathematical facts, to count as knowledge, and knowledge about the future does not require backward causation. Consider then *K*[*P*]–*P*, where *P* concerns events that have not yet occurred, but are only expected. How evaluable is *K*[*P*]–*P* in worlds where the expectation turns out to be false?

One certainly sees how the remainder could be false. It is false if conditions obtain that ensure the truth of *P*→¬*K*[*P*] in a *P*-friendly way.[17] Conditions like that are easily imagined. Maybe the thinker doesn't understand *P*, or her source is Madame Zelda at the Psychic Hotline. The remainder is true if conditions obtain that ensure the truth of *P*→*K*[*P*] in a *P*-friendly way. This is trickier. We need a case where the one and only obstacle to knowing of some future event is that the event does not in fact occur. Remove that obstacle and the believer cannot help but know.

The world is not about to end, in Alma's view. The belief is true and, I would think, knowledgeable. Imagine, though, a world that agrees with actuality so far, but is about, through some bizarre quantum coincidence, to pop out of existence. Alma does not know in that scenario that tomorrow will come, because in that scenario it does not come. Is that the only reason she fails to know? Was her belief arrived at in such a way that if you transplant it and its background into a world that does *not* end—the

---

[16] Hornsby (1980a) is an excellent discussion. See also Hornsby (1980b).

[17] Unless conditions like that obtain also for *P*→*K*[*P*]. I treat the proviso as implicit.

Chapter 9

Table 9.3 Remainders in Propositional Calculus

X	Y	$X - Y$
$p \& q$	q	p
p	$p \lor q$	$p \& \partial(p \lor q)$
$p \leftrightarrow q$	$p \to q$	$q \to p$
$p \mathbin{\dot\lor} q$	$p \lor q$	$\neg(p \& q)$
$p \& q$	$p \leftrightarrow q$	$(p \lor q) \& \partial(p \leftrightarrow q)$
$pq \lor r$	$p \lor r$	$q \lor r$
$pq \lor rs$	$p \lor r$	$pq \lor rs \lor qs$

actual world, as it might be—the belief becomes (must become) not only true but knowledgeable? I am far from sure about this, but I submit that Alma is bound to know, or the example can be filled out so that she is bound to know, in a world where the belief is not mistaken. If the example is granted, then *Tomorrow will come* is two-sidedly extricable from *Alma knows that tomorrow will come*; the remainder is true in some away-worlds and false in others.

Some implications are perfectly extricable from their impliers; others are partly extricable; others are not extricable at all (A–B is defined only on B-worlds). All these possibilities arise already in a propositional calculus setting.[18] So, for instance, q is wholly extricable from $p \& q$, and $p \lor q$ is wholly extricable from $p \mathbin{\dot\lor} q$ ($\dot\lor$ is exclusive disjunction). $p \lor q$ is wholly inextricable from p, and $p \leftrightarrow q$ is wholly inextricable from $p \& q$.[19] Results along these lines are collected in Table 9.3.[20]

---

[18] Minimal models and countermodels play the role of truthmakers and falsemakers. A minimal model of S is a partial valuation minimal among those whose classical extensions all verify S. A minimal countermodel of S is a minimal model of $\neg S$. The minimal models of $p \leftrightarrow q$, for instance, are $\{p \to 1, q \to 1\}$, and $\{p \to 0, q \to 0\}$. Its minimal countermodels are $\{p \to 1, q \to 0\}$ and $\{p \to 0, q \to 1\}$.

[19] Gappy remainders require one new bit of notation. If X and Y are PC sentences, then $X \& \partial Y$ is defined just where Y is true, and has the same truth-value as X where it is defined. The ∂-notation is from (Beaver 2001).

[20] A word about the last row. $pq \lor rs \lor qs$ is not part of $pq \lor rs$ even though $p \lor r$ is part of $pq \lor rs$. (No minimal model of $pq \lor rs$ extends the minimal model of $pq \lor rs \lor qs$ that assigns truth to q and s.) This runs counter to the mereological principle of *Supplementation*. That principle is satisfied, however, by "inner" remainders, defined so that subtracting a part always leaves a part. $X{\sim}Y$ is obtained by restricting X–Y to worlds where it has a truthmaker (falsemaker) implied by some truthmaker (falsemaker) for X. $X{\sim}Y$ agrees with X–Y except

158

9.8 SUBTRACTION AS A PHILOSOPHICAL TOOL

I mentioned that philosophy has tended to approach elusive contents from below, asking how they might be reached by conjoining weaker contents. What are the prospects for "analysis from above," in which we characterize a content by first overshooting the mark and then pulling back? One large difference, of course, is that conjunctions are always well-defined, while remainders may or may not be, depending on how extricable the subtrahend is from the minuend. Certainly there have been some spectacular failures in this area.[21] But there have also been some prima facie successes. Note that full extricability is not always required, for the target notion may itself be defined only in our corner of logical space. Rather than getting into the weeds on this, let me list for your consideration some *attempted* analyses from above. Some we have seen before, others not; some are implausible, others perhaps less so.

Trying to raise my arm = raising it, except it might not go up.

A lawlike statement = a law, except it may or may not be true.

Prehension is comprehension, except maybe not intellectual.[22]

Judgment = what is left of belief when phenomenal quality is subtracted.[23]

Quasi-remembering = remembering, but it might not have been me.[24]

Solipsistic jealousy is jealousy, minus the target's existence.[25]

Fragility = what breaking adds to being dropped.[26]

A thing looks red iff I see it is red, minus the implication of being red.

To be green is what looking green adds to being under observation.

An act is "courageous" iff it is courageous, apart from being admirable.

Warrant = whatever distinguishes knowledge from true belief.[27]

I am responsible for φing if I am to blame, not to say φing is wrong.[28]

---

on the last row. The inner remainder when $p \vee r$ is subtracted from $pq \vee rs$ is $(pq \vee rs)$ & $\partial(qs \to (p \vee r))$.

[21] See Williamson (1998) on factorization.
[22] From a commentary on Whitehead, *Process and Reality*.
[23] Chalmers (1996, 174)
[24] Shoemaker (1970, 4).
[25] Putnam (1975).
[26] Goodman (1983).
[27] Plantinga (1993).
[28] Gideon Rosen suggested this as a possible view, not necessarily his own.

These are again analyses that have been *attempted*, not necessarily suc-
cessful analyses. Subtraction is a delicate operation that may not come off
as planned or hoped. One then has to decide whether it is the analysis that
is faulty, or the analysandum; if this is what it means to be *F*, then so much
the worse for the notion of being *F*. It is because warrant and square-quoted
courage are rightly defined that they are rightly viewed with suspicion.

That being said, it is not always clear why suspicion falls where it does.
Enormous weight may be laid on notions superficially analogous to pseudo-
notions that are considered unfit for serious work. Take the dogmatism
debate in epistemology. Does the fact of a sock's looking red give me non-
inferential justification for believing it to be red, or am I supposed to *infer*
its color from how it looks? Both sides take themselves to understand what
it means to look red. But, if a sock's looking red to me is defined as my
seeing it to be red, but for the implication of veridicality, then the notion
is problematic. Why should there be a state that makes up the difference
between *P* and seeing that *P*, when there is nothing like that for knowing
that *P* or bringing it about that *P*? Maybe looking red can be explained
in some other way; maybe we can confine ourselves to paradigm cases of
looking red. I do not at all mean to be saying that the debate is confused,
just that philosophers are strangely unbothered about the issue.[29]

A second area where subtraction might potentially shed some light
is metaontology. Some existence questions are hard, or harder, to take
seriously than others. (That a question is hard to take seriously does not
make it automatically misguided. A thing that is hard to do may be
nevertheless worth doing.) Special efforts are called for with, for instance,
numbers and fists and arbitrary mereological sums. We can all agree on
this, I hope, even if we think the effort worth making.

A world with bachelors in it seems clearly distinguishable from a world
where it is clear what bachelors are supposed to be like: they should not be
married, and so on. Imagine now a world with facts about what numbers
are supposed to be like; there should dwell among them one that is least
but none that is greatest, and so on. How a world like that differs from one

---

[29] Williamson is again an exception. "Neither the equation 'Red = coloured + X'
nor the equation 'Knowledge = true belief + X' need have a non-circular solution"
(Williamson 2000, 3).

where objects of the supposed type exist is not obvious. Still less, perhaps, do we understand

> how the truth of a mathematical statement may be ensured by the concepts employed rather than by the objects described. Whether with a more developed understanding of these notions we can, to use a Wittgensteinian phrase, "divide through" by the objects of mathematics, be they abstract objects or mental constructs, is a question that remains open (Lear 1977, 102).

Let's pursue this question a little. The dividing-through metaphor is attractive but mysterious. Here is a suggestion about how to cash it out.

Division by n, the function taking x to $x \div n$, is the inverse of multiplication by n, the function taking x to $x \times n$. Insofar as conjunction is the logical counterpart of multiplication, "logical division" is the operation on X that undoes conjunction with N. This operation we know as X–N; let's write it now as $X \div N$ in light of the stated analogy.

What does it mean to "divide through by the objects of mathematics," on this picture, if the objects are numbers and the claim at issue is $A = $ *The number of planets is ten times the number of stars*. To say that we can divide through by the numbers is to say that the operation leaves A in relevant respects unchanged; numbers aside, it says the same as before.

Now, A cannot literally be divided by numbers; division as we are conceiving it is an operation on statements or hypotheses. What is available as a divisor is the hypothesis N that numbers exist. We can divide through by N if $A \div N$ says the same about the non-numerical world (viz, that there are ten times as many planets as stars) as A itself. $A \div N$ says the same as A, numbers aside, just if N is perfectly extricable from A. The Wittgensteinian line of thought can now be reconstructed as follows: it is moot whether numbers exist if the hypothesis of their existence is perfectly extricable from claims (like A) that appear to incorporate that hypothesis.[30]

---

[30] It is actually in connection with sensations that Wittgenstein speaks of dividing through. " 'But you will surely admit that there is a difference between pain-behaviour accompanied by pain and pain-behaviour without any pain?'—Admit it? What greater difference could there be?—'And yet you again and again reach the conclusion that the sensation itself is a nothing.' — Not at all. It is not a something, but not a nothing either! The conclusion was only that a nothing would serve just as well as a something about which nothing could be said" (Wittgenstein 1953, 304). Lear evidently sees a connection. Reck (1997) agrees and traces the connection back to Frege. See also Ricketts (1986).

Chapter 9

I have been characterizing subtraction as a way of *cancelling* the subtrahend's content, rather than *negating* its content. On some views, negation is itself just a cancellation device. Here is Strawson in *Introduction to Logical Theory*:

> Suppose a man sets out to walk to a certain place; but when he gets half way there, he turns round and comes back again. This may not be pointless. But, from the point of view of change of position it is as if he had never set out. And so a man who contradicts himself may have succeeded in exercising his vocal chords. But from the point of view of imparting information, or communicating facts (or falsehoods), it is as if he had never opened his mouth. The standard function of speech is frustrated by self-contradiction. Contradiction is like writing something down and erasing it, or putting a line through it. A contradiction cancels itself and leaves nothing.
> (Strawson 1952, 2)

Strawson seems to suggest that a speech starting with *A* and following up with ¬*A* has no effect on the conversational score: it is as if the speaker had never opened her mouth. Is it just me, or is Strawson wrong about this? Even if we grant that ¬*A* erases the earlier assertion of *A*, why think that *A* returns the favor, erasing the later assertion of ¬*A*?

The idea that negation is, or can be, a cancellation device raises in any case an interesting question. What *does* one do to wipe the slate clean after an improper assertion? What goes in for *X* in the update rule

(i) $A + X =$ nothing asserted?

¬*A* is too strong; it reverses our stand on *A* rather than nullifying it. If strength is the worry, perhaps *X* should be a logical triviality like $A \vee \neg A$. But, although $A \vee \neg A$ might conceivably in some contexts *implicate* that the speaker is backing off of *A*, it can equally be heard as leaving *A* in place (perhaps he is inferring $A \vee \neg A$ from *A*). What we need, it seems, is a statement that (unlike $A \vee \neg A$) has enough substance to it to dislodge *A*, but (unlike ¬*A*) is not so substantial as to put an opposing claim in *A*'s place. I can think of only one form of words that does this. To cancel *A* cleanly, one says, *hold on, it might be that* ¬*A*. Putting $\Diamond \neg A$ in for *X* in (i),

(ii) $A + \Diamond \neg A =$ nothing asserted.

162

This is interesting, because we know of one *other* operation that returns us from *A* to the nothing-asserted state: the operation of *subtracting A*.

(iii) *A* minus *A* = nothing asserted.

(ii) and (iii) suggest a hypothesis about what is accomplished by adding a might-statement to the conversational record:

(iv) adding $\Diamond \neg A$ = subtracting *A*,

or, rearranging a bit,

(v) adding $\Diamond A$ = subtracting $\neg A$.

This is just the shell of a theory of "might," but one worth exploring, I think, because of the help it gives with two puzzles.

Recall my complaint in the first chapter about the traditional view of epistemic modals—"Bob might be in his office" is true in my mouth iff my information (or information available to me) is consistent with his being there. I said that it gets the subject matter wrong; I am talking about Bob and his office, not the extent of my information. It was unclear, at the time, how any theory of "might" could hope to avoid this result. Now we see how the thing might be possible. Negating *A* does not, we saw, change its subject matter; and disavowing something, as opposed to asserting it, wouldn't appear to change the subject matter either. Attaching "might," on the present theory, is ringing those changes in sequence; it is disavowing the negation of *A*. If two operations are individually subject-matter-preserving, then the result of composing them ought to be subject-matter-preserving as well.

Now a puzzle due to Seth Yalcin (2007). The following argument is very clearly invalid:

> It might be the case that $\neg A$.
> _____
> Therefore $\neg A$.

X therefore Y is invalid, one would think, only if the conclusion can be false while the premise is true, that is, there is a possible scenario where $\neg Y \& X$. In the present case, $\neg Y = A$ and $X = \Diamond \neg A$, so there ought to be a possible scenario where $A \& \Diamond \neg A$. And a scenario like that makes no sense. The problem is not just unassertability, as with *A but I do not know that A*. Unassertible hypotheses can still be hypothesized, say, in the antecedent of a conditional; if this dish has been unbeknownst to me poisoned, then I'm in trouble. And it makes no sense to say, *If it's raining out, but it might not be raining out, then we'll get wet.* What if "might" is a cancellation device? *It might be the case that* ¬A, *therefore* ¬A is invalid, not because the truth of ◇¬A does not force ¬A to be true, but because disavowing A does not force me to assert that ¬A. A&◇¬A is incoherent, even as a supposition, because the instructions it gives to the would-be supposer are self-contradictory: she is to suppose that A, while at the same time not supposing that A.

9.9 SUMMING UP

Who is right, the logician or the mysterian? Not the logician, it seems, for her recipe doesn't work; B→A is a terrible candidate for the role of A–B. No recipe *could* work, one might think, for we know of cases where B cannot be cleanly excised from A. What is the remainder supposed to be when *Tom is red* is subtracted from *Tom is crimson*, or *Tom is red or green* is subtracted from *Tom is red*? Not the mysterian either, for she thinks that a recipe is impossible, and we have attempted to give one. That being said, the logician is right, insofar as a remainder always exists. And the mysterian is right, insofar as A–B may not extend very far out of the B-region. Possible applications include analysis from above, metaontology, and epistemic modality.

- 10 -

Pretense and Presupposition

10.1 SEMANTIC NOVELTY

A great puzzle of twentieth-century philosophy of language was, how are finite beings able to understand a potential infinity of sentences? The answer is supposed to be that understanding is recursive: infinitely many sentences can be constructed out of finitely many words combined according to finitely many rules; we understand a sentence by understanding the words in it and knowing the relevant rules. If this is right, then meaning, defined as whatever you have to grasp to understand, had better be compositional, too. A sentence's meaning should be determined by the meanings of the individual words in it and by how they are put together.

A great puzzle of twenty-first-century philosophy of language is shaping up to be this: how do we reconcile the solution to the previous puzzle with what sentences actually strike us as *saying*? It's a puzzle because *S*'s compositionally determined meaning is not always a very good guide to what *S* intuitively says, or to its contribution to what is said by sentences in which *S* is embedded. A sentence's felt content is often something that you would not have expected, or even thought possible, given just a grasp of its meaning.

It is familiar, of course, that *speakers* say things you would not have expected from the meanings of the sentences they utter. "That is not such a great idea" is used to say that it's a *bad* idea, a reading that would seem hard to generate compositionally. But I am talking, or trying to, about contents lodged in the words—ones a sentence retains when it is not asserted, as in the antecedent of a conditional.[1] How are these unexpected contents determined?

To appreciate the kind of problem this is, we need to think about the grades of semantic unexpectedness. In the first grade, emphasized by

---

[1] Unfortunately for this way of putting it, content passed up the compositional chain of command is not necessarily semantic content. See Levinson (2000), Geurts (2009), and Simons (2010) on "intrusive implicature."

Chapter 10

Kaplan, a sentence's meaning doesn't tell you *all by itself* what it says in a particular context of utterance; the meaning of "I am thirsty," for instance, doesn't all by itself tell you whether the one said to be thirsty is Smith or Jones. This is a weak form of unexpectedness, because the meaning of "I am thirsty" can be seen in advance to generate *Jones is thirsty* and *Smith is thirsty* as possible readings in the appropriate context, and in the second place, it is the meaning itself that tells you how context singles out one of these readings as correct.

A second possibility is that S's meaning doesn't make it transparent *how* context singles out a certain reading as correct. The meaning of "Smith's book is on the table" offers little guidance as to why it is a book Smith *owns* we're talking about, as opposed to one she *wrote*, and so on. One can understand "Jones cut the grass" perfectly well while having not the slightest idea of how it comes about that cutting the grass is *mowing* it, as opposed to cutting individual blades with a scalpel.[2] This is a stronger form of unexpectedness, because one doesn't know of a rule that determines which of two allowed readings is correct in context. But it is not as strong as all that. Our difficulty in articulating *how* context determines what is said does not mean the determination doesn't occur. The problem could be one of semantic self-consciousness.

A third possibility, prominent in relevance theory and truth-conditional pragmatics,[3] is that S's meaning does *not* determine what is said, even in context.[4] An essential role is played by agent-driven pragmatic processes ("free enrichment," e.g.) not mandated by anything in the sentence.[5] "She ran to the edge and jumped" says in context that she jumped *off the* building

---

[2] Searle (1980), Kissine (2011).

[3] Recanati (1989, 2011), Bach (1994), Bezuidenhout (2002), Sperber and Wilson (1986), Carston (2002).

[4] Context had better not be understood too expansively, lest it determine what is said all by itself. One way of drawing the line is suggested by Brandom: "What I want to call 'genuine' semantic indices are features of utterances that can be read off without knowing anything about what the utterance means. Time, place, speaker, and possible world are properties of tokenings that can be settled and specified before one turns one's attention to the content expressed by those tokenings.... [They] can be determined independently of [the context-sensitive expression's] semantic value and then appealed to as input from which the value could then be computed by a character-function" (Brandom 2008, 58). Whether "and" conveys temporal order depends, by contrast, on the sentences it connects.

[5] "[S]aturation is a 'bottom-up' process in the sense that it is signal-driven, not context-driven. A 'top-down' or context-driven process is a pragmatic process which is not triggered by an expression in the sentence but takes place for purely pragmatic reasons—in order to make

166

(the example is from Saul 2012). "He's not ready" says in context that he's not ready to stay home alone.[6] There may be nothing in the sentence's standing meaning to suggest or even play host to such an interpretation. This is a still stronger form of unexpectedness, because what is said is to some extent a free creation. But it is not as strong as can be imagined. A reading underdetermined (even in context) by a sentence's meaning might still be fully *consonant* with that meaning; the meaning points in the right direction, it just doesn't take you all the way there.

I am interested in the more radical case where a sentence says something its meaning *positively disallows*. If we use "real content" for what the sentence is (rightly) taken to say on some occasion, and "semantic content" for anything worked up in context from its standing compositional meaning, then I am talking about the case where a sentence's real content is not a possible semantic content.

Everyone will have their own favorite example. Here is one that Saul Kripke considers in his 1973 Locke Lectures.[7] Imagine someone climbing onto a raft and pushing off into the ocean. You remain on the beach, following her progress, until she is hardly visible. When it comes time to write this up in your journal, you say,

> I watched her drift slowly out to sea, until she became a dot on the horizon.

Taken at face value, this seems incomprehensible. "*What?*," Kripke said. "She turned into a *DOT*!?" Whatever exactly "dots" are, people never really turn into them. Insofar as the sentence nevertheless strikes us as true, we are not reading it in a way licensed by its ordinary meaning.

Donnellan gives the example of Jones, who has been falsely accused of murdering Smith (Donnellan 1966, 285–286):

---

sense of what the speaker is saying. Such processes I also refer to as 'free' pragmatic processes—free because they are not mandated by the linguistic material but respond to wholly pragmatic considerations. For example, the pragmatic process through which an expression is given a nonliteral (e.g. a metaphorical or metonymical) interpretation is context-driven: we interpret an expression nonliterally in order to make sense of the speech act, not because this is dictated by the linguistic materials in virtue of the rules of the language." (Recanati 2012, 142)

[6] This is disputed in Cappelen and Lepore (2008). See also Borg (2006).

[7] The ultimate source may be Austin (1962). See also Azzouni (2010).

> Imagine that there is a discussion of Jones's odd behavior at his trial. We might sum up our impression of his behavior by saying, "Smith's murderer is insane." If someone asks to whom we are referring, by using this description, the answer here is "Jones." ... We were speaking about Jones even though he is not in fact Smith's murderer and, in the circumstances imagined, it was his behavior we were commenting upon. Jones might, for example, accuse us of saying false things of him in calling him insane and it would be no defense, I should think, that our description, "the murderer of Smith," failed to fit him.

If the sentence too counts as saying, in context, that Jones is insane, then this is a second case in which a sentence says what its meaning disallows. Donnellan has a description ("Smith's murderer") acting, in its contribution to what is said, like a demonstrative. Scott Soames in *Beyond Rigidity* notes that an indexical can sometimes act like a description.

> I am in an auditorium, attending a lecture. Two university officials enter the room, interrupt the lecturer, and announce, "There is an emergency. We are looking for Professor Scott Soames. Is Professor Soames here?" I stand up, saying, as I do, "I am Scott Soames." My intention in saying this is to indicate that I am the person they are looking for. Although this is not the semantic content of the sentence I uttered, they immediately grasp this, and the three of us leave the auditorium. Later, another member of the audience reports what happened to a third party. He says . . . "Professor Soames said [told them] he was the person they were looking for, and the three of them left." (Soames 2002, 74–75)[8]

The unexpected readings, or contents, in these examples raise two kinds of problem. One is about the contents themselves. When you throw the door open to content-assignments not generated in the ordinary compositional way, you would appear to have thrown the door open to everything. What makes *these* readings the right ones? Second, supposing the right readings or contents have somehow been singled out, there is the

---

[8] "If mother goat knocks on the door of her hut, and the seven little goats open immediately without even asking who's there, she might say: 'Are you crazy, to open the door like this?! I could have been the wolf!'" (Irene Heim, reported in Büring 1998, 16). *I could have been the wolf* says, in context, that it could have been the wolf that was knocking.

cognitive problem of saying how people are able to hit on them in actual speech situations. I am interested more in the first problem—what makes these the right readings?—but they will both figure to some extent in what follows.

10.2 ROUTES TO THE UNEXPECTED

I know of two main quasi-systematic ways in which unexpected readings can be generated. One route is via figurative speech. Ken Walton has a famous example.

(1) Crotone is in the arch of the Italian boot.

The sentence says something true, in a charmingly efficient way. Taken literally it says that a Crotonean is some kind of Mother Hubbard–like character who lives in a shoe.[9] That the literal content is must be ridiculous is a good sign that the real content must be something else.

Here our judgment that we are dealing with an unexpected content is confirmed by the clash of truth-values. But the judgment can often stand on its own; it can be independently clear that one of the contents is unexpected, even if both are true. Another of Walton's examples:

(2) It was Grand Central Station around here this morning.

Normally this is true at best on a figurative reading, but imagine it uttered in Grand Central Station on Xmas Eve. The fact that both readings are true does not make it particularly difficult to tell them apart.[10]

That was the striking and dramatic route to compositionally unexpected content. There is also a homely and undramatic route, discussed by linguists and philosophers of language more than literary theorists. Imagine that the so-called "King" is a usurper, but we decide for safety's sake to talk

---

[9] Michigan's Lower Peninsula is roughly hand-shaped, which lets Michiganders indicate where they live by pointing to the corresponding spot on an upheld appendage. Imagine someone taking this at face value—"*What*, you live on your hand?"

[10] Cohen (1976) introduced the idea of twice-true metaphor. Examples include, "No man is an island," "That guy is an animal," "The rain beat down without mercy," and "Singapore is an island of efficiency in Southeast Asia" (the last from Goatley 1997).

as if he is indeed king.[11] Then if the usurper is in the counting house,

(3) The King is in the counting house

might well be heard as saying something true—even if its semantic content is false, since the King properly so-called is in prison. (3)'s real content concerns, not the actual king, but the one who is king in the world we are treating as actual. Stalnaker sums the situation up as follows:

> If there is no one person who is presupposed to fit the description, then reference fails (even if some person does in fact fit the description uniquely). But if there is one, then it makes no difference whether that presupposition is true or false. The presupposition helps to determine the proposition expressed, but once the proposition is determined, it can stand alone. (Stalnaker 1999, 43)

Here, as in (1), there is a difference in truth-value (remember, the king is in prison) to bolster our judgment that the real content is not the compositionally expected one. But as before, the contrast may be directly evident. Consider

(4) My cousin is not a boy anymore.[12]

This would normally be heard to say that my cousin is now a man. But that is because he is presumed to be still a male human being. He could in principle have left the boys' room by a different door: death, surgery, deification, and so on.[13] The same sentence can, in a context where all other doors are blocked, "mean" that he is now a girl, or pillar of salt, or that he has been converted by some Parfitian device into five boys. Likewise, *My neighbor is a bachelor* says ordinarily that my neighbor is unmarried, it being presumed, and not asserted, that my neighbor is an adult male. I will call this the *presuppositional* route to unexpected content, since we

---

[11] Donnellan (1966).
[12] Langendoen (1971).
[13] Langendoen: "[I]f the presupposition-assertion distinction for nouns is appropriate, there is a considerable degree of freedom that one has in shifting various aspects of their meaning from the assertive side to the presuppositional side, and back again" (Langendoen 1971, 342).

access the content by pivoting somehow on a background assumption. The assumption influences what is said, without *entering into* what is said.

10.3 PIGGYBACKING ON A GAME

Two routes to unexpected content have been sketched: one relatively dramatic, by way of metaphor, studied by English professors; the other humdrum, prosaic, a matter primarily for linguists, by way of presupposition. You might have thought, from that description, that we had a better grip on the second route than the first; and you would have been right, if you'd thought it in 1992. Walton's "Metaphor and Prop Oriented Make-Believe" (Walton 1993) appeared in 1993. Here very briefly is Walton's view of metaphorical content.

He starts with make-believe games, conceived as rules for the imagination. The rules for "Cops and Robbers" specify that gunplay is to be imagined (pretended, posited, daydreamt, simulated, etc.). We are not to think of ourselves as doing surgery or walking the plank. A game's *content* is whatever it is that players are supposed to imagine to be the case.

How is the content determined? The simplest way would be to lay it out explicitly. Players are to imagine that they are in a gunfight, pinned in a corner, almost out of bullets—PERIOD. They are to do this directly, without regard to the physical setting, or where their fingers are pointing, or who might be pointing a finger at them. A game like that would be boring and is unsurprisingly never played. Content is a function rather of real world events. You are firing at me in the game only if your finger is pointing at me outside the game. You do not count as having me in your sights if you can't see any part of me. The stash is buried wherever the sack of marbles was left.

"Props" is the word Walton uses for the things whose game-independent properties determine the content of a particular game G. If γ is the function taking hypotheses X about the props to whatever it is that players are supposed to imagine to be the case when X really is the case, then here is Walton's basic idea. Often in our engagement with make-believe games, we are focused on the content; we look to X (the state of the props) just for the light it sheds on $\gamma(X)$ (the game's content, what we are to imagine). That is content-oriented make-believe, in Walton's terminology. But we might also

171

be interested in the game's content for what it says about the props. That
Y is supposable indicates that the props must be in a condition to license
that particular supposition. This is *prop*-oriented make-believe, or since the
props might be anything, *world*-oriented make-believe.

Prop-oriented make-believe is the kind that is supposed to provide a
model for metaphor. *Crotone is in the arch of the Italian boot* invites us to
take a certain perspective on Italy, namely, seeing it as a boot. Seeing-as is
allowing our imagination to be guided down certain paths by facts about
the thing seen. The fact in question here is that Crotone is in a certain place.
Which place? We know it by its fruits. Crotone is in the place it would need
to be, to make it acceptable in the game that Crotone is in the arch of the
Italian boot. Adapting a device from Kaplan, the sentence acquires as its
real content that Crotone is in *dthat* (the place that makes it supposable
that it sits in the arch).[14]

Now, Walton does not really mean to be laying out a general theory of
how metaphorical contents are generated. But suppose we were young and
headstrong and wanted to do just that. Then we might proceed as follows.

46 A's real content, in the context of game G, is the R such that A is to
   be imagined true just when R really is true.

If γ is the associated generation function—the function taking hypotheses about the props to specifications of what is to be imagined—one can
state this as follows:

47 A's real content, in the context of game G, is $\gamma^{-1}(A)$.

Exploiting a make-believe game in the way (**46**) suggests, imposing on
A a truth-conditional content coinciding with A's enabling conditions in
the game, has been called *piggybacking* on the game, and I will borrow that
terminology.[15]

A picture may be helpful. We start out with A, the sentence uttered, or
the proposition that A (let's not be fussy about the distinction), represented
as a region in logical space: the gray diagonal on the bottom left. A invites

[14] Exploiting a game in this way is not the same as playing it, though the two may be done in
tandem. To appreciate what would make the utterance correct, "construed as an act of verbal
participation in the game," one has to grasp the rules, not necessarily follow them.
[15] Richard (2000).

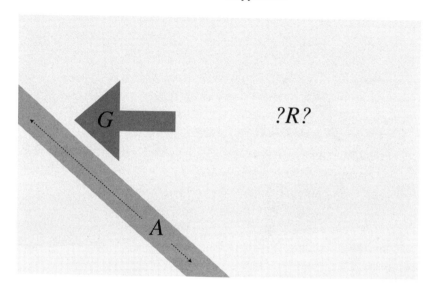

Figure 10.1 *A*'s real content is whatever γ maps to *A*

or suggests a game *G*. The generation function γ is represented by the left-pointing arrow. *A* and γ together are supposed to induce a real content *R*, written initially (in Figure 10.1) as a question mark.

How do they do it? *R* is supposed to be real-world hypothesis that makes *A* imaginable in the game—the minimal input to γ that gets us *A* in the output. That minimal input is something like the inverse image of *A* under γ. It is represented in Figure 10.2 as the string of diamonds at the base of the game-arrow pointing to *A*.

This may be illustrated with another Walton example: "The Metropolitan Museum borrows a portrait of Napoleon from the Louvre for a special exhibit and has it shipped to New York on the Queen Mary.... One might observe that Napoleon is a 'passenger' on the Queen Mary, thus invoking a possible game in which the presence of a portrait on a ship makes it fictional that the subject of the portrait is a passenger" (Walton 1993, 41).

The sentence uttered is *A* = *Napoleon is a passenger on the Queen Mary*. *A*'s compositional content, containing the worlds where Napoleon is indeed on board, is the diagonal at the lower left. The game is as Walton describes it. A portrait in the hold makes it pretendable that the portrayed individual is a passenger. The string of diamonds contains the *R*-worlds: the

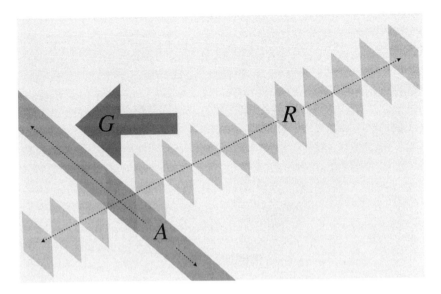

Figure 10.2 A's real content is $R = \gamma^{-1}(A)$

ones where it is legitimate to pretend that Napoleon is a passenger, because Napoleon is portrayed by some portrait on the ship. Each of the diamonds corresponds to a different possible portrait, all equally legitimating the pretense that Napoleon is a passenger on the *Queen Mary*.[16]

10.4 PIVOTING ON A PRESUPPOSITION

Let's turn now from piggybacking on a pretense to pivoting on a presupposition. The two have a certain amount in common. Both have us treating certain hypotheses as true, not because we believe them, but in pursuit of some expressive goal. (We *may* believe them; but that is not why we are at the moment treating them as true.) The goal is to draw a line through logical space, in order to characterize our world as lying on one side of that line and not the other.

---

[16] The diagonal bar overlaps the string of diamonds because *Napoleon is a passenger* could be literally and figuratively true at the same time; he could be delivering the portrait to the Metropolitan Museum himself. The area of overlap is the region of twice-true metaphor.

The strategy adopted, in both cases, is to draw a *different* line from the one that's intended, or maybe I should say, to *gesture at* or *lightly sketch* a different line. One takes this indirect route because drawing the line directly is for some reason not an option—one doesn't know how to draw it directly, or it is dangerous to do so, or inconvenient, or drawing it directly is suboptimal for some other reason. Indicating it indirectly *is* an option, however, for the intended line is recoverable from the one lightly sketched.

A further analogy is on the score of reusability. The real-world facts that make *A* pretendable in one game may not do so in another; its metaphorical content varies accordingly. There was an example on the radio, the morning I wrote this. The newscaster started by saying, in a metaphorical vein, that the senators on a certain committee were "all over the map" on the new immigration bill—meaning that they had a wide range of views on that bill. He then said that the senators in question were also *literally* all over the map, in that they came from different parts of the country, a fact that was supposed to explain their differing views on immigration.

But of course, the far-apart-spatially reading of *all over the map* is as metaphorical as the far-apart-doctrinally reading. (None of the senators lives on a map, any more than Michiganders live on their hands.) The one reading corresponds to a game in which your map position is a function of what you *believe*, the other to a game in which it is a function of the *state* you represent. A sentence's possible metaphorical contents are all over the map, too, and the potential to shift between them is a boost to the language's expressive power.[17]

A sentence's real content can shift too, as we pivot on different presuppositions. Let *A* be *My cousin is not a boy any more*—uttered this time on a park bench as we watch my cousin fooling around on the monkey bars. Where before we assumed that my cousin was still male, it now becomes common ground that he/she is still a child. How does the real content change when we pivot, not on gender, but age? *A*'s real content is the condition *R* that

---

[17] "Productivity emphasizes the possibility of using ever more complex expressions to describe things around us. But what is important . . . is that expressions, whether simple or complex, can be recycled, can be used over and over again by in different ways, . . . by different people, to say different things. This is what we mean by the *efficiency* of language" (Barwise and Perry 1983, 32).

distinguishes worlds where my eight-year-old cousin is no longer a boy from those where he is (still) a boy. What sets the first off from the second is, I take it, that is now a girl in those worlds. That "he" is now a girl supplants his growing up as the sentence's real content.

Or imagine the mother of the groom announcing, *I regret that the wedding is cancelled.* Quite likely we hear this as saying simply that it is cancelled. Obviously this is going to be a matter for regret. Suppose, though, that it is the cancellation that is obvious; we are the bride and groom and called it off ourselves. Now the claim is quite different. Events have taken a bad turn, in her view. She was not opposed to the marriage, as we seem to imagine.[18]

With so much in common, could it be that pivoting and piggybacking are the same phenomenon, or inessential variants of each other? It's a nice idea, which, it seems, can't possibly work. What is the content that A acquires through pivoting on a presupposition? It corresponds to the feature of certain P-worlds whereby they verify A as opposed to $\neg A$. This is what in the last chapter we called $A\text{–}P$. But, $A\text{–}P$ as defined by (**40**) is implied by A. Pivoting as defined by (**40**) can only *weaken A*. Piggybacking on the other hand can generate any contents you like; it is just a matter of finding the right game. The great majority of figurative contents are *independent* of A, as *There's a portrait of Napoleon on board* is independent of *Napoleon is on board*. None of these independent contents can be obtained by the kind of pivoting defined above.

10.5 SUMMING UP

Readings are more or less unexpected according to the difficulty of working them up from a sentence's standing meaning. The meaning might underdetermine the proper reading, or it might positively disallow it. I know of two main quasi-systematic ways in which radically unexpected readings may be generated: piggybacking on a pretense (Walton 1993), and pivoting

---

[18] An example from David Beaver. *Have you ever noticed that your belly button lint is the same color as your clothing?* (Beaver 2010). Compare, *Have you ever known me to lie?*, said first by a friend asking to be trusted, then a CIA trainer interested in your powers of detection. "[T]here is a considerable degree of freedom that one has in shifting various aspects of... meaning from the assertive side to the presuppositional side, and back again" (Langendoen 1971, 342).

on a presupposition (Stalnaker 1999). The second appears to involve logical subtraction. *A* is interpreted in light of some background assumption *B*, and is heard to say that *A–B*. The problem, to which we'll be returning, is that *A–B* has been defined only for a certain special case, where the subtrahend *B* is implied by the minuend *A*. *A–B* is always weaker than *A* in that case. Unexpected readings or contents may well be independent of *A*, as in some of the examples above.

- 11 -

The Missing Premise

Bear with me as I bring in an unrelated-seeming topic from introductory logic. Students are taught about valid arguments. Validity is a pretty demanding standard, they learn, rarely met outside of logic class. They are not to despair, however, for validity may be achieved by plugging in additional premises. Arguments in need of that kind of completion are called *enthymemes*, and plugging the premise in is called *completing the enthymeme*. The simplest sort of enthymeme may be depicted as follows:

$$B$$
$$\underline{?R?}$$
$$\therefore A$$

The problem, in any particular case, is what to put in for R, to make the argument valid. Or rather, what *best* to put in for R, for there will be lots of options ($B \rightarrow A$, for starters), and the argument may cry out to be completed in a particular sort of way. That some Rs are better than others is indeed sometimes written into the definition.

> An enthymeme is a deductive argument *with an unstated assumption* that must be true for the premises to lead to the conclusion.

It's that unstated assumption, sometimes called the missing, or implied, or suppressed, premise, that we are typically looking for. The tagline for Smucker's jam is, "With a name like 'Smucker's,' it's got to be good." *Smucker's jam has a funny name* combines with some unstated R to imply that *Smucker's is good jam*. Any number of things could be put in, if the goal were just a valid argument.

178

Smucker's jam would not exist, were it not good.
Only good jams have names beginning with "*S*".
Smucker's is good jam, and a passable adhesive.
All jam is good, and good for you.
Smucker's is good jam, its funny name notwithstanding.

The proper assumption, I take it, is that funnily named jam has to be good (to compensate). A second example comes from Mark Twain: "There is no law against composing music when one has no ideas whatsoever. The music of Wagner, therefore, is perfectly legal." Twain is expecting us to solve the following enthymeme for *R*.

> Music based on no ideas whatever is not illegal.
> ....*R*...............
> ∴ Wagner's music is not illegal.

Again, if a solution is whatever makes the argument valid, there are lots of them:

> If music based on no ideas is legal, then Wagner's music is legal.
> Wagner's music is legal, profound, and based on no ideas whatever.
> Wagner's music is based on bad ideas.
> Music is always legal.
> Music is always legal if it is composed by Wagner.

The intended solution, of course, is *Wagner's music is based on no ideas whatever*. Here, finally, is a suggestive passage from Bush's 2003 "Mission Accomplished" speech.

> The battle of Iraq is one victory in a war on terror that began on September the 11th, 2001, and still goes on. With those attacks, the terrorists declared war on the United States. And war is what they got.

There may be various enthymemes here, but the one of interest to us is this:

> Our enemy in the war on terror is the 9/11 attackers.
> ....*R*...............
> ∴ Defeating Iraq is a victory in the war on terror.

Any number of validity-restoring *R*s can be imagined.

Defeating anyone is a victory in the war on terror.

Victory over our 9/11 attackers is achieved by defeating Iraq.

Iraq is our enemy in every war.

We were not attacked on 9/11.

The war on terror is a war against everyone.

Odd as some of the commentary was on Bush's speech, none of these were suggested as "what he must have been thinking." He was thinking that Iraq attacked us on 9/11.

An R that *interpolates* between B and A is evidently preferred to one that blocks the combination of B with $\neg A$ as such. Such a preference makes sense, given the notion's dialectical roots.

> In order to make a target group believe that A, the orator must first select a sentence B that is already accepted by the target group; secondly he has to show that A can be derived [with the help of plausible auxiliary premises] from B.[1]

Imagine that we are trying to win acceptance of A from an interlocutor who admits only B. A is not implied by B, so there are B-worlds where A is false. Who is to say that our world is not among them? This is where R comes in. A ought to inherit whatever plausibility attaches to R, for A is implied by R and B, and B is common ground. More carefully, A inherits whatever *independent* plausibility attaches to R. R makes a case for A only insofar as it is plausible in its own right.

Our preferences can to some extent be explained on this basis. One isn't going to persuade anyone of A by first getting them to agree that $\neg B$, if they have already signed on to B. Still less am I going to persuade you of A by getting you first to agree that A. What about $B \to A$? A conditional whose antecedent is already accepted will be judged by its consequent, in this case, A. If $B \to A$ is only as plausible as A, one is not going to persuade anyone of A by getting them first to agree that $B \to A$. An R that interpolates between B and A is going to be more persuasive than one that contradicts B or derives whatever plausibility it may possess from A.

---

[1] "Aristotle's Rhetoric," *Stanford Encyclopedia of Philosophy.*

11.2 BAD CHOICES

Some candidate enthymeme-completers are worse than others. The question is how to pick out the bad ones. All we have so far is a label—R should "interpolate" between B and A—and a few shared judgments. We don't know the factors driving these judgments. An example that wears its logical form on its face will help us to sort these out.

> All and only firefighters are goalkeepers.
> ....R...............
> ∴ No firefighters are horticulturalists.

The following seem like *bad* things to put in for R:

(R_1) No firefighters are phrenologists.

(R_2) No firefighters are horticulturalists or phrenologists.

(R_3) All and only firefighters are goalkeepers and no goalkeepers are horticulturalists.

(R_4) If the firefighters are the goalkeepers, then no firefighters are horticulturalists.

(R_5) No firefighters are horticulturalists.

That is, abbreviating in the obvious way,

(R_1) $\forall x(Fx \rightarrow \neg Px)$
(R_2) $\forall x(Fx \rightarrow \neg(Hx \lor Px))$
(R_3) $\forall x(Fx \equiv Gx)$ & $\forall x(Gx \rightarrow \neg Hx)$
(R_4) $\forall x(Fx \equiv Gx) \rightarrow \forall x(Fx \rightarrow \neg Hx)$
(R_5) $\forall x(Fx \rightarrow \neg Hx)$

are bad things to put in for R in

> $B : \forall x(Fx \equiv Gx)$
> ....R...............
> $A : \forall x(Fx \rightarrow \neg Hx)$

So, then, what is wrong with R_1–R_5? One should not expect a single answer to this; there are lots of ways of not taking the shortest path from B to A.

Chapter 11

R_1 doesn't even make it to A. R_2 upon reaching A keeps on going. R_3 goes over ground already covered. R_4 threatens to destroy ground already covered. R_5 begins at the finish line. The next section spells this out.

11.3 BRIDGING THE GAP

The least we expect of R is to deliver a valid argument. R_1 fails even at that basic task. $\forall x(Fx \rightarrow \neg Px)$ does not combine with $\forall x(Fx \equiv Gx)$ to imply $\forall x(Fx \rightarrow \neg Hx)$. Our first requirement on R is

Sufficiency R suffices, with B, for A.[2]

R_2 has the opposite problem. $\forall x(Fx \rightarrow \neg(Hx \vee Px))$ does in some sense bridge the gap, but it is a bridge too far.[3] R_2 goes too far by postulating, unnecessarily, that firefighters are not phrenologists. The next requirement is

Necessity R is necessary, given B, for A.[4]

Neither complaint applies to R_3. $\forall x(Fx \equiv Gx) \& \forall x(Gx \rightarrow \neg Hx)$ is necessary and sufficient, given B, for $\forall x(Fx \rightarrow \neg Hx)$. Where it goes wrong is in repeating material already present in B. It picks up *before* B leaves off, which makes it, if you like, a bridge too near.

How do we test for this? If R repeats something in B, it will have falsemakers (targeting the repeated element) that force B too to be false. B and R might be p and $p\&q$. That $p\&q$ covers old ground shows up in its having a falsemaker, $\bar{p}$, that implies the falsity of p.[5] Our third condition on R is

Originality No falsemaker for R should force B to be false.

---

[2] That is, R implies $B \rightarrow A$.
[3] To vary the metaphor slightly.
[4] Meaning, B implies $\neg R \rightarrow \neg A$; or, $\neg R$ implies $B \rightarrow \neg A$.
[5] R here entails B, which is the paradigm case. But it is not the only case. R, to be repetitive, does not even need to entail part of B, or B part of R. For instance: $(p\&q) \vee r$ is repetitive with respect to p, since its falsemaker $\bar{p}\&\bar{r}$ forces p to be false; likewise $p \equiv q$, due to its falsemaker $\bar{p}\&\bar{q}$.

Now $R_4 = \forall x(Fx \equiv Gx) \rightarrow \forall x(Fx \rightarrow \neg Hx)$, which amounts in the present case to $B \rightarrow A$. Does $B \rightarrow A$ have falsemakers forcing B too to be false? On the contrary, any falsemaker for $B \rightarrow A$ forces B to be *true*. $B \rightarrow A$ is not unoriginal, then. Nor is the problem one of sufficiency or necessity: $B \rightarrow A$ is equivalent to A in B-worlds.

The problem with $B \rightarrow A$ is that, although it leaves A no *alternative* but to be true in B-worlds, it plays no role in how A *comes* to be true in such worlds. Forgive me the following strained analogy. The cereal brand Wheaties used to bill itself as the Breakfast of Champions. *Why*, one might wonder, is it the Breakfast of Champions? Jerry Fodor distinguishes two possible answers.

1. Wheaties contains performance-boosting vitamins and minerals.
2. Wheaties is eaten by a non-negligible number of champions.

Our situation now is, R is billing itself as that which yields A when added to B. Why, one might wonder, is it the R-type B-worlds that are also A-worlds? Again there are two styles of answer.

1. They have such and such additional A-promoting features.
2. They are the ones which do not fail to be A-worlds.

To complete the enthymeme with $B \rightarrow A$ is like answering in the second way. $B \rightarrow A$ tells us *that* the only allowable B-worlds are A-worlds. But it doesn't tell us *what it is* about certain B-worlds that makes them moreover A. The reason a *Snow is cold*-world w is moreover such that snow is cold and white is not that: snow is cold and white in w, if it is cold there. Snow by hypothesis *is* cold in w, and we want to know why, *given* that it is cold, it is cold and white. Just so, the reason a world where *The Fs = the Gs* would be furthermore such that *No Fs are Hs* is not that *No Fs are Hs, if the Fs = the Gs*. The *Fs* by hypothesis *are* the *Gs* in this world; the question is why, *given* this identity, it would then be the case that no *Fs* are *Hs*. (It's got to do with none of the *Gs* being *Hs*.)

Now, R cannot capture what it is about certain B-worlds, that makes them moreover A-worlds, unless its reasons for being true *obtain* in B-worlds. A truthmaker holding only in $\neg B$-worlds is irrelevant to the distinction between B-worlds in which A is true and those where A is false.

This is the thinking behind our fourth condition:

Combinability No truthmaker for R should force B to be false.

The problem with $B \rightarrow A$ is that, since one way to verify a conditional is to falsify the antecedent, among its reasons for being true are some that force B to be false.

Our fifth bad candidate for the gap-bridging role is R_5 ($=\forall x(Fx \rightarrow \neg Hx)$), which says that no firefighters are horticulturalists. This is necessary and sufficient for the conclusion A, simply because it is that conclusion. Originality and combinability are satisfied, too. What is wrong with it, then? B is utterly wasted; R_5 implies A all by itself. Our fifth requirement is that R should leave B with as much responsibility as possible for the fact that the two together imply A.

Efficiency R should use as much of B as it can.

How do we tell if R is "using as much of B as it can"? This may be the trickiest question, logically speaking, in the whole book. Let us proceed carefully.

Any truthmaker for R will imply the truth of $B \rightarrow A$, simply because B and R imply A.[6] If it also implies $B^- \rightarrow A$, for B^- a proper part of B, it will have *wasted*, so to speak, B's surplus content relative to B^-. A candidate truthmaker is *efficient* insofar as it is not wasteful. Likewise any falsemaker for R will imply the truth of $B \rightarrow \neg A$.[7] Candidate falsemakers become more efficient as they come to imply fewer and fewer conditionals of the form $B^- \rightarrow \neg A$ (B^- ranging again over B's parts).[8] R uses as much of B as it can if the facts controlling its truth-value are *efficient* in the sense just indicated.[9]

---

[6] By *Sufficiency*. I assume, and treat it as implicit in *Sufficiency*, that R's truthmakers accomplish this by making $B \rightarrow A$ true.

[7] By *Necessity*. R's falsemakers are assumed moreover to make $B \rightarrow \neg A$ true.

[8] Suppose A and B are pqr and qrs. An example of an inefficient truthmaker for $pqr \rightarrow qrs$ is rs (the fact that r and s). That rs does not take full advantage of B can be seen from the fact that it also implies $B^- \rightarrow A = pq \rightarrow qrs$. A better (more efficient) choice would be s.

[9] Here is the definition in full, with R ranging over potential truthmakers for R.

1. R′ *uses more of* B *than* R iff $\{B^- \mid R', B^- \nvDash A\} \subsetneq \{B^- \mid R, B^- \nvDash A\}$.

2. R is B-*wasteful* in w iff some R′ holding in w uses more of B than R does.

To review, an enthymeme-completer should combine with B to imply A, and it should not be stronger than needed for that purpose. *Sufficiency* speaks to the first issue, by requiring R to imply $B \to A$. *Necessity* speaks to the second, since if R was stronger than needed, there would be B-worlds where it failed though A was true, hence B would not imply $\neg R \to \neg A$.

Now, R's implication relations have not, strictly speaking, been specified any further than this; we don't what else it implies besides $B \to A$, and what implies it, besides $B \& A$. These implication relations depend, presumably, on R's truth- and falsity-makers, as set out in the three remaining conditions, but how?

The simplest course is to let R imply whatever the disjunction of its truthmakers does, and be implied by whatever implies that disjunction; $\neg R$ would imply the disjunction of R's falsity-makers, and be implied by impliers of *that* disjunction. Shall R then be counted true *and* false in worlds where both disjunctions obtain? That has a certain elegance, and it preserves the principle that R is implied by R's truthmakers, and $\neg R$ by R's falsity-makers. Not to get bogged down in technicalities, we adopt the convention that R has neither truth-value in such worlds, even though it officially ought to have both. Our final condition is

Simplicity R is true (false) where it has a truthmaker (falsemaker),

where it is understood that opposing truth-values, like particles and antiparticles, destroy each other when they collide.

11.4 INTERPOLATION = EXTRAPOLATION

So, to finally put it all in one place, these are the conditions R should meet to count as completing the enthymeme $B, ?R? \therefore A$:

Sufficiency R implies $B \to A$.
Necessity B implies $\neg R \to \neg A$.

---

3. R is *B-wasteful* (period) iff it is *B*-wasteful in every *B*-world where it obtains.

4. R is *B-efficient* iff it is not *B*-wasteful.

Originality No falsemaker for R forces B to be false.
Combinability No truthmaker for R forces B to be false.
Efficiency R's truthmakers are B-efficient truthmakers for $B \rightarrow A$.[10]
Simplicity R is true (false) where it has a truthmaker (falsemaker).[11]

These conditions do not determine a unique gap-filling *sentence*, but that was never to be expected. Between two *R*s expressing the same thought (ones that differ, say, only in the order of their conjuncts), there is not much to choose. The six conditions do pin down the *thought* a gap-filling sentence should express. That is all we asked of the conditions defining extrapolants and that is all we ask here.

Remainders were portrayed in chapter **9** as the result of continuing A from the B-region into the rest of logical space. That sort of model makes sense if A implies B, for then the A-region is included in the B-region, as extrapolation would seem to require. Now the door has been opened, though, to Bs that A does not imply. What could extrapolation mean in that more general case? The idea of extending one region beyond the confines imposed by another is none too clear, if the one was not confined to begin with.

A new model is needed, now that A and B are allowed to be logically independent. Our discussion of enthymemes in the last section suggests one. The missing premise in B, ?R? $\therefore$ A, makes intuitive sense whether A implies B or not.[12] Once an extrapolant, A–B is in the general case to be conceived as an interpolant.

For this to work, the models had better agree in the original case, where B is implied by A. There is so far no reason to expect this. The (six) conditions defining interpolants do not line up in any obvious way with the (four) conditions defining extrapolants. To count as extrapolating A beyond B, R would have to possess the following features. It would have to be

Agreement . . . true (false) in the same B-worlds as A.
Rectitude . . . true (false) at home for the same reasons as $B \rightarrow A$ ($\neg A$).

---

[10] Similarly for its falsity-makers.
[11] A slight reordering yields the mnemonic SCONES.
[12] Compare vector subtraction. $\vec{a}$ and $\vec{b}$ don't have to point in the same direction for there to be an $\vec{r}$ which, added to $\vec{b}$, yields $\vec{a}$.

Integrity . . . true (false) away for the same reasons as at home.
Determination . . . true (false) away if that is all it has reason to be.[13]

Also the motivation was different. Extrapolation links up with Wittgensteinian worries about going on in the same way. Interpolation harks back to Aristotelian rhetoric by way of introductory logic. Extrapolation is based on the quasi-geometrical idea of extending a pattern into new territory. Interpolation draws us further into old territory, as we attempt to bridge the gap between two extant hypotheses.

This makes it all the more interesting that the two -polations agree, given some minor fiddling, when A implies B. Interpolation is what you get when extrapolation is extrapolated to the case where A does not imply B. They agree also when B is not implied, if the truthmakers in **Rectitude** are required to be B-efficient. (As could easily have been required; see note 2 in section **9.2**). If there is anything like a "result" in this book, it's that

48 Interpolation comes to the same as extrapolation.

Let me wave my hands at why this is so. Please skip ahead to the next section unless you are enthralled by such issues.

The combined effect of **Necessity** and **Sufficiency** is to make R equivalent, in the B-region, to A. That is the same as A and R agreeing on B-worlds, as per **Agreement**.

The combined content of **Originality** and **Combinability** is that R's truth- and falsity-makers do not force B to be false. This makes them (assuming B is bivalent) B-compatible. R's truth- (falsity-)makers are characterized by **Efficiency** and **Integrity** as truthmakers for $B \to A$ ($B \to \neg A$) that "use all of B that they can." The four together require R's truthmakers (falsemakers) to be B-friendly, B-efficient truthmakers for $B \to A$ ($B \to \neg A$). This is also the requirement laid down by **Rectitude** and **Integrity**.

Now, what **Simplicity** officially says is that R is true where it has a truthmaker and false where it has a falsemaker. A convention was adopted for worlds where it has both: R shall be seen as neither true nor false in such worlds. R is true, then, according to our convention, where it has a truthmaker and no falsemaker, and false where it has a falsemaker but

---

[13] The acronym: ARID.

no truthmaker. These are the truth-value assignment rules laid down by *Determination* as well.

11.5 SUMMING UP

Extrapolation is hard to make sense of if A does not imply B. Sense can be made, however, of *interpolating* between B and A: finding an R to complete the enthymeme, B, $?R?$, $\therefore$ A. Interpolation is the more general procedure since the initial premise in an enthymeme need not be weaker than the conclusion. It turns out to agree with extrapolation, however, when the initial premise *is* weaker. The two agree indeed across the board, if the home-style truthmakers in *Rectitude* are understood to be targeted (section **9.2**, footnote 2).

- 12 -

What Is Said

I want to return now to the comparison begun in section **10.4** between piggybacking on a game and pivoting on a presupposition. The two have a lot in common, we said. *A* can take on different figurative contents, for instance, as we vary the game, and different incremental contents as we vary the presupposition. Could it be that pivoting and piggybacking are one and the same phenomenon, or inessential variants of each other? This was rejected on the following grounds (repeated from chapter **10**).

> If the content *A* acquires through pivoting on *B* is *A–B*, then pivoting can only *weaken* *A*'s literal content; for *A–B* as defined so far is always implied by *A*. Piggybacking thus looks like the more powerful operation; the contents it generates can be *independent* of *A*.

To illustrate with an example from above, *Napoleon is a passenger on the Queen Mary* (= *A*) can through piggybacking come to express that there is a portrait of Napoleon on board (= *R*). In the diagram, repeated as Figure 12.1, *A*'s compositional content, comprising the worlds where Napoleon himself is on board, is the diagonal at the lower left. The string of diamonds contains the *R*-worlds—the ones where a Napoleon-portrait is traveling on the *Queen Mary*. Each of the diamonds corresponds to a different possible portrait, all equally legitimating the pretense that Napoleon himself is a passenger. That the diamondy region is not contained in the diagonal, or vice versa, testifies to *A* and *R*'s independence.

But, this only shows piggybacking to be more powerful than pivoting on an *entailed* presupposition. The question has to be revisited now that we have found an enthymematic construal of *A–B* that allows *B* to be independent of *A*. As the difference between independent vectors points in a third direction, independent of both, the difference between independent hypotheses is independent of both. Let me illustrate with *A = The king is in the counting house* and *B = The king is Nigel*, represented respectively by the diagonal and vertical bars in Figure 12.2.

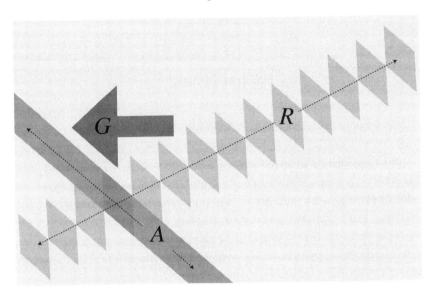

Figure 12.1 *A*'s real content is $R = \gamma^{-1}(A)$.

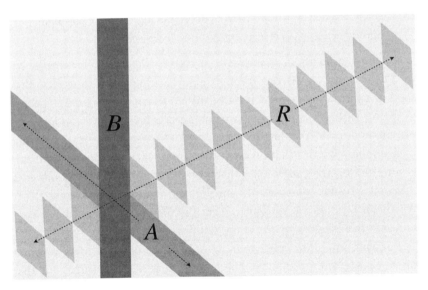

Figure 12.2 *A*'s real content is $R = \beta^{-1}(A)$.

To complete the enthymeme we need to find an *R* independent of both that agrees with *A* in the *B*-region, and "goes on in the same way" outside it. This *R* in graphical terms should continue the diamond pattern set by the diagonal's overlap with the vertical bar into the rest of logical space.

So then, at the risk of some repetition, the content A acquires through piggybacking on a game G is the condition that reality has to satisfy for A to be "assertible" in G. If γ is the rule specifying what is assertible as a function of how the world is, then

49 A's real content, piggybacking on a game G, is $\gamma^{-1}(A)$.

The content A acquires through pivoting on B is the premise that B needs to supplemented with, to obtain a valid argument for A. If β is the function mapping hypotheses X to their conjunction with B, then

50 A's real content, pivoting on a presupposition B, is $\beta^{-1}(A)$.[1]

The two approaches are starting, once again, to bear a certain resemblance. Both have us uttering A to convey a content R that differs from A's semantic content. Both frame the utterance against a certain backdrop: as a move in game G if we're piggybacking, under the assumption that B if we're pivoting. G and B are content-*fixers*, not ingredients in the content that gets fixed. Both employ a booster device—the game's generation rules if we are piggybacking on G, the function taking X to $X\&B$ if we're pivoting on B. Both characterize A's real content as what must be fed into the booster device to obtain output A. The devices are themselves analogous, in that each B has associated with it a game G whereby X makes it fictional that Y just if Y follows from $X\&B$.

Consider a Walton-style explanation of how a pretend assertion of *Holmes wrote a learned monograph on cigar ash* acquires the serious content that *According to the book, Holmes wrote a learned monograph on cigar ash*. The book is a prop: players are to pretend that it is factual, that what it says is true. What property must the book have to make it pretense-worthy that Holmes wrote a monograph on cigar ash, if we are pretending that the book is true? The book should *say* that he wrote a monograph on cigar ash. The real content thus becomes *According to the book, Holmes wrote a learned monograph on cigar ash*.

---

[1] This is a bit misleading because, as already discussed, $\beta : X \to X\&B$ is a many-one function. One should think of β^{-1} as taking A to the "best" X such that $X\&B = A$; the best such X is $A{-}B$.

A pivoting-style explanation has not been tried, to my knowledge. How would it go? Readers of fiction are not wrestling with doubts about the document's veracity. The phrase "suspension of disbelief" is misleading insofar as it suggests an effortful, deliberate undertaking. One simply takes the statements on board without subjecting them to any particular scrutiny; there is a presumption of accuracy. The real content of *Holmes wrote a learned monograph on cigar ash*, pivoting on this presumption, is the missing premise R in

What the book says is true.

...........R...........

Holmes wrote a learned monograph on cigar ash.

The premise that suggests itself is: *The book says that Holmes wrote a learned monograph on cigar ash*. This is the same result that Walton gets, but arrived at with regular issue, off-the-shelf equipment.

Walton-inspired hermeneutic fictionalism has been tried in a huge lot of problem areas in recent years: truth, paradox, attitude ascriptions, properties, fictional characters, nonexistence, mathematics, and morality. These applications have often been found objectionable, but the objections turn, for the most part, on features of pretense that are not shared by presupposition. If piggybacking and pivoting are variations on a theme, one might hope to pick up with the second some of the load dropped by the first.

12.2 TROUBLES WITH PRETENSE

Philosophers get interested in unexpected content, in many cases, because among the statements they cannot bring themselves to believe are some that cannot easily be renounced, either. An explanation is needed of why falsehoods would be treated as true, and pretense appears to provide it. Speakers are not *really* asserting that A, they are *making as if* to assert it, in order to really assert a different thing which is more in keeping with the philosopher's worldview. One makes as if to assert that that the rate of star formation is decreasing in order to really assert that fewer and fewer stars are coming into existence. Piggybacking is called in to explain how the one is a way of doing the other.

Piggybacking is one possible explanation of why we'd assert an untruth, or what might for all we knew was an untruth. But is it a plausible explanation, or an illuminating one? There have been doubts on this score. They can be grouped under three main headings: incredulity, opportunism, and honest toil.

Incredulity: The idea that speakers are *making as if* to believe in mathematical objects can seem just fantastic. If they were pretending, wouldn't they know it? They seem to know, if anything, the opposite.

> Competent users of arithmetical discourse will certainly deny that they
> are pretending when they discuss arithmetic. (Stanley 2001, 46)

The denial seems all too credible. Pretending is not the sort of thing to be done behind our back. Also speakers may positively *believe* in numbers; why pretend what one takes to be genuinely the case?

Opportunism: The fictionalist might respond that pretense is a theoretical notion. It's for the theorist to decide who is pretending; speakers have no authority in the matter. But, if speakers' judgments are so easily overruled, then

> nothing appears to prevent the hermeneutic fictionalist from simply
> declaring, when faced with an ontologically loaded discourse, that its
> users, when engaged in it, employ principles of generation that link the
> discourse up with ontologically innocent truth-conditions. (Stanley
> 2001, 43)

This links up with the first worry. To use the method responsibly, we would need some objective check on when speakers are really pretending. And it is hard to think what test there could possibly be that ignores their self-reports.

Honest Toil:[2] Semantics has an explanatory job to do. There is a long-standing puzzle of how finite beings are able to understand an unlimited range of sentences (section **10.1**).

> Linguists and philosophers have long held that the type of systematic-
> ity required to explain this ability requires attribution to language users
> of a compositional semantic theory. (Stanley 2001, 40).

---

[2] This goes back, of course, to Russell's remark about the method of postulation having all the advantages of theft over honest toil.

The fictionalist seems to have forgotten her responsibilities here. Her theory specifies A's real content, relative to a game G, as $\gamma^{-1}(A)$, where γ is the associated generation function ((**49**) in section 12.1). It is hard to see γ as anything but a semantic skyhook plopping A down on what is deemed the proper interpretation.[3] Fictionalist "semantics" *stipulates* what linguists and philosophers have considered it their business to explain.[4]

Not to say that I agree with all of these objections,[5] they look serious and might be thought decisive. The question then becomes, are presupposition-based theories similarly problematic?

Take first *Incredulity*. Asked if they are *pretending* there are numbers, people will deny it. But suppose we ask instead whether they are taking it for granted as they pursue other matters. Will they deny this, too? I doubt it.[6] That seems, in fact, to capture the phenomenology pretty exactly. And the conversational role. A physicist might tell her class that spin takes integer and half-integer values. The students do not take themselves to have been told that integers exist. Nor would the professor expect to be described as testifying to this effect.

---

[3] A skyhook is defined by Dennett as "a 'mind first' force or power or process, an exception to the principle that all design, and apparent design, is ultimately the result of mindless, motiveless mechanicity." (Dennett 1996, 74).

[4] "[I]t is difficult to see how, on a pretense account of arithmetic, the real-world truth-conditions of arithmetical sentences are a function of the meanings of the parts of the sentence. But we are able smoothly to grasp the truth-conditions of novel arithmetical sentences on the basis of our familiarity with their parts. This ability of ours is mysterious, if our understanding of such discourse involves the mechanism of pretense" (Stanley 2001, 41).

[5] See the appendix to Yablo (2001). The squabbling is partly terminological. Walton uses "pretend" in an extraordinarily wide sense, and hermeneutic fictionalists have followed him in this. "Shallow" pretense is "not the sort of pretense that draws us into imaginative play" (Crimmins 1998, 3). All it involves is that "to understand me, ... you have to distinguish what's so from what's [as if] so" (Crimmins 1998, 3). I would add that what is as if so is not necessarily false; the speaker may even believe it to be true, as long as the belief is not why it is being treated as true. *Incredulity* from this perspective relies on an overheated conception of pretense. A self-knowledgeable speaker should, perhaps, know whether she is treating B as true, and whether she believes that B. But pretending is to do with the relations between these two; would she still, for instance, treat B as true if she stopped believing it? The idea that one must first investigate these matters, before treating B as true, is like insisting that to smile one must first decide whether it is out of politeness or genuine friendly feeling.

[6] "Presupposes" is so much the natural term here that Putnam reaches for it even when his dialectical purposes are better served by "asserts": "This type of argument stems, of course, from Quine, who has for years stressed both the indispensability of quantification over mathematical entities and the intellectual dishonesty of denying the existence of what one daily *presupposes*" (Putnam 1971, 347, italics added).

Another question the objector raises is, why would anyone go to the trouble of pretending that *P*, if she already believed it? One could equally ask why anyone would go to the trouble of *exempting P* from the pretense. Dostoevsky would not be much fun if we had to be constantly on the lookout for statements that were independently plausible, lest we extend to some *P* the unneeded courtesy of *supposing* it to be true.[7]

Anyway, there is not even the *appearance* of a clash when it comes to presupposing. What I presuppose in saying, *Neither of my children is a lion-tamer*, namely that I have two children, I also believe. Nor does presupposing look like a deliberate act. You didn't "decide" to accommodate the presupposition just mentioned, it just quietly slipped on board.

Opportunism was the worry that if speakers have no say in the matter, we can impute whatever pretense we like. But there is plenty to prevent us from imputing whatever presupposition we like. Presupposition is a load-bearing notion in linguistics, and something we know, within limits, how to test for.

One test, due I think to Frege, is that presuppositions are preserved under denial. To deny *The discoverer of the elliptical motions of the planets died in misery*, one says, *The discoverer did not die in misery*, not that followed by... *or else nobody discovered the elliptical motions of the planets*. Another test grows out of the fact that "new information" should not in most cases be presupposed. This is why it sounds better to say, *He came to think the tank was empty, and he was right*, than to say, *He came to think the tank was empty, and what is more, came to realize it was empty*.

A third test turns on the way surprising presuppositions are challenged Told that *The oldest Finnish bullfighter is starring in a new movie*, you may respond, *Hey, I didn't know Finland had bullfighters*, but not, *Hey, I didn't know a bullfighter was going to be starring in a movie*. (Of course not, that is what I was telling you.) A fourth test is that presuppositions are not typically imported into the content of attitude ascriptions. Robespierre wanted the king of France to be called before the tribunal. For him to be called before the tribunal presupposes that France has a king. But Robespierre did not want France to have a king. (See von Fintel (2004) for the tests just mentioned.)

---

[7] I thought first of Tolstoy, who sticks in lots of truths, but *War and Peace* is indeed not much fun.

The tests are not perfect, but they're something. Let's try them out on the presuppositions we are contemplating here.

To deny *The number of Martian moons is two*, one says *The number of Martian moons is not two*, not *The number of Martian moons is not two, or else Mars doesn't exist, or there is no such thing as the number of its moons.*

Suppose I say, *The king is coming this way*, when we're postulating, for fear of the secret police, that Nigel is the king. *Hey, I didn't know that Nigel was the king* is a much better response than *Hey, I didn't know anyone was coming this way.*

I know what is meant by *Dogs exist, moreover the set of them is nonempty*, but it sounds terrible. *Dogs exist, and what is more, there exists such a thing as the set of dogs* is fine, reflecting the fact that *The set of them contains some dogs* presupposes what *There is such a thing as the set of dogs* asserts.

Imagine a nominalist who tries to *make* her position true by destroying all the abstract objects. Initially the number of abstracta is infinite. She brings it down on Monday to 1,000,001, on Tuesday to 100,001, on Wednesday to 10,001, on Thursday to 1,001,... on Sunday to 1. Tuesday morning she wakes up with a terrible hangover. She may by now have destroyed the one remaining abstract object, but can't be sure. She *wonders* whether the number of abstract objects has fallen finally to zero. She *hopes* that the number is zero. But she does not wonder whether there is such a thing as zero; it was destroyed last week. Still less does she hope that zero exists. Her desire is quite the opposite.

The *Honest Toil* objection accuses fictionalists of stipulating what real semanticists seek to explain. Presuppositionalism has the outlines of a reply: pivoting-induced real content, even if not compositional, is systematically enough *related* to compositional content to keep us honest. It is compositional content minus a bit: minus operative presuppositions. What determines the presuppositions, though? Some of them are generated compositionally by way of hard-wired presupposition triggers ("too," "managed," "stopped").[8] But not all; there is nothing in the semantics of *The king is in the counting house* to suggest that by "the king," we have in mind Nigel.

Pragmatic presuppositions are an unruly lot, and which we are actually pivoting on is a further question. I *wish* I could now pull out a road-tested

---

[8] See Abrusán (2011) for an aboutness-based explanation of why certain sorts of terms predictably, cross-linguistically, give rise to certain sorts of presuppositions.

diagnostic. So, for instance, as it might be, the parties to a speech exchange are pivoting on P if the audience can go on to say, after "Hey, I didn't know that P," things like

> Oh, you mean *supposing* that P.
> Pardon *me*, I happen actually to *care* about the question.

and if the audience *cannot* say, without alarming the speaker, things like

> Hold on, how do *you* know that P?
> Fine, I'll take your word for it.

As you can see, we are not quite there yet. Having tagged this as an open question, I will proceed on the assumption that it can be answered. Pivot presuppositions are not pulled out of thin air; they are genuine discourse features no less respectable than, say, focal stress, or domain restriction, or the question under discussion.

12.3 MOONLIGHTING

Pivoting offers certain advantages over piggybacking. If the metaphorical route to unexpected content were just a scenic alternative to the presuppositional route, taking us to the same place in more style, then we could perhaps just drop pretense and do it all with presupposition. How does *Planetary motion is described by a function of the form* $ax^2 + by^2 = r^2$ acquire the content that planets move elliptically? It's not because we *pretend* there are real-valued functions, on this view, it's that we *assume* there are real-valued functions.

This might be right about the elliptical motion example. But is it true in general that the expressive work done by pretense can be taken over by presupposition?

Nelson Goodman considered metaphor a kind of linguistic moonlighting. One takes a word or phrase that was already gainfully employed, and finds additional work for it—work it can do while still holding onto its day job, indeed, work that often *depends* on its day job. What this means at the sentential level is that an A already endowed with truth-conditions is fitted out with new ones, informed by the original truth-conditions, but departing from them in some way. The question is whether metaphorical truth-conditions can depart further than incremental truth-conditions. Is it the case that for every game G, a presupposition B_G can be found such that the content A acquires through piggybacking on G is the content it acquires through pivoting on B_G?

It is not the case. Piggybacking is a strictly more powerful method. This may not come as a huge surprise to you. But the reasons are interesting; they tell us something about our theoretical options in particular cases. A's metaphorical content can in principle be anything we want; it is just a matter of finding the right game. *Not* any old R can be A's incremental content, however, even if we are allowed complete freedom in the choice of which presupposition B to pivot on. A and R have got to stand in certain relations for R to fit snugly into the gap between B and A.

This can be seen as follows. A truthmaker for R is *at least* a B-friendly truthmaker for $B \to A$. B-friendliness means that it has got to obtain in at least one B-world. A B-world with a truthmaker for $B \to A$ obtaining in it is clearly also an A-world. Each truthmaker for R thus holds in an at least one A-world, and similarly each falsemaker for R holds in at least one $\neg A$-world. This gives us a constraint on presuppositionally induced contents. A is *open* to R, let's say, just if R's truthmakers are one and all compatible with A, and its falsemakers are one and all compatible with $\neg A$. The constraint is this:

51   R cannot be A's incremental real content unless A is open to R.

Once again, figurative contents are not constrained in this way. Consider a simple game: we pretend that *Judy is sailing around the world* just when Judy is riding her bike around a puddle. *Judy is riding around the puddle* then becomes the metaphorical content of *Judy is sailing around the world*. Could it also be the incremental content of *Judy is sailing around the world*, relatively to some cleverly chosen B?

Some of R's truthmakers are A-friendly; the nearest puddle could be on the deck of a world-circling schooner. But that is not the usual case. Judy cannot ride around a puddle in Boston Common while simultaneously circling the globe on a sailboat. *Judy is sailing around the world* is therefore *not* open to *Judy is riding around the puddle*. It follows by (**51**) that *Judy is riding around the puddle* cannot be an incremental real content of *Judy is sailing around the world*, relative to any presupposition.

Our conclusion so far is that metaphorical contents—contents obtainable by piggybacking on a game—cannot always be reconstrued as incremental contents—contents obtained by pivoting on a suitably related presupposition. Pivoting is a limited operation, compared to piggybacking.

But the argument for this had a limitation, too; it applies just when A is closed to its metaphorical content. It could be, for all we have shown, that piggybacking on a game G *can* always be simulated by pivoting on a corresponding presupposition, *provided* that every A is open to its G-induced metaphorical content. I do not know that this is really so, but we can adopt it as a working hypothesis.

Now, wholes are certainly open to their parts. The part's truthmakers are compatible with the whole's, for they are nontrivially implied by the whole's. The part's falsemakers are compatible with the whole's, too, for the same reason. Let us look, then, at games where the truth of a part licenses us in pretending the whole. Games of this type have players in a broad sense *exaggerating*—saying more than they mean—so let's call them *hyperbolic*.

The contents generated by hyperbolic games do not fall afoul of (51) for the reason already mentioned; wholes are open to their parts. As far as the openness requirement is concerned, it *could* be that for each hyperbolic game G, there is a presupposition B_G that "duplicates" it; piggybacking on the one yields the exact same real contents as pivoting on the other.

And now I make a conjecture: most, if not all, of the philosophically controversial games—the games invoked by fictionalists about numbers, sets, properties, mereological sums, other times and worlds, and so on—are hyperbolic. The facts that make A pretendable are included in the facts that would make it true. I shall illustrate, as will not surprise you, with number fictionalism.

One version of the number game has us pretending, for any bunch of Fs, that there is such a thing as their number, subject to the condition (Hume's Principle) that the number of Fs = the number of Gs iff there are exactly as many Fs as Gs. Another version tells us to pretend that there is a number 0 such that, when there are no Fs, the number of Fs = 0; that there is a number 1 such that when there is a unique F, the number of Fs = 1; and so on. The game is hyperbolic in either version. Part of what it takes for the number of dogs to equal the number of cats is for there to be exactly as many dogs as cats. Part of what is involved in the literal truth of *the number of Fs* = 1 is that there is an *F* such that nothing else is an *F*.

Where does this leave us? Hyperbolic fictionalism can, it seems, be replayed in the key of presupposition. And, the kinds of fictionalism one ordinarily thinks of are hyperbolic; they have us imagining a richer set of circumstances than perhaps obtains. I do not want to leave the impression that this works *only* for hyperbolic games; it works, we're speculating, whenever *A* is open to *R*. For *A* to actually include *R* is just a special case of that.[9] I *certainly* don't want to leave the impression that incremental contents must be included in, or even implied by, literal contents. Sense can be made of "what *A* adds to *B*" whether *A* implies *B* or not. Now we argue that "what *A* adds to *B*" is in many cases a good candidate for the role of what is said or alleged in an assertive utterance of *A*, where *B* is the operative presupposition.

12.4 UNEXPECTED INCREMENTAL CONTENT

Allow me to reset the scene from section **10.1**. One utters a sentence *S* that is heard as saying that BLAH; BLAH is its "real content" on the occasion of utterance. Real contents may be more or less unexpected relative to *S*'s standing meaning. Four grades of unexpectedness were distinguished.

BLAH is unexpected$_1$ if it is not determined by the sentence's standing meaning. What the meaning gives us is an intelligible *rule* by which to determine real content as a function of context. BLAH is unexpected$_2$ if, although real content may still be a function of context, the function is not defined by a rule that speakers are expected to know. BLAH is unexpected$_3$ if *S*'s meaning does *not* determine its real content as a function of context; at most it puts BLAH on a list of possible readings. BLAH is unexpected$_4$ if the meaning of *S disallows* BLAH as a possible reading. Our proposed

---

[9] As one sees by comparing the definition of *A includes B*—each of *R*'s truthmakers (falsemakers) is implied by a truthmaker (falsemaker) for *A*—to that of *A is open to B* (rewritten to facilitate the comparison)—each of *R*'s truthmakers (falsemaker) is compatible with a truthmaker (falsemakers) for *A*. The difference is that "implied by" in the first definition becomes "compatible with" in the second.

model for this last kind of unexpected content is

52 *S*'s real content, pivoting on presupposition *P*, is *S–P*.[10]

Recall Soames's example of campus security announcing to a large lecture hall that they're looking for Scott Soames. He says, *I am Scott Soames*, and this seems a good reply despite the triviality of its compositional semantic content. *I am Scott Soames* does not mean that *I am the one you're looking for*, and yet that is what we hear it to say.[11] *My cousin is not a boy any more* cannot have as its compositional semantic content *My cousin is now grown up*; yet that is how it would ordinarily be understood. Likewise for the other examples. *Smith's murderer is insane* does not mean *That guy* [pointing] *is insane*. *She became a dot on the horizon* does not mean *She came to look like a dot on the horizon*. And so on.

Which of the above-mentioned unexpected contents can be understood as incremental, that is, as propositions that "bridge the gap" between *S* and some salient presupposition *P*?[12]

Donnellan's protagonists are assuming that *that* guy is Smith's murderer. The incremental content of *Smith's murderer is insane* relative to this assumption is the *R* that completes

> That guy is Smith's murderer
> ....*R*............
> ∴ Smith's murderer is insane.

If we ask what goes in for *R* here, the answer seems clear: *That guy is insane*. Which is what we hear *S* as saying, according to Donnellan, and intuitively as well. So here is a case where incremental content does seem to coincide with real or assertive content.

[10] I am not saying the model *doesn't* apply to *lesser* forms of unexpectedness. Recanati suggested the possibility of obtaining *She mowed the grass* (which is only unexpected₃) from *She cut the grass* by pivoting on the widely held assumption that grass is cut by mowing it rather than slicing individual blades with a scalpel.

[11] Another possible reading is *The present speaker is Scott Soames*. This is unexpected, too, but less so than the reading in the main text. A type-shifting account might be tried here.

[12] *Can* be understood. We seek a 'proof of concept' for the idea of obtaining unexpected contents from semantic contents by the device of pivoting on a presupposition. The device in its present form may overgenerate; still we see how the trick *could* be pulled.

Soames's example is in some ways the opposite of Donnellan's. Soames uses *I am Scott Soames* to convey that he is the one they're looking for. This time the operative assumption, I take it, is that Scott Soames is the one they are looking for; after all, the last sentence uttered before Soames speaks is *We are looking for Scott Soames*. The incremental content of *I am Scott Soames*, relative to this assumption, is the *R* that slots into:

> Scott Soames is the one you're looking for.
> ....*R*............
> ∴ I am Scott Soames.

The missing premise would seem to be *I am the one you're looking for*—which, again, is what we hear *S* as saying.[13]

What about *My cousin is not a boy any more*? Its real content can shift, we noticed, as one pivots on different presuppositions. Normally, one is assuming the cousin is still male, and the real content is *My cousin is grown up*. Is this what the theory predicts? Well, what is the *R* that completes

> My cousin is still a male human being.(*P*)
> ....*R*...........
> ∴ My cousin is not a boy any more.(*S*)

It's *My cousin is now grown up*. That is what has to be added to *He is still male* to reach *He is no longer a boy*. Now imagine we utter the same sentence (*My cousin is not a boy any more*) while, to re-set the scene, sitting on a park bench watching my eight-year-old cousin swing on the monkey bars. Where before it was assumed that my cousin is still male, now it is assumed that my cousin is still a child. What we're looking for this time is the *R* that completes

> My cousin is an eight-year-old human being.(*P*)
> ....*R*............
> ∴ My cousin is not a boy any more.(*S*)

---

[13] It might be objected (e.g., by Scott Soames) that *I am Scott Soames* is a trivially necessary truth which is implied by everything. This may be so in one sense of implication. But not a theoretically neutral sense.

What else do you need to know, to get from *My cousin is an eight-year-old human being* to *My cousin is not a boy anymore?* You need to know that the cousin is no longer male, hence presumably female.[14]

Next, the Kripke/Austin example: *She became a dot on the horizon.* I should probably let the example follow her over the horizon, because it is somewhat bewildering. But pivoting is not entirely helpless even with as weird a case as this. The background assumption is that things look the way they are. The real content obtained by pivoting on that assumption is the missing premise in

How she looks is how she is.(*P*)

..........*R*..........

∴ She became a dot on the horizon.(*S*)

The missing premise, I suggest, is that she came to *look* like a dot on the horizon.[15] Compare the use of *Holmes wrote a learned monograph about cigar ash*, pivoting on the story's supposed truth, to say that he wrote a monograph on that topic according to the story. Examples with a similar flavor: *The moon is huge tonight, There are twenty-five students in our class picture.*[16]

12.5 THE PLAIN AND THE PHILOSOPHICAL

The 2006 Hempel lectures were on the philosophy of philosophy, which got me to wondering what the implications of this material might

[14] I suggested early on that *S*'s unexpected content is not just what the *speaker* says, if *S* carries it into larger grammatical contexts. *My cousin is not a boy any more* contributes different propositions depending on whether the cousin is understood still to be eight years old. David Hills makes this sort of point regarding metaphorical content (Hills (1998)). Stanley considers it "good evidence to take [the] paraphrase as part of what is expressed, rather than simply what is pragmatically communicated" (Stanley 2001, 46).

[15] A thing looks to me like an *F* if I see it as an *F*. This does not require me to know how it would look if it really were *F*. One can see a horse as a unicorn, or a harbinger of doom. Thanks here to Sally Haslanger.

[16] Exercise: Explain in each case how the pivot point should change, to bring on the indicated shift in assertive content. *The bank stopped bothering me* says, pivoting on one assumption, that the bank stopped calling; pivoting on another, that I have come to enjoy the calls. *You aren't getting any younger* expresses, pivoting on one assumption, that you are getting older, on another, that the rejuvenation machine is broken. *They are shooting at us* expresses, on one assumption, that they don't recognize us, on another, that we should stop negotiating and start shooting at them.

be for philosophical theory-building. (Grandiose metaphilosophical speculation alert.)

A physical theory need not be true to be good, Field has argued, and I agree. All we ask of it truth-wise is that its physical implications should be true, or, in my version, that it should be true about the physical. What about philosophical theories? Should we be willing to settle for a philosophy that is only *partly* true?

Those of us raised in the David Lewis tradition of systematic theorizing, answerable to every datum in sight, will say *NO*. Lewis himself suggests a negative answer, when he objects to a theoretical outlook that defies common sense that

> unless we are doubleplusgood doublethinkers, it will not last. And it should not last, for it is safe to say in such a case that we will believe a great deal that is false. (Lewis 1983, xi)

A theory that defies common sense will contain some falsity, and that, it seems, is intolerable. That is from the Preface to the first volume of his *Philosophical Papers*. In the Preface to the *second* volume, however, he says that

> what I uphold is not so much the truth of Humean supervenience as the tenability of it. If physics were to teach me that it is false, I wouldn't grieve...What I want to fight are philosophical arguments against Humean supervenience. (Lewis 1986, xi)

Now the goal seems to be a theory that, although perhaps false, is not false for *philosophical* reasons. "I am not ready to take lessons in ontology from quantum physics as it is now," he says (Lewis 1986, xi). Falsity for *scientific* reasons now apparently *can* be tolerated, until the physicists get their act together.

That is one goal, the goal of a philosophical system-builder: one seeks a theory that is false for scientific reasons, perhaps, but not philosophical reasons.[17] But not all of us are theory-builders. Another kind of philosopher (the self-hating kind?) thinks we need sometimes to acquiesce in

---

[17] I don't know how Lewis would want to distinguish *philosophical* ways of being false from scientific ones. See Hawthorne and Michael (1996) for some interesting thoughts on threats to truth that only a philosopher could care about.

appearances, rather than trying always to penetrate them. The goal might even be to sweep philosophical theory aside and return to the plain truths we had in common before getting so curious. At that point we would face a choice: either give up philosophy, as Wittgenstein recommended, or depart from the plain truths only as necessary to clear up tempting confusions, as Wittgenstein actually did, or tried to do.

Either way, our first step should be to identify the facts that no one really disagrees about, though we may end up putting different philosophical construals on them. This turns out to be a difficult problem. It is the problem that led the positivists to despair of finding a neutral observational language in which to formulate protocol sentences (Carnap 1987, Neurath 1959). Should the language speak of experience? Or of nearby middle-sized objects? Should it be an operationalist language that confines itself to our tests and tracking methods? Right from the start, there are theoretical choices to be made of a kind we were hoping to be done with. It seems the words do not exist any longer to state the facts in a way that arouses no philosophical suspicions. (The distinction here—"plain" versus "philosophical"—is from Clarke 1972.)[18] One inevitably winds up saying more than one had meant to.

This ought to sound familiar, however. It is one more instance of the phenomenon we've been studying all along, in which truths come to us wrapped in larger falsehoods, or what may be falsehoods—claims anyway that court unnecessary controversy from our perspective, that go beyond what we really wanted to say. The strategy we have adopted is to go with the flow, letting *A* carry us past our destination with the idea of then backing up to the part of *A* that we care about: the part about the plain, in this case, as opposed to the philosophical. This requires us to *identify* the plain, however. And, as already remarked, we have no real conception of that subject matter.

Or is it that we have no real *positive* conception of it? Maybe we know the plain only as the part of our doctrine that is not vulnerable to certain worries. Where Lewis sought a story that was not false for philosophical reasons, we in our Wittgensteinian moments are after the opposite: a story that is false, if it is, *only* for philosophical reasons. (Reasons of the kind raised by idealists, or bundle theorists, or nominalists, or mereological

---

[18] I am not using the terms in quite his sense. See also Stroud (1984).

nihilists.) Our advocacy extends only to the part R of what we say that is not philosophically exposed.

The framework we've been developing is admittedly pushed beyond its limits here. R is meant to be the part of S that is not about the philosophical. To model the philosophical would require a version of logical space with worlds in it answering to Plato's picture of things, and Berkeley's, and van Inwagen's, and so on. It would also require a way of deciding when worlds are alike in "ordinary" respects, even though only one of them contains macro-objects, or enduring things, or what have you. But although the idea of plain truths may not be capturable with these methods, they do seem to bring it into some kind of relief. Maybe we need better methods. Or maybe, as Clarke maintained,[19] the plain is not a self-contained matter; it contains the seeds of the philosophical.

---

[19] With a nod to Kant on reason setting problems for itself that reason cannot solve.

Appendix

NOMENCLATURE

$A, B, \ldots$	sentences
$p, q, \ldots$	atomic sentences
w	a possible world
$\equiv$	an equivalence relation
$[x]_{\equiv}$	x's cell in the partition: the set of y equivalent to x
$\approx$	a similarity relation
$[x]_{\approx}$	x's cell in the corresponding division: the set of y similar to x
m	a subject matter considered as an entity in its own right
m(w)	how matters stand in w where m is concerned
m $\geq$ n	subject matter m includes subject matter n
$A{\uparrow}$	a truthmaker for A
$A{\downarrow}$	a falsemaker for A
{p}	the fact that p
{p̄}	the fact that $\neg p$
a	the subject matter of sentence A
ā	the subject anti-matter of sentence A
â	A's overall subject matter, a + ā
$<A>$	another term for A's overall subject matter
$A \geq B$	A includes B, B is part of A
X	a set of worlds
X/m	the "quotient set" when X is divided by m
A_{m}	the part of A about m, what A says about m
A	A's truth-conditional content
$|A|$	A's truth-conditional content again

$\mathcal{A}$ the directed proposition that A, $\texttt{A} + \hat{\texttt{a}}$

$||A||$ the directed proposition that A again, $|A| + <A>$

$B \nearrow A$ A, supposing that B

$A - B$ what A adds to B, the remainder when B is subtracted from A

$A \Vdash B$ the fact that A makes it true that B

$A \& \partial B$ a sentence agreeing with A in B-worlds, otherwise undefined

Bibliography

Abrusán, Marta. Predicting the presuppositions of soft triggers. *Linguistics and Philosophy*, 34(6):1–45, 2011.

Adams, Ernest W. Remarks on wishes and counterfactuals. *Pacific Philosophical Quarterly*, 79(3):191–211, 1998.

Alonso-Ovalle, Luis. Counterfactuals, correlatives, and disjunction. *Linguistics and Philosophy*, 32(2):207–244, 2009.

Alxatib, Sam and Francis J. Pelletier. The psychology of vagueness: Borderline cases and contradictions. *Mind & Language*, 26(3):287–326, 2011.

Anderson, Alan R. A reduction of deontic logic to alethic modal logic. *Mind*, 67(265):100–103, 1958.

Anderson, Alan R. and Nuel D. Belnap. Tautological entailments. *Philosophical Studies*, 13(1):9–24, 1962.

Armstrong, David M. *Truth and Truthmakers*. Cambridge University Press, 2004.

Armstrong, Joshua and Jason Stanley. Singular thoughts and singular propositions. *Philosophical Studies*, 154(2):205–222, 2011.

Atlas, Jay D. What are negative existence statements about? *Linguistics and Philosophy*, 11(4):373–394, 1988.

Austin, J. L. *Sense and Sensibilia*. Oxford University Press, 1962.

Azzouni, Jody. *Talking about Nothing: Numbers, Hallucinations and Fictions*. Oxford University Press, 2010.

Bach, Kent. Conversational impliciture. *Mind & Language*, 9:124–162, 1994.

Bar-Hillel, Yehoshua and Rudolf Carnap. Semantic information. *British Journal for the Philosophy of Science*, 4(14):147–157, 1953.

Barwise, Jon and John Perry. *Situations and Attitudes*. Bradford Books/MIT Press, 1983.

Beaver, David. *Presupposition and Assertion in Dynamic Semantics*. CSLI, 2001.

———. Have you noticed that your belly button lint colour is related to the colour of your clothing? *Presuppositions and Discourse: Essays Offered to Hans Kamp*, 21:65, 2010.

Beaver, David I. and Brady Z. Clark. *Sense and Sensitivity: How Focus Determines Meaning*. Wiley-Blackwell, 2009.

Beckett, Samuel. *Watt*. Grove, 1959.

Belnap, Nuel D. Conditional assertion and restricted quantification. *Noûs*, 4(1): 1–12, 1970.

Bezuidenhout, Anne. Truth-conditional pragmatics. *Noûs*, 36:105–134, 2002.

Borg, Emma. *Minimal Semantics*. Oxford University Press, 2006.

Brandom, Robert. *Between Saying and Doing: Towards an Analytic Pragmatism*. Oxford University Press, 2008.

Brentano, Franz. *Psychology from an Empirical Standpoint*. Psychology Press, 1995.

Bibliography

Büring, Daniel. Identity, modality, and the candidate behind the wall. In *Proceedings of SALT*, 8:36–54. Citeseer, 1998.

Cappelen, Herman and Ernest Lepore. *Insensitive Semantics: A Defense of Semantic Minimalism and Speech Act Pluralism*. Wiley-Blackwell, 2008.

Carnap, Rudolf. On protocol sentences. *Nous*, 21(4):457–470, 1987.

———. *The Logical Syntax of Language*. Open Court, 2002.

Carston, Robyn. *Thoughts and Utterances*. Blackwell, 2002.

Cartwright, Nancy. *How the Laws of Physics Lie*. Clarendon, 1983.

Chalmers, David J. *The Conscious Mind*. Oxford University Press, 1996.

Christensen, David. What is relative confirmation? *Nous*, 31(3):370–384, 1997.

Clarke, Thompson. The legacy of skepticism. *Journal of Philosophy*, 69(20):754–769, 1972.

Cohen, Stewart. Basic knowledge and the problem of easy knowledge. *Philosophy and Phenomenological Research*, 65(2):309–329, 2002.

Cohen, Ted. Notes on metaphor. *Journal of Aesthetics and Art Criticism*, 34(3):249–259, 1976.

Colyvan, Mark. Conceptual contingency and abstract existence. *Philosophical Quarterly*, 50(198):87–91, 2000.

———. *The Indispensability of Mathematics*. Oxford University Press, 2003.

Correia, Fabrice. Generic essence, objectual essence, and modality. *Nous*, 40(4):753–767, 2006.

Crimmins, Mark. Having ideas and having the concept. *Mind & Language*, 4(4):280–294, 1989.

———. Hesperus and phosphorus: Sense, pretense, and reference. *Philosophical Review*, 107(1):1–47, 1998.

Crimminsm, Mark and John Perry. The prince and the phone booth: Reporting puzzling beliefs. *Journal of Philosophy*, 86(12):685–711, 1989.

Cross, Troy. Skeptical success. *Oxford Studies in Epistemology*, 3:35–62, 2010.

Davidson, Donald. Causal relations. *Journal of Philosophy*, 64(21):691–703, 1967.

———. True to the facts. *Journal of Philosophy*, 66(21):748–764, 1969.

———. Reality without reference. *Dialectica*, 31(3–4):247–258, 2007.

Demolombe, Robert and Andrew Jones. On sentences of the kind "sentence p is about topic t": Some steps toward a formal-logical analysis. In *Essays in Honor of Dov Gabbay*, 115–138. Kluwer, 1998.

Dennett, Daniel. Beyond belief. In *Thought and Object*, 1–95. Clarendon, 1982.

———. *Darwin's Dangerous Idea: Evolution and the Meanings of Life*. Simon & Schuster, 1996.

Donnellan, Keith. Reference and definite descriptions. *Philosophical Review*, 75:281–304, 1966.

Dorr, Cian. Of numbers and electrons. *Proceedings of the Aristotelian Society*, 110:133–181, 2010.

Dretske, Fred. Contrastive statements. *Philosophical Review*, 81(4):411–437, 1972.

Earman, John. *Bayes or Bust?* MIT Press, 1992.

Field, Hartry. *Science Without Numbers*. Princeton University Press, 1980.

———. The conceptual contingency of mathematical objects. *Mind*, 102(406):285–299, 1993.

Bibliography

Fine, Kit. Analytic implication. *Notre Dame Journal of Formal Logic*, 27:169–179, 1986.

———. Essence and modality (volume 8: Logic and language). *Nous Supplement*, 8:1–16, 1994.

———. A difficulty for the possible worlds analysis of counterfactuals. *Synthese*, 189(1):1–29, 2012.

———. A note on partial content. *Analysis*, 73(3):413–419, 2013.

———. Truth-maker semantics for intuitionistic logic. *Journal of Philosophical Logic*, 1–29, 2013.

———. Angellic content. Forthcoming.

Fodor, Jerry A. *Psychosemantics: The Problem of Meaning in the Philosophy of Mind*. No. 2 in Explorations in Cognitive Science. MIT Press, 1987.

Fuhrmann, André. *An Essay on Contraction*. University of Chicago Press, 1996.

———. When hyperpropositions meet. *Journal of Philosophical Logic*, 28(6):559–574, 1999.

Funkhouser, Eric. The determinable-determinate relation. *Nous*, 40(3):548–569, 2006.

Gajewski, John. NPI any and connected exceptive phrases. *Natural Language Semantics*, 16(1):69–110, 2008.

Gemes, Ken. Horwich, Hempel, and hypothetico-deductivism. *Philosophy of Science*, 57(4):699, 1990.

———. A new theory of content I: Basic content. *Journal of Philosophical Logic*, 23(6):595–620, 1994.

———. A new theory of content II: Model theory and some alternatives. *Journal of Philosophical Logic*, 26(4):449–476, 1997.

———. Hypothetico-deductivism: The current state of play. *Erkenntnis*, 49(1):1–20, 1998.

———. Hypothetico-deductivism: Incomplete but not hopeless. *Erkenntnis*, 63(1):139–147, 2005.

———. Verisimilitude and content. *Synthese*, 154(2):293–306, 2007a.

———. Carnap-confirmation, content-cutting, and real confirmation. Manuscript, 2007b.

Gettier, Edmund. Is justified true belief knowledge? *Analysis*, 23:121–123, 1963.

Geurts, Bart. Scalar implicature and local pragmatics. *Mind & Language*, 24(1):51–79, 2009.

Goatley, Andrew. *The Language of Metaphors*. Routledge, 1997.

Goodman, Nelson. About. *Mind*, 70(277):1–24, 1961.

———. *Fact, Fiction, and Forecast*. Harvard University Press, 1983.

Grimes, Thomas. Truth, content, and the hypothetico-deductive method. *Philosophy of Science*, 57(3):514–522, 1990.

Gundel, Jeanette. Shared knowledge and topicality. *Journal of Pragmatics*, 9(1):83–107, 1985.

Hajicová, Eva, Barbara Hall Partee, and Petr Sgall. *Topic-Focus Articulation, Tripartite Structures, and Semantic Content*. Kluwer, 1998.

Hare, Caspar. Voices from another world: Must we respect the interests of people who do not, and will never, exist? *Ethics*, 117(3):498–523, 2007.

Bibliography

Harman, Gilbert. *Thought*. Princeton University Press, 1973.

Hawthorne, John. *Knowledge and Lotteries*. Clarendon Press, 2004.

——. The case for closure. In Matthias Steup, editor, *Contemporary Debates in Epistemology*, 26–43. Blackwell, 2005.

Hawthorne, John and Michaelis Michael. Compatibilist semantics in metaphysics: A case study. *Australasian Journal of Philosophy*, 74(1):117–134, 1996.

Hazen, Allen P. and Lloyd Humberstone. Similarity relations and the preservation of solidity. *Journal of Logic, Language and Information*, 13(1):25–46, 2004.

Heim, Irene. Presupposition projection and the semantics of attitude verbs. *Journal of Semantics*, 9:183–221, 1992.

Hellman, Geoffrey. *Mathematics without Numbers: Towards a Modal-Structural Interpretation*. Clarendon Press, 1989.

Hempel, Carl G. Review: Janina Lindenbaum Hosiasson, Induction et analogie: Comparison de leur fondement. *Journal of Symbolic Logic*, 7(1):40–41, 1942.

——. A purely syntactical definition of confirmation. *Journal of Symbolic Logic*, 8(4):122–143, 1943.

——. Studies in the logic of confirmation (I). *Mind*, 54(213):1–26, 1945a.

——. Studies in the logic of confirmation (II). *Mind*, 54(214):97–121, 1945b.

——. Inductive inconsistencies. *Synthese*, 12:439–469, 1960.

——. Rudolf Carnap, logical empiricist. *Synthese*, 25:257–268, 1975.

Hills, David. Aptness and truth in verbal metaphor. *Philosophical Topics*, 25:117–154, 1998.

Hornsby, Jennifer. *Actions*. Routledge and Kegan Paul, 1980a.

——. Arm raising and arm rising. *Philosophy*, 55(211):73–84, 1980b.

Hosiasson-Lindenbaum, Janina. On confirmation. *Journal of Symbolic Logic*, 5(4):133–148, 1940.

Hudson, James L. Logical subtraction. *Analysis*, 35(4):130–135, 1975.

Humberstone, Lloyd. Logical subtraction: Problems and prospects. *Typescript*, 1981.

——. Scope and subjunctivity. *Philosophia*, 12:99–126, 1982.

——. Wanting as believing. *Canadian Journal of Philosophy*, 17:49–62, 1987.

——. Parts and partitions. *Theoria*, 66(1):41–82, 2000.

——. False though partly true—An experiment in logic. *Journal of Philosophical Logic*, 32(6):613–665, 2003.

——. *The Connectives*. MIT Press, 2011.

Husserl, Edmund G. *The Crisis of European Sciences and Transcendental Phenomenology: An Introduction to Phenomenological Philosophy*. TriQuarterly Books, 1970.

Hutchins, John. On the problem of "aboutness" in document analysis. *Journal of Informatics*, 1:17–35, 1977.

——. The concept of "aboutness" in subject indexing. In *ASLIB Proceedings*, 30:172–181. MCB UP, 1978.

Jackson, Frank. *Perception: A Representative Theory*. Cambridge University Press, 1977.

Jaeger, Ronald. Action and subtraction. *Philosophical Review*, 82(3):320–329, 1973.

——. Logical subtraction and the analysis of action. *Analysis*, 36(3):141–146, 1976.

James, William. *The Will to Believe and Other Essays in Popular Philosophy*. Harvard University Press, 1979.

Bibliography

Kagan, Shelly. The additive fallacy. *Ethics*, 99(1):5–31, 1988.

Kissine, Mikhail. Misleading appearances: Searle on assertion and meaning. *Erkenntnis*, 74(1):115–129, 2011.

Kripke, Saul. *Naming and Necessity*. Harvard University Press, 1980.

———. *Wittgenstein on Rules and Private Language: An Elementary Exposition*. Harvard University Press, 1982.

———. Nozick on knowledge. In *Philosophical Troubles: Collected Papers*, 1:162–224, Oxford University Press, 2011a.

———. *Philosophical Troubles: Collected Papers*. Vol. 1. Oxford University Press, 2011b.

Lange, Marc. A tale of two vectors. *Dialectica*, 63(4):397–431, 2009.

Langendoen, Terence. Presupposition and assertion in the semantic analysis of nouns and verbs in English. In *Semantics: An Interdisciplinary Reader in Philosophy, Linguistics and Psychology*, 341–344. Cambridge University Press, 1971.

Lasersohn, Peter. Pragmatic halos. *Language*, 75(3):522–551, 1999.

Lear, Jonathan. Sets and semantics. *Journal of Philosophy*, 74(2):86–102, 1977.

Levinson, Stephen. *Presumptive Meanings: The Theory of Generalized Conversational Implicature*. MIT Press, 2000.

Lewin, Leonard C. *Report from Iron Mountain: On the Possibility and Desirability of Peace*. Free Press, 1996.

Lewis, David. Counterparts of persons and their bodies. *Journal of Philosophy*, 68:203–211, 1971.

———. Scorekeeping in a language game. *Journal of Philosophical Logic*, 87:339–359, 1979.

———. *Philosophical Papers*, Vol. 1. Oxford University Press, 1983.

———. *Philosophical Papers*. Vol. 2. Oxford University Press, 1986.

———. Relevant implication. *Theoria*, 54(3):161–174, 1988a.

———. Statements partly about observation. In *Papers in Philosophical Logic*, 125–155. Cambridge University Press, 1988b.

———. *Parts of Classes*. Blackwell, 1991.

———. Elusive knowledge. *Australasian Journal of Philosophy*, 74:549–567, 1996.

Locke, John. *An Essay Concerning Human Understanding*. Oxford University Press, 1706.

Miller, David. Popper's qualitative theory of verisimilitude. *British Journal for the Philosophy of Science*, 25(2):166–177, 1974.

Moore, G. E. *Principia Ethica*. Cambridge University Press, 1903.

Moretti, Luca. The tacking by disjunction paradox: Bayesianism versus hypothetico-deductivism. *Erkenntnis*, 64(1):115–138, 2006.

Muller, F. A. and B. C. van Fraassen. How to talk about unobservables. *Analysis*, 68(299):197–205, 2008.

Neurath, Otto. Protocol sentences. In A. J. Ayer, editor, *Logical Positivism*, 199–208. Macmillan, 1959.

Niiniluoto, Ilkka. *Truthlikeness*. Vol. 185. Springer, 1987.

Peacocke, Christopher. Principles for possibilia. *Noûs*, 36(3):486–508, 2002.

Perry, John. Possible worlds and subject matter. In *Possible Worlds in Humanities, Arts and Sciences. Proceedings of Nobel Symposium*, 65:173–191. Walter De Gruyter, 1989.

Bibliography

———.Frege on identity, cognitive value, and subject matter. Manuscript, 2011.
Plantinga, Alvin. *Warrant: The Current Debate*. Oxford University Press, 1993.
Popper, Karl. *Objective Knowledge: An Evolutionary Approach*. Clarendon Press, 1972.
Putnam, Hilary. Formalization of the concept "About." *Philosophy of Science*, 25(2):125–130, 1958.
———. *Philosophy of Logic*. Harper and Row, 1971.
———. The Meaning of "Meaning". In *Mind, Language and Reality*, 215–272. Cambridge University Press, 1975.
———. Models and reality. *Journal of Symbolic Logic*, 45(3):464–482, 1980.
Putnam, Hilary and Joseph Ullian. More about "about". *Journal of Philosophy*, 62(12):305–310, 1965.
Quine, Willard Van Orman. On what there is. *Review of Metaphysics*, 2(5):21–38, 1948.
———. A way to simplify truth functions. *American Mathematical Monthly*, 62(9):627–631, 1955.
———. *Word and Object*. MIT Press, 1960.
———. Ontological relativity. In *Ontological Relativity and Other Essays*, 26–68. Columbia University Press, 1996.
Rayo, Augustin. The construction of Logical Space. Oxford University Press, 2013.
Recanati, Francois. The pragmatics of what is said. *Mind and Language*, 4(4):295–329, 1989.
———. *Truth-Conditional Pragmatics*. Oxford University Press, 2011.
———. Contextualism: Some varieties. In Keith Allan and Kasia M. Jaszczolt, editors, *Cambridge Handbook of Pragmatics*, 135–149. Cambridge University Press, 2012.
Reck, Erich. Frege's influence on Wittgenstein: Reversing metaphysics via the context principle. In *Early Analytic Philosophy: Frege, Russell, Wittgenstein*, 123–185. Open Court, 1997.
Richard, Mark. Semantic pretense. In Anthony J. Everett and Thomas Hofweber, editors, *Empty Names, Fiction and the Puzzle of Non-Existence*, 205–232. CSLI, 2000.
Ricketts, Thomas G. Objectivity and objecthood: Frege's metaphysics of judgment. In *Frege Synthesized*, 65–95. Springer, 1986.
Ripley, David. Contradictions at the borders. In Rick Nouwen and Robert van Rooij, editors, *Vagueness in Communication*, 169–188. Springer, 2011.
Rosen, Gideon. The limits of contingency. In *Identity and Modality*, 13–40. Oxford University Press, 2006.
Roush, Sherrilyn. Précis of tracking truth. *Philosophy and Phenomenological Research*, 79(1):213–222, 2009.
Russell, Bertrand. Pragmatism. In *Philosophical Essays*, Longmans, Green, 1910. 79–111.
Ryle, Gilbert. About. *Analysis*, 1(1):10–12, 1933.
Sartorio, Carolina. Disjunctive causes. *Journal of Philisophy*, 103(10):521–538, 2006.
Sauerland, U. The computation of scalar implicatures: Pragmatic, lexical or grammatical? *Language and Linguistics Compass*, 6(1):36–49, 2012.
Saul, Jennifer Mather. *Lying, Misleading, and What Is Said: An Exploration in Philosophy of Language and in Ethics*. Oxford University Press, 2012.

214

Bibliography

Schaffer, Jonathan. Knowing the answer. *Philosophy and Phenomenological Research*, 75(2):383–403, 2007.

Schaffer, Jonathan and Zoltán Gendler Szabó. Epistemic comparativism: A contextualist semantics for knowledge ascriptions. *Philosophical Studies*, forthcoming.

Scheffler, Israel and Nelson Goodman. Selective confirmation and the ravens. *Journal of Philosophy*, 69(3):78–83, 1972.

Schlenker, Philippe. The lazy frenchman's approach to the subjunctive: Speculations on reference to worlds and semantic defaults in the analysis of mood. In I. van Ginneken, T. Geerts, and H. Jenken, editors, *Romance Languages and Linguistic Theory 2003*, 269–309. John Benjamins, 2005.

Schoubye, Anders J. Descriptions, truth value intuitions, and questions. *Linguistics and Philosophy*, 32(6):583–617, 2009.

———. Ghosts, murderers, and the semantics of descriptions. *Noûs*, 32:583–617, 2011.

Schurz, Gerhard. Relevant deduction and hypothetico-deductivism: A reply to Gemes. *Erkenntnis*, 41(2):183–188, 1994.

Searle, John. The background of meaning. In *Speech Act Theory and Pragmatics*, 221–232. Springer, 1980.

Searle, John and Stephan Körner. Symposium: On determinables and resemblance. *Proceedings of the Aristotelian Society*, 33:125–158, 1959.

Shoemaker, Sydney. Persons and their pasts. *American Philosophical Quarterly*, 7(4):269–285, 1970.

Sider, Theodore. The ersatz pluriverse. *Journal of Philosophy*, 99(6):279–315, 2002.

Simons, Mandy. A Gricean view on intrusive implicatures. In *Meaning and Analysis: New Essays on Grice*, 138–169. Palgrave Studies in Pragmatics, Language and Cognition Series. Palgrave, 2010.

Soames, Scott. *Beyond Rigidity: The Unfinished Semantic Agenda of Naming and Necessity*. Oxford University Press, 2002.

Sober, Elliott. Constructive empiricism and the problem of aboutness. *British Journal for the Philosophy of Science*, 36(1):11–18, 1985.

Sperber, Dan and Deirdre Wilson. Loose talk. *Proceedings of the Aristotelian Society*, 86:153–171, 1985.

———. *Relevance: Communication and Cognition*. Blackwell, 1986.

Sprenger, Jan. Hypothetico-deductive confirmation. *Philosophy Compass*, 6(7):497–508, 2011.

Stalnaker, Robert C. *Context and Content*. Oxford University Press, 1999.

———. Comments on "From contextualism to contrastivism." *Philosophical Studies*, 119(1):105–117, 2004.

Stanley, Jason. Hermeneutic fictionalism. *Midwest Studies in Philosophy*, 25(1):36–71, 2001.

Stine, Gail C. Skepticism, relevant alternatives, and deductive closure. *Philosophical Studies*, 29(4):249–261, 1976.

Strawson, Peter Frederick. *Introduction to Logical Theory*. Wiley, 1952.

Stroud, Barry. *The Significance of Philosophical Scepticism*. Oxford University Press, 1984.

Tappenden, Jamie. Extending knowledge and "fruitful concepts": Fregean themes in the foundations of mathematics. *Noûs*, 29(4):427–467, 1995.

Bibliography

Tarski, Alfred. The semantic conception of truth and the foundations of semantics. *Philosophy and Phenomenological Research*, 4(3):341–376, 1944.

Tennant, Neil. On the necessary existence of numbers. *Nous*, 31(3):307–336, 1997.

Tichỳ, Pavel. On Popper's definitions of verisimilitude. *British Journal for the Philosophy of Science*, 25(2):155–160, 1974.

Ullian, Joseph and Nelson Goodman. Truth about Jones. *Journal of Philosophy*, 74(6):317–338, 1977.

van Fraassen, Bas C. Facts and tautological entailment. *Journal of Philosophy*, 66(15):477–487, 1969.

Veltman, F. Defaults in update semantics. *Journal of Philosophical Logic*, 25(3):221–261, 1996.

Vogel, Jonathan. Are there counterexamples to the closure principle? In Michael David Roth and Glenn Ross, editors, *Doubting: Contemporary Perspectives on Skepticism*, 13–27. Kluwer, 1990.

von Fintel, Kai. Exceptive constructions. *Natural Language Semantics*, 1(2):123–148, 1993.

———. Would you believe it? The King of France is back! (Presuppositions and truth-value intuitions). In Marga Reimer and Anne Bezuidenhout, editors, *Descriptions and Beyond*, 315–341. Oxford University Press, 2004.

Walton, Kendall. Metaphor and prop oriented make-believe. *European Journal of Philosophy*, 1(1):39–57, 1993.

Weslake, Brad. The problem of disjunctive explanations. Unpublished.

Williamson, Timothy. *Identity and Discrimination*. Blackwell, 1990.

———. The broadness of the mental: Some logical considerations. In James Tomberlin, editor, *Language, Mind, and Ontology*, volume 12 of Philosophical Perspectives, 388–410. Blackwell, 1998.

———. *Knowledge and Its Limits*. Oxford University Press, 2000.

Windschitl, Paul D. and Gary L. Wells. The alternative-outcomes effect. *Journal of Personality and Social Psychology*, 75(6):1411, 1998.

Wittgenstein, Ludwig. *Philosophical Investigations*. Blackwell, 1953.

———. *Remarks on Color*. Blackwell, 1977.

Woods, John. On species and determinates. *Nous*, 1(3):243–254, 1967.

Wright, Crispin and Bob Hale. Nominalism and the contingency of abstract objects. *Journal of Philosophy*, 89(3):111–135, 1992.

Yablo, Stephen. Cause and essence. *Synthese*, 93(3):403–449, 1992.

———. Go figure: A path through fictionalism. *Midwest Studies in Philosophy*, 25(1):72–102, 2001.

———. Abstract objects: A case study. *Nous*, 36(s1):220–240, 2002.

———. Causal relevance. *Philosophical Issues*, 13(1):316–329, 2003.

———. No fool's cold: Notes on illusions of possibility. In M. Garcia-Carpintero and J. Macia, editors, *Two-Dimensional Semantics*, 327–345. Oxford University Press, 2006a.

———. Non-catastrophic presupposition failure. In *Content and Modality: Themes from the Philosophy of Robert Stalnaker*, 164–190. Oxford University Press, 2006b.

———. A problem about permission and possibility. In Andy Egan and Brian Weatherson, editors, *Epistemic Modality*, 270–294. Oxford University Press, 2011.

Yalcin, Seth. Epistemic modals. *Mind*, 116(464):983–1026, 2007.

———. Probability operators. *Philosophy Compass*, 5(11):916–937, 2010.

———. Figure and Ground in Logical Space. Manuscript, 2011.

Zwart, Sjoerd and Maarten Franssen. An impossibility theorem for verisimilitude. *Synthese*, 158(1):75–92, 2007.

Index